ADMIRAL BYNG

And the Loss of Minorca

BY

BRIAN TUNSTALL

LECTURER IN HISTORY AT THE
ROYAL NAVAL COLLEGE
GREENWICH

LONDON

PHILIP ALLAN & CO. LTD.

QUALITY HOUSE, GREAT RUSSELL STREET

First Edition in 1928

Made and Printed in Great Britain by
The Camelot Press Limited,
London and Southampton

PREFACE

ONE hundred and seventy-two years ago to-day, at about two o'clock in the afternoon, Admiral Byng was pacing the quarterdeck of the *Ramillies*, considering how best to bring his fleet into action with the French fleet lying to, awaiting his attack, under M. de la Galissonnière. Ships were rarely sunk in sailing-ship actions during the eighteenth century, chiefly because the smooth-bore, muzzle-loading guns of the time, throwing solid shot, were strictly limited in range and destructive power. Nowadays, explosive shells not only do enormous damage, but the increased range of gunfire enables many ships to concentrate their fire on a single opponent, whereas in the eighteenth century the effective range was so short, that it was often impossible for ships to do more than engage each other in pairs. The main object was to kill the enemy's crew, and board and capture his ship, which was afterwards used in the victor's fleet, as in a game of reversi.

In Byng's action off Minorca no ships were sunk on either side, but the injuries which some of his received seemed to demand a return to Gibraltar for repairs. While there, he was superseded from his command and sent home. On arrival he was put under arrest, imprisoned, tried by court martial, and shot by a party of marines on the quarterdeck of the *Monarque*.

Ever since, his name has been a household word. But although he is mentioned in hundreds of books, historians, and others who should know better, have shown a surprising ignorance of his case, and their comments seldom go beyond the epithet 'fool,' 'coward,' and 'scapegoat.'

Byng's failure to 'relieve' Minorca, and his subsequent trial and death following the surrender of St. Philip's Castle, and the loss of the whole island, agitated England for the best part of a year. Everyone remembers that it happened, but nobody knows how or why. His ship, the *Ramillies*, has still an honourable descendant in the British line of battle, but even in the Navy his case is hardly understood.

In this book I have attempted, for the first time, to present at full length a truthful and complete account of the whole affair, which, from its tragic end alone, must always rank as one of the most amazing incidents in British Naval History.

The official printed version of the trial, of which there are several editions, thoroughly explains the details of the battle and contemporary naval opinion with regard to the strategy of the campaign, but it is full of technicalities, and is not easy reading for the layman. The Admiralty In and Out Letters in the Public Record Office give the official despatches, and the Newcastle and Hardwicke Papers, included in the *Additional MSS.*[1] in the British Museum, throw a somewhat lurid light on the political machinations lying behind the combined strategy of the Admiralty and War Office.

[1] Referred to as 'Add.' in notes.

The contemporary pamphlets, despised by some authorities, throw even more light on the feelings of the civilian public at large, and are characteristic of the ignorance of Englishmen about their Navy. Moreover, they show that close connection between party politics and journalism which has often had such an evil influence on the personnel of the service.

I am especially indebted to Professor Geoffrey Callender for his valuable advice in dealing with the data and arrangement of the story, and for his most helpful criticisms. I have received great assistance in the preparation of the material from Lady Corbett, Mr. Richard Corbett, Mr. L. Cranmer-Byng, and Professor R. M. Dawkins. Captain E. W. Denison, R.N., Professor T. Holland Rose, and Mr. W. G. Perrin have been most helpful in drawing my attention to various authorities.

Through the courtesy of His Excellency Señor Don Miguel Cabanellas, Military Governor-General of Minorca, I was able to make a close inspection of the site of St. Philip's Castle, which was especially valuable to me in estimating its potentialities as a fortress during the eighteenth century. Señor Don Alberto Garcia Diaz, Capitan de Artilleria, commanding the Spanish garrison now quartered there, most kindly conducted me all through the underground passages used during the siege, and across St. Stephen's Cove to Fort Marlborough, which is still fairly intact.

I am deeply indebted to Señor Don Bartolomé Escudero, M.V.O., British Vice-Consul at Port Mahon, who made my brief visit to Minorca so pleasant and fruitful, to Señor Don Hernandez and Señor Don Antonio Victory, President of the Athenæum, Port Mahon, whose excellent life of General Kane has been at my disposal, and to Messrs. T. H. Parker for their permission to reproduce the mezzotint of General Blakeney.

Royal Naval College,
Greenwich,
20th May, 1928.

W. C. B. T.

CONTENTS

ILLUSTRATIONS

PLANS

ADMIRAL BYNG

CHAPTER I

THE LEGEND

En causant ainsi ils abordèrent à Portsmouth. Une multitude de peuple couvrait le rivage, et regardait attentivement un assez gros homme qui était à genoux, les yeux bandés, sur le tillac d'un des vaisseaux de la flotte ; quatre soldats, postés vis-à-vis de cet homme, lui tirèrent chacun trois balles dans le crâne, le plus paisiblement du monde ; et toute l'assemblée s'en retourna extrêmement satisfaite.

" Qu'est-ce donc que tout ceci ? " dit Candide ; " et quel démon exerce partout son empire ? "

Il demanda qui était ce gros homme qu'on venait de tuer en cérémonie.

" C'est un amiral," lui répondit-on.

" Et pourquoi tuer cet amiral ? "

" C'est," lui dit-on, " parce qu'il n'a pas fait tuer assez de monde ; il a livré un combat à un amiral français, et on a trouvé qu'il n'était pas assez près de lui."

" Mais," dit Candide, " l'amiral français était aussi loin de l'amiral anglais que celui-ci l'était de l'autre ! "

" Cela est incontestable," lui repliqua-t-on ; " mais

dans ce pays-ci il est bon de tuer de temps en temps un amiral pour encourager les autres."

'CANDIDE.'

EVERYONE has heard of Admiral Byng, who failed to relieve Minorca, because Voltaire has made him famous by a single sentence. To his contemporaries Byng was an object of universal pity. Opinion was divided as to his conduct in the Minorca campaign, but all agreed that he was the brave victim of an incompetent Ministry. Horace Walpole, the most reliable and well-informed diarist of his age, had no hesitation in speaking his mind about him. 'I can appeal to God,' he writes, 'that I never spoke to Mr. Byng in my life, nor had the most distant acquaintance with any of his family. The man I never saw but in the streets, or in the House of Commons, and there I thought his carriage haughty and disgusting . . . from the clamours of the world, I was carried away with the multitude in believing he had not done his duty. . . . When his pamphlet appeared, I read it, and found he had been cruelly and scandalously treated. . . . He was, if I may be allowed the expression, a coward of his glory, not of his life; with regard to that, poor man, he had an opportunity of showing he was a hero.'

John Charnock, the naval biographer, wrote in 1796: 'Reviewing the whole transaction, future ages can scarcely avoid considering Mr. Byng as a true victim to the mistakes of others, bestowing on them the lightest term. In whatever respect he might be deficient as a commander, the blame certainly attaches, in a much stronger degree, to those who sent him on such a service.'

Dr. Robert Beatson in his *Naval and Military Memoirs* of about the same date, said: '. . . The lapse of more than thirty years has thrown much light on this tragedy; there being now the best reasons for presuming . . . that the misconduct of Admiral Byng did not deserve so severe a punishment as death; and that, so far from considering him as a victim to public justice, he will be regarded by posterity as a martyr to the resentment of an Administration of whose conduct their country had too much reason to be ashamed.'

Again more than thirty years elapsed; Nelson fell, the French were beaten, the Navy assumed for all time its true place in the British system, and truth lay at the mercy of Lord Macaulay. In 1834 he announced that 'Admiral Byng was sent from Gibraltar to throw succours into Port Mahon; but he did not think fit to engage the French squadron, and sailed back without having effected his purpose.' The untruthfulness of the first two statements is of course aggravated by the obvious truth of the third, but the public never questioned any of the three, and in 1913 Mr. Guedalla was able to add a neat little note to that particular essay, stating that Byng's 'conduct at Minorca was militarily wise as it was politically foolish.' Macaulay doubtless only wished to paint a vivid picture, and Mr. Guedalla to say something clever, but during the last twenty years Byng has become the victim of another kind of truth improver. A number of intelligent persons suddenly discovered that Chatham was a very great man, and that it was time that the twentieth century realised it. Several biographies appeared, deifying Chatham, calling his worst speeches oratory and his stupidest actions patriotism. Everyone knew that Chatham had made a half-hearted effort to save Byng, and this was soon represented as a magnanimous attempt defeated by unscrupulous opponents. In such accounts Byng's character inevitably suffered, Mr. Frederic Harrison stating that 'the unlucky Byng made a poor fight with the French and sailed away in the night, though he had more ships than the enemy.'

Horace Walpole was decried because he refused to make gods out of men, and Byng became a miserable creature, whose death was only useful as a means of displaying the generosity of Chatham.

In 1907 Dr. Albert von Ruville published the most balanced life of Chatham that has yet appeared, and in which Horace Walpole was praised for his trustworthiness as a contemporary authority, and Byng was given something like a fair hearing. The book was, of course, violently criticised by the Chatham enthusiasts, but soon they received another attack. A strong attempt was made to restore the reputation of the Newcastle-Hardwicke Government. Horace Walpole was again decried, and Byng was treated worse than ever; for this time it became the special object of such writers to prove that he failed entirely through his own fault, and was treated with absolute fairness afterwards. Luckily, the partisans of Chatham and Newcastle were not very interested in the sea, and confined their researches to the public and private correspondence of their heroes, so that a rich harvest was still open to those who could give an unbiased view of statesmanship in terms of naval warfare. An official copy of Byng's trial, 'As taken by Mr. Charles Fearne, Judge Advocate of His Majesty's Fleet,' was published by order of the Admiralty in 1757, and was used by Admiral Mahan and other pioneers of naval history, but it was not till 1907 that Sir Julian Corbett, in his *England in the Seven Years' War*, gave a clear and convincing account of Byng's strategy and tactics.

The Admiralty instructions, Byng's despatches, the fighting instructions, and the logs of the ships engaged, were set side by side with the diplomatic and political correspondence. Moreover, the best French authorities were consulted, the most reliable of whom had already described Byng's death as '*cette exécution barbare et inutile*.' Sir Julian Corbett's narrative is contained within a very few pages, and makes no attempt to carry the story beyond Byng's supersession and return to England. How he was tried, the debates in Parliament on the sentence, and the whole influence of his career on the fate of the Newcastle Ministry still remain to be told. His imprisonment, trial and death produced a large crop of pamphlets, ballads and lampoons which throw an important light on the attitude of the public towards the Navy. Some are by such well-known men as Dr. Johnson, Paul Whitehead of the Hell Fire Club, and David Mallet the poet, while others are by the unknown hacks of Grub Street. Sir John Laughton, in his article on Byng in the *Dictionary of National Biography,* treated these pamphlets with great contempt. It is true that only a few of their authors show any knowledge of naval matters, but they are indispensable as evidence of the methods used to give publicity to important topics, and for giving Byng his proper place in our national history.

After his execution, a Parliamentary enquiry was held to discover to what extent the late Ministers had been responsible for the loss of Minorca, and papers were called for; but the result was an anti-climax. Reports and intelligences were sent to the House of Commons dealing with the supposed object of French naval and military preparations in 1755 and 1756. Our ambassadors at Madrid and Turin, our consuls at Nice, Leghorn, Genoa, Cartagena and Berne, naval officers in the Mediterranean and Channel, and hosts of unknown and lesser persons, had all contributed scraps of information. The late Ministers saw to it that a mass of documents was collected, sufficiently unwieldy and indigestible to deter the researches of their most relentless critics, while a short statement by way of an apologia accompanied each separate batch. Those who hoped to discover something definite in the papers were at first confused, then baffled, and finally bored. In 1913 the dossier was edited for the Navy Records Society, and the effect of the papers on the editor and the public was identical to what it had been in 1757.

CHAPTER II

THE MAN

THE Hon. John Byng was the fourth son of Sir George Byng, Lord Torrington, victor in the famous action off Cape Passaro in 1718. Coming in the middle of a period of comparative peace, his success received more than its full share of praise, and, during the failures and disappointments of the next war, was often looked back to with feelings of envy and regret, when the less brilliant but more solid triumphs of Rooke and Leake were already long forgotten. Byng had certainly acted with speed and vigour, but against a very inferior and demoralised foe. Yet from that moment his reputation was made. He had already rendered valuable service to the cause of the Glorious Revolution by canvassing the support of the Fleet for William of Orange, and twice helping to defeat the efforts of the Old Pretender.[1] He had fought at Beachy Head, Barfleur and Malaga, and had led the attack at the capture of Gibraltar. Later, as the only sailor lucky enough to achieve distinction after the Peace of Utrecht, he basked in the full blaze of Whig sunshine. He was made Admiral of the Fleet in 1718, created Viscount Torrington in 1721, and given the lucrative office of Treasurer of the Navy. George II, on his

[1] In 1708 by preventing his sailing from Dunkirk and in 1715 by cutting off the Jacobites' supplies.

BB

accession, appointed him First Lord of the Admiralty, recognising by this popular act his ability as an officer, and his devotion to the Protestant Succession.

Naturally the ample patronage of the father was used to promote the public career of his children. The eldest, Henry Pattee Byng, succeeded his father as second Lord Torrington and also as Treasurer of the Navy, later becoming Vice-Treasurer of Ireland and Captain of the Yeomen of the Guard. Of Torrington's other children, Robert became Extra Commissioner of the Navy, Comptroller of the Store-keeper's Accounts and Governor of Barbados, Edward reached the rank of Colonel in the Army, while Sarah married Admiral Henry Osborn.

John Byng was born in 1704, and entered the Navy in 1718, receiving a memorable introduction to the service by being present in the *Superb*, 60 guns, at his father's victory, and helping to board the Spanish flagship. He passed his examination for lieutenant in 1722, after serving in the *Orford*, *Newcastle*, *Nassau* and *Torbay*, as midshipman, able seaman or captain's servant. He was not, however, pushed forward too quickly, and continued to be rated as able seaman in the *Dover* and *Solebay* till 1724, when he became second lieutenant of the *Superb*, his original ship.

He served in her two years, and then between 1726 and 1727, became fourth, third and second lieutenant of the *Burford* (70), which formed part of Sir Charles Wager's squadron in the Mediterranean. Soon after, he was transferred to the *Torbay* (80), and on 8th August, 1727, was made captain of the *Gibraltar*, a twenty-gun frigate. He commanded the *Princess Louisa* (40) from 1728-31, and the *Falmouth* (50) from 1731-6; two short commissions followed in the *Augusta* (60) and the *Portland* (50), after which he commanded the *Sunderland* (60) in the Mediterranean.

The War of the Austrian Succession had begun in 1740, but Byng was not to take part in any of the earlier operations, and in 1742 he was sent out in the *Sutherland* (50) to supervise the Newfoundland fisheries.[1] As senior naval officer on the station he held the formal post of Governor of Newfoundland, which was then customary, and next year returned to command the *Winchester* (50) in the Channel. In 1744 he was made flag captain to Sir Charles Hardy in the *St. George* (90)—an ominous appointment, for it was in this ship, twelve years later, that he was tried for his life. But nothing of any importance befell him during this commission, and after escorting the Lisbon Convoy, he returned to join the Channel Fleet under Sir John Norris.

He received his flag as Rear-Admiral of the Blue on 8th August, 1745, at the age of forty-one, and after being twenty-seven years in the service. Such an advancement was rapid, but by no means phenomenal, and hardly to be compared with the promotions of Forbes, Boscawen and Northesk when still in the thirties. But, considering that he had seen so little fighting, he might be considered distinctly lucky to obtain his flag so soon.

[1] Burrows, in his life of Hawke, tries to magnify this purely routine appointment into a post of immense importance, specially secured for him by family influence.

Meanwhile stirring events had been taking place in the Mediterranean. The combined fleets of France and Spain had left Toulon and had been brought to action by Admiral Matthews, which resulted in more mutual recriminations and courts martial than have been provoked by any naval battle before or since. Byng, who was lucky enough to have been absent from the Mediterranean on this disastrous occasion, was now made a member of the court by which Lestock was tried, and apparently concurred in the extraordinary verdict which acquitted the vice-admiral, in keeping to the absolute letter of the fighting instructions.

In the autumn of 1745, Byng in the *Kinsale* (40), was appointed to command one of the small squadrons, collected in home waters under Admiral Vernon, to prevent the French assisting the Young Pretender. In September and October we hear of him in the Firth of Forth, co-operating vigorously with the land forces, and constantly receiving his orders from the land officers. His assistance was invaluable, as the English troops might have become demoralised had any French force made a landing immediately after Preston Pans.

Next year, as a member of the court which tried Matthews, he again concurred in a yet more extraordinary verdict, which found the commander-in-chief guilty of 'divers breaches of duty,' which were 'a principal cause of the miscarriage of His Majesty's Fleet.' It would seem impossible to have devised a better method of turning an officer into a hidebound formalist than by making him sit on two such courts;

and we know that these events made a lasting impression on his mind, and haunted him in his last battle.

In October 1746 he was ordered to hoist his flag in the *Superb* (60) and proceed to the Mediterranean as second in command to Admiral Medley. This appointment was one of considerable importance, as the Mediterranean Fleet totalled more than thirty sail, and was actively engaged in preventing the French attacking our Austrian allies in Italy either by sea or land. Byng's reception of his good fortune was remarkable. In a private letter to the Duke of Bedford,[1] he expressed his thanks for the new command, but added, 'I do not think myself equal to the task I am going to undertake.'[2]

However, in February 1747 he set sail and joined Medley in Vado Bay,[3] where he was immediately given the task of protecting the Lerins Islands against the French. Our successful blockade of Toulon forced the enemy to advance by the Riviera coast road in order to enter Italy, and the islands, now in Austrian hands, formed a useful base from which to harass their lines of communication.

Byng at once began enumerating the difficulties involved in opposing the French: 'I cannot flatter myself that I shall have it in my power to prevent them,'[4] and again, 'All I can do is to keep ships plying about the islands.'[5] Eventually he was driven off his station by a gale, and the islands were lost. No fault seemed to have been found with him for

[1] Then First Lord.
[2] 25th October. Correspondence of the Fourth Duke of Bedford, Vol. I., pp. 164–5.
[3] 17th April. [4] 9th May. Ad. In Letters. [5] 27th April.

this unfortunate reverse, and on 15th July he was promoted to Vice-Admiral of the Blue. Three weeks later Medley died, and he succeeded to the command, shifting his flag to the *Boyne* (80). The Government now saw fit to order home about a third of his fleet, so that, owing to lack of small craft, he was forced to spread his ships over a very wide area.[1] By next spring the situation was such that he had enough ships either to seal Toulon completely, or else to maintain a general blockade of the whole coast, but not to do both, and so he decided to adopt the second alternative.[2]

On 12th May he was promoted to be Vice-Admiral of the Red, and was ordered home on 12th July, at the conclusion of the war, leaving only seven ships as a permanent Mediterranean squadron.

Such was the public career of the man who at the age of forty-three had risen to the exalted rank of vice-admiral, during a war lasting nine years, without ever once commanding a squadron or even a single ship in any important action. But if Byng had never distinguished himself he had certainly never failed, and in the tragic collapse of reputations which the war produced, the Government was only too willing to recognise the merits of an officer who through no fault of his own had had little chance of making any gross mistakes.

In an age when eccentricity was encouraged, admirals were expected to be peculiar, but the nature of their profession restricted their behaviour to

[1] Byng to Newcastle, 15th September.
[2] Byng to Admiralty, 13th February, 1748.

well-defined limits. Byng was 'by no means popular,' 'a very strict disciplinarian,' 'austere and rigid, almost to a degree of undue oppression.' This was quite satisfactory and all that might be expected from the imperious figure painted by Hudson. His expression is aggressive and contemptuous, and we hardly need to be told that he was addicted to duelling. His wig is ceremonial in volume, a splendid waistcoat sheathes his large frame, over which he wears a magnificent admiral's coat, richly decorated with gold, the cuffs of enormous width and ending well above the wrist, to allow the display of delicate lace ruffles. No wonder that the man who wore such a uniform was thought 'haughty and disgusting.' There was nothing, however, in Byng's exterior to create any public uneasiness, and it was only when he turned philosopher, and spoke with undue modesty of his own powers, that the illusion was shattered and people became alarmed.

After all, what was the use of such a uniform, if the man inside it did not act the part? But in the years after the Peace of Aix-la-Chapelle he had not yet been found out; on the contrary, he was in high favour. He represented the Borough of Rochester, and strutted to the House of Commons with even more contempt for landsmen written on his face than was then considered absolutely necessary for a naval officer.

CHAPTER III

THE NAVY, POLITICS AND PUBLIC OPINION

ANY day in the year 1755 a silent man might have been seen working at the Admiralty. The man was Lord Anson, and his work the reconstruction of the battle fleet. The old illogical jumble of 'rates' was to go, and in future the fleet was to be threefold, consisting of battleships, frigates and light craft forming the flotilla. Anson had sailed round the world, defeated a French squadron in the last war, captured its convoy, worth £3,000,000, married the Lord Chancellor's daughter, and was now First Lord. He had once been handsome, and was still well favoured though a trifle sleek, but he was always very silent. Reform was in the air; the Navy had sometimes failed in the last war through vague strategy and sluggish tactics. Officers as well as ships must be improved, and Anson hoped in the future to conduct a war for the King in which there would be no courts martial.

The worth of the Navy was generally appreciated, but its fighting traditions were those of the Dutch Wars, and the classic epoch was still to come which should give it a true position in the British system. Meanwhile the Duke of Newcastle considered that the exercise of naval patronage on political grounds was quite compatible with service efficiency. Should there be a vacant post in the Victualling Office, he

LORD ANSON

From the picture after Sir J. Reynolds in the National Portrait Gallery

[*p.* 14

would be bound to hear of it and at once recommend 'a very pretty young man,' whom Anson would promptly reject as merely 'adding to the useless people already encumbering that office.'

So the struggle went on, Anson trying to bring in 'men of business,' and Newcastle continually pressing the claims of nonentities. The Duke was the butt of the age and ridiculed by every humorist from Chesterfield to Toby Smollet, but at any rate he was very successful. Lord Chamberlain at twenty-four, and Secretary of State at thirty-one, he had been in office ever since, and was now in his sixty-second year. Though by nature nervous and irresolute, he was by no means devoid of political common sense, while long experience, wide patronage,[1] and able friends supplied that stability which his character otherwise lacked. His supporters, the Pelham, or as they afterwards were called, the Newcastle Whigs, were those who believed that society had been saved in 1688. The sanction for Whig supremacy was the Hanoverian settlement, which placed the exercise of the chief functions of

[1] Newcastle was perpetually besieged by applicants for ecclesiastical preferment and posts in the Treasury and Exchequer. A large part of his correspondence is filled with letters urging with every kind of fulsomeness the claims of the writers or their friends. The following (*Add. MSS.*, 32862, f. 48) is a good example of an ending:

'That your grace will permit me to subscribe myself with the inviolable duty and attachment to your grace

'My Lord Duke
'Your Grace's
'Most devoted
'Most obliged
'Most obedient
'and ever faithfull
'humble servant
'W. SHARPE.

'8th January, 1756.'

sovereignty in the hands of men whose ideas of good government were based on 'Revolution Principles.' The strength of the Whig position was to be found in the continued threat of a Stuart restoration; and while Scotch peers and Tory squires, branded by the common name of 'Jacobite,' skulked in political obscurity, the great Whig magnificoes calmly apportioned the spoils of office, and meted out the heritage of their German king. Associated by 'ties of blood and friendship,' 'honourable connections,' and 'mutual obligations,' they formed a solid phalanx of ability and culture which was the marvel of all Europe; while their ample fortune, derived alike from private purse and public perquisite, gave them the appearance of men to whom life was the exercise of a godlike power.

The main business of government, apart from finance, was in the hands of the two 'Principal Secretaries of State.' They controlled every act of war, every detail of foreign policy and domestic administration, and they alone had authority to give orders in the name of the Sovereign. The First Lord of the Admiralty, the 'Secretary at War' and all other heads of departments, except those of the Treasury and Exchequer, were bound to secure their written authority for all acts of more than office routine. They divided foreign affairs between them; one taking Germany, Russia, Scandinavia and Scotland, while the other took the colonies and the rest of the world. Apart from foreign affairs, their powers were equal and concurrent, each being able to act singly and with full authority. In practice this apparent anomaly was generally solved by mutual goodwill, and the dominance of the stronger character over the weaker.

Unfortunately, the most recent appointment had not been a success. Sir Thomas Robinson was a veteran diplomatist, but unused to political life, and as the other Secretary, Lord Holderness, and Newcastle himself were both peers, he suffered many rebuffs in trying single-handed to lead the Government in the House of Commons. Mr. Pitt and Mr. Fox were his chief persecutors. The future Earl of Chatham, who among his contemporaries was chiefly remarkable for his great eloquence and patriotism, was at this moment acquiring notoriety by his intense individualism and devotion to ' clean politics.' Being Paymaster-General, and therefore not in a position of great responsibility, he was able to indulge in several Parliamentary frolics at Robinson's expense. Henry Fox was ' Secretary at War ' and, like Pitt, was at little pains to disguise his contempt for Newcastle and all his arrangements, so that the great Whig system was already endangered by the mutinous conduct of two of its ablest men. The mainstay of the ministry was the Chancellor, Lord Hardwicke, who began life as a lawyer's clerk, and left a family which soon became distinguished in every branch of public life. The Georgian Whigs, despite their grandiose manners, were always ready to strengthen their ranks by discovering fresh talent, and never stagnated within the formidable barriers of a noblesse. Hardwicke's unrivalled legal knowledge and great general ability were always at

Newcastle's disposal, and he regularly spent many hours of the day and night returning methodical answers to the excited queries of the poor Duke.

Finance is the bugbear of all Governments, and in the eighteenth century there was added the problem of how to secure the large supplies of ready cash then necessary in order to conduct a war. This could only be done by a close understanding with the City merchants, and they in turn demanded substantial concessions. If they were to open subscription lists and raise loans, the great trading fleets must be protected. The goods they imported were not, as now, the necessaries of life, but rather luxury products from the East and West Indies, which could be re-exported to Europe and so produce that balance of bullion in our favour which the mercantile system seemed to demand. Consequently we could no more fight a successful war then, without protecting our imports of sugar and spices, than we could now without protecting our imports of raw materials.

The City magnates were well aware of the power they wielded, and though only sparsely represented in the House of Commons, they had many unofficial channels through which to make their wishes felt, and a petition to the House from the Common Council was received with as much respect as a message from the Throne. This meant that in every war a large part of the fleet had to be devoted to commerce protection before any thought could be given to offensive action against the enemy's main forces.

Newcastle was on good terms with the merchants,

but it was to Pitt that they opened their hearts, and knowing his zeal for their interests, entrusted him with exclusive information on colonial topics, derived from their unrivalled intelligence service. Unfortunately, like other commercial gentlemen, their judgment was sometimes at fault, and though generally stout-hearted in the day of trouble, they were liable to fits of sudden panic. At such times they would react fiercely, accuse the Government of fraud, and demand scapegoats. Actually these outbursts meant very little, for the princes of the East India House and the much chastened South Sea Company were the staunchest champions of Whig Protestantism, and had helped it ride out many heavy storms. But beyond the offices of the merchants were those of the brokers, and it was in their ranks and those of the public that the worst exhibitions of panic generally took place, with a resultant fall of the stocks. The 'public' consisted of all those whose occupations were either polite or lucrative, and could be conveniently divided into those who owned carriages and those who hired them. In the year 1755 the public possessed many distinguished persons ready to instruct and to please. Mr. Wesley, a St. Francis in breeches, was having a severe passage of arms with his 'Conference.' Dr. Johnson was publishing his dictionary, and Edward Gibbon was at Lausanne being snatched from Rome, into whose clutches he had strayed after being utterly bored with Oxford, where 'the deep potations of age excused the brisk intemperance of youth.' Joshua Reynolds had just returned from Italy, and (as the

Dictionary of National Biography quaintly expresses it) was about ' to put all rivals at a distance ' ; while David Garrick had recently provoked a riot at Covent Garden by introducing a troupe of French dancers. And besides, there were Government lotteries, and fashionable suicides, routs at Ranelagh, hangings, gambling and cockfights.

But publicity was in its infancy, for London, though important, was small, and when the public wanted news it went to the coffee-houses. Debates in Parliament could not be published, and such newspapers as there were, confined themselves chiefly to routine announcements. Consequently when the public wished to know more than gossip could tell of certain interesting topics, it had to be instructed by pamphlets. These were the work of paid hacks, rising authors and simple-minded fanatics. Recently there had been a tendency for great names to desert the trade, as Walpole and the Pelhams preferred to rely on permanent writers of small ability, seeing that there was now no public question of sufficient interest to attract the talents of a Swift or a Dryden. Moreover, Pope and Johnson had begun to encourage a new policy in authorship by going themselves to strike bargains with the publishers rather than by relying on the fickle patronage of some literary peer.

Nevertheless, it only required a really sensational affair, such as Byng's arrest and trial, to bring the best writers in with the worst, when Paul Whitehead of the Hell Fire Club, David Mallet the poet, Carteret Webb the antiquary, and even Johnson himself, did not disdain to cross swords with the baser hirelings. Their productions were chiefly read in London, but there was also a London which only received these genteel opinions second hand; it was the London of Hogarth's 'Gin Alley' and 'Beer Lane.' For beneath the descending orders of smug tradesmen and lean apprentices there was a degraded urban population, conveniently referred to as 'the mob,' and this unlovely proletariat was an ideal instrument for political intimidation, because if once thoroughly roused, its excesses were difficult to check. The police did not exist, there was no tradition of law or order, and the Government of England was in serious danger wherever ten thousand men could be gathered together with any pretence of a grievance. Luckily, disorders seldom reached a ferocious climax, and were generally confined to booing, carriage-pelting and burning in effigy; but occasionally the mob broke out badly, the magistrates were overawed, and the resulting saturnalia of lawlessness could only be quelled by troops, and was sure to involve lavish hangings and transportations.

Titus Oates, the Seven Bishops and Dr. Sacheverell were now only dim traditions; and the mob's most recent opportunity for a demonstration had been Walpole's Excise Bill. In later years John Wilkes and Lord George Gordon were to stage some masterpieces of disorder, but for the moment all was quiet, until suddenly the country found itself in the throes of an invasion scare and war with France.

CHAPTER IV

THE SEVEN YEARS' WAR

The fighting began on the Ohio, where the French were attempting to build a chain of forts from the Great Lakes to New Orleans, thus shutting our colonists into the area along the coast. 'Cavalier liberties' had been taken, and a certain George Washington had been captured in trying to hold the French up. All the territory where fighting had occurred was still *sub judice,* and for a year both Governments confined themselves to reinforcing their colonists with ships and regular troops. To our own Ministers there seemed very good reasons for isolating the approaching war as much as possible, and making it naval and colonial rather than military and European.

Our cardinal principle ever since the fifteenth century had been to prevent the Rhine delta falling into the hands of any great power. In recent years the Triple Alliance of England, Austria and the Dutch had been formed for this purpose against the continual aggressions of France. But the Dutch were now so weak as to be hardly capable of sustaining a land war, and it was doubtful if they could even hold the barrier fortresses against a sudden *coup de main.* Austria too, whom we had learnt to look on as the great military counterpoise to France, was showing signs of undergoing a complete 'diplomatic revolution,' and the 'monstrous propositions of Count Kaunitz' for a French alliance were gaining ready acceptance at Vienna and Versailles. It certainly looked like the collapse of the 'good and old system' by which England had fought every war since the Peace of Nimwegen.

The possible defection of our chief allies was bad enough, but it could hardly have appeared so disquieting to the Ministry, if we had not been so deeply committed to the defence of Hanover. Her geographical position and her *rôle* in previous history gave her a position at once symbolic and sentimental, and no Minister of the first two Georges ever failed to recognise the intimate connection between English and Hanoverian interests. She had been a member of the Grand Alliance and was the birthplace of the Whig's Protestant substitute for the Francophile Stuarts. But it was no mere tenderness for the King's personal property which gave our Government such anxiety, but rather a clear perception of the importance of maintaining a strong north German opposition to France, in consequence of the gradual decline of Austria and the Dutch. Of course, this apparent illogical attachment to continental interests provided an excellent handle to any group of skilful opponents, who, by calling themselves 'patriots,' could upbraid the Ministers for betraying true British interests. The young men who continually attempted to pierce the solid defences of Sir Robert Walpole, and obtain some share of the political spoils, were soon able to point to a further argument. There had long been an idea amongst merchants and politicians that the interests of England would be better served by complete detachment from European politics, and a vigorous concentration on colonial and maritime expansion. This theory, which found definite expression in the War of the Spanish Succession, was now at the height of its popularity and enabled its champions to draw a very definite though quite irrational distinction between a war which would assist British trade, and a war which would merely send a few thousand more troops and a few thousand more pounds to be lost in the cockpit of Europe.

Intentionally, in many cases, these critics refused to recognise that operations of war must be considered as a whole, and that unless a method were found of draining French resources in Europe, it would be impossible to rival her beyond the seas. With the War of the Austrian Succession it became increasingly clear that without some diplomatic and strategic centre on the Continent, England could never hope to carry out her colonial projects, since she would be compelled at the end of each war to barter her choicest overseas conquests in order to regain the territory lost in defence of her cause by allies on the Continent, whose military assistance was indispensable.

At the Peace of Aix-la-Chapelle, France was able to recover Louisburg and Cape Breton Island in return for surrendering her grasp on the Netherlands, without which England could not feel secure, thus retrieving the key to the St. Lawrence, and frustrating one of the main English objectives of the war. With such considerations in their minds, English Ministers might well look to Hanover with something more than royal sentiments, realising that there, ready to hand, was a lever for the overturning of French power.

Factious criticism, if it meant anything at all, aimed at preventing continental operations from becoming the major partner in combined strategy, and so allowing the maritime objective to become merely a containing diversion. Pitt had long been the great accuser of the partisans of Hanover, and it was perhaps as well that there was at least one man of irreproachable character to give the lead to maritime interests, and point the way to the true goal, otherwise sheer distance might have tempted the public to forget it altogether.

Meanwhile, in America and the Atlantic the French had been remarkably successful. All the squadrons protecting their transports had come and gone just as they liked, and Boscawen's unfortunate capture of the *Alcide* and *Lys* had only made matters worse. Public opinion talked gaily of first blood, but the Ministers knew better, and Newcastle was in despair. Boscawen, without realising it, had done 'either too little or too much'; too little to prevent the French reinforcing their colonists, and too much towards provoking a full dress European war. The King was abroad, negotiating for the protection of Hanover, and a Council of Regency exercised the full powers of 'the King in Council.' By the end of June it was considering whether or not to let Sir Edward Hawke take the Western Squadron to sea.

If this were done, what instructions should Hawke be given? The question was a critical one, as in it there lay all the difference between a precautionary measure and a war in European waters.

The Duke of Cumberland[1] and Henry Fox were in favour of vigorous measures against French warships and trade, while Lord Granville was absolutely against meddling with trade—he called it 'vexing your neighbours for a little muck,' and Newcastle struggled to find a formula that would satisfy all. 'I own I tremble,' he writes to Hardwicke, 'when I reflect we shall begin a war in Europe without one single ally . . . suppose they should in revenge take the King prisoner!' However, Boscawen's news settled the question, and on 18th July Hawke sailed with nineteen of the line, and instructions to take any French ships of the line, to prevent the junction of the Mediterranean and Atlantic squadrons, and de la Motte's ships returning from America. The result was unlucky, for Hawke was driven into Plymouth by a north-west gale at the end of September.

On land our position was far worse; Braddock was defeated and killed, and the fourfold attack on French Canada had failed everywhere but at Beauséjour. There was a rapid hunt for scapegoats, but only two could be found. It was useless to attack the awe-inspiring Cumberland, so a shower of abuse

[1] Cumberland was Commander-in-Chief of the Army at the moment, and his good sense and ability were always recognised. 'It is no disparagement of other members of the Royal Family to say that he was the ablest man which it has produced during the two centuries of its reign in England' (Fortescue's *History of the British Army*, Vol. II., p. 576).

was rained on his unfortunate minion Braddock, who, despite his obstinacy and uncouthness, had acted with moderate efficiency and great courage. Hawke, the other victim, being alive and in favour with the King, replied to the Admiralty in kind. "I . . . am extremely sorry to find," he wrote,[1] "that their lordships think any of my squadron could have stayed out any longer. I hope they will be of another opinion when they reflect that most of the men had been pressed, after long voyages, cooped up in tenders and ships at Spithead for many months, and the water in general long kept in new casks, which occasioned great sickness—besides the number of French prisoners, and the men required to navigate them into port. . . . Upon the whole, I am conscious of having used my utmost endeavours to answer the end of my being sent out, and of having never once lost sight of the principal object of my course. If their lordships should be of another opinion, I am ready and willing to resign my command to anyone else in whose abilities they have more confidence." The Board at once apologised.

All this time war was undeclared and both sides were keeping up a pretence of negotiations, the French accusing us of naval piracy, while we accused them of unprovoked attacks in America. Although our naval operations had so far been a failure, there was no reason why we should not use the few remaining weeks of tolerable weather to damage French trade as much as possible, and so the Western Squadron was again ordered to sea, with the sole

[1] Spithead, 1st October; Ad. In Letters.

object of commerce destruction, and this time under the command of John Byng. Rear-Admiral Temple West was appointed as his second-in-command, having served in the same capacity under Hawke. He was nine years junior to Byng, and, although he had been temporarily suspended after the battle of Toulon, he had earned high praise at the first battle of Finisterre as Sir Peter Warren's flag captain, and had recently been promoted to rear-admiral.

Byng hoisted his flag in the *Ramillies* (90), and West in the *Buckingham* (68), and they put to sea on 14th August, and acted with such energy that by 21st November, when they returned, three hundred French merchantmen had been captured. Moreover their presence off Brest and in the Bay not only endangered all the French incoming Atlantic trade, but protected our own as it drew towards the focal area between Cape Clear and Ushant. They also captured the *Esperance*, a seventy-four, armed *en flûte*, but she was much damaged and the weather was so bad that they had to burn her. Instead of selling the three hundred prizes and their cargoes outright, they were detained in port as pledges which might be returned if the French were willing to remain at peace. Unfortunately, the cargoes consisted in many cases of fish and other perishable goods, so that although 'the Ministry acted with great delicacy in relation to them,' their eventual sale realised a far smaller sum than their value at the time of capture.

The King had come home on 15th September, having concluded two treaties, one with the Czarina of Russia, and the other with the Landgrave of Hesse. The first secured the protection of Hanover against attack by Prussia or any other power, and the second arranged for 8,000 Hessians to serve anywhere in the British dominions for a sum of £300,000 a year. The treaties produced a revolt in the Cabinet. The Leicester House party saw a chance to embarrass Newcastle, Legge refused to sign the warrants for the Hessians, Pitt was only to be reconciled by additional power, and Fox by additional profit. Clearly it was a time to enforce discipline even at the expense of buying the support of the principal malcontents. Pitt, on being approached, demanded 'an office of advice as well as execution,' and remained unconvinced that the Russian treaty was the crowning triumph of four years of strenuous negotiations. Finally, Newcastle took courage and made a great purge. Pitt and Legge were dismissed, and Sir Thomas Robinson returned to the safe and lucrative pastures of the Wardrobe. Fox was made Secretary of State, and given dictator's powers so far as leadership of the House was concerned. Lord Barrington quitted the Wardrobe and relieved Fox at the War Office, and Lord Lyttelton deserted the 'Cousinhood' to receive the Exchequer.

Although Horace Walpole and the wits of the day could wring many good jokes out of these political disturbances, public business was carried on with commendable zeal, and to the French we appeared united and resolute. Parliament voted a million 'upon account, to enable His Majesty to concert and take all such measures as may be necessary to disappoint or defeat the designs of his enemies,' and fifty thousand seamen in place of the existing twelve.

At Versailles, Louis XV ruled without the inconvenience of a Parliament, but his Ministers, being independent of party ties and majorities, intrigued against each other, and the requirements of Madame de Pompadour exceeded the English Civil List. Rouillé, who had lately been succeeded at the Admiralty by Machault, was now Foreign Minister, and judged it the right moment to issue a stern memorial to England. He was bent on branding us as the aggressors and so ruining our last chance of getting the Dutch to fight under the terms of the Triple Alliance. Spain too was if anything pro-English at the moment, and there were great hopes of using some 'incident' to expose our well-known perfidy and bring about a Franco-Spanish dynastic 'family compact.' Hence these diplomatic quadrilles, often misunderstood by historians, and impatiently described as 'drift.' Rouillé boldly accused us of piracy; 'the attack and capture in July last, of two of the King's ships in open seas, and without a declaration of war, was a public insult to His Majesty's flag.' The King had waited to see if England would disavow this action, and likewise the acts of piracy on Frencn commerce, 'but seeing that the King of England, instead of punishing the robberies committed by the English navy, on the contrary encourages them . . . His Majesty would fall short of what he owes to his own glory

. . . if he deferred any longer demanding a signal reparation for the outrage done to the French flag.' He then demanded restitution of all ships of war or commerce, including their personnel and cargoes, adding that if such demand were complied with, the French were willing to negotiate about America, but that an unsatisfactory reply would be regarded 'as the most authentic declaration of war . . . to disturb the peace of Europe.'

Unfortunately, the launching of the ultimatum was slightly premature. Frederick the Great, alarmed at the text of the Russian treaty, had quickly decided to guarantee the neutrality of Hanover himself, and on 16th January, 1756, the Convention of Westminster clinched the bargain with a Prussian subsidy. This last-minute change of front was artfully concealed from the French, while the English Government hardly realised that they would now have to back Prussia in a great war against Maria Theresa.

The French were completely deceived by Frederick, and at the same time they learnt that our Government had sold the captured ships and cargoes, bad fish and all. So this was the answer to their ultimatum. A few days later, Fox wrote 'that His Majesty continues desirous of preserving the public tranquillity,' and took the precaution to circulate to all European Courts 'a strong and masterly representation' showing the 'differences' between the two nations. English perfidy had again succeeded.

One of those numerous schemes for the invasion of England was already in the air, and realising that their army could not for the moment be used against Hanover, the French determined to make the scheme a reality. It was not to be a crude attempt to conquer all England, after the Spanish Armada type, but rather a sudden stroke at London, our 'nerve centre,' quite modern in conception, and aimed at destroying our credit system and *morale*, creating a panic, and so preventing the Government sending reinforcements to America.[1]

By the end of January, Marshal Belleisle was appointed Commander-in-Chief from Dunkirk to Bayonne, and was busy collecting troops and transports all along the north coast. His general idea seems to have been a direct invasion of England across the Channel, covered by the main fleet from Brest and Rochefort, and assisted by feints at attacking Scotland and Ireland, the whole to be combined with an elaborate diversion against Halifax[2] and the island of Minorca. The scheme certainly had its attractions, and being directed from interior lines, was capable of confusing our strategy and bringing about a dispersal of our forces. But far stronger than these solid reasons for its adoption was the overwhelming desire to strike us some sudden and crippling blow, which should make up for our recent diplomatic success.[3] 'The moderation of the French King is at an end,' writes our intelligencer, 'and is followed by all the passion and resentment that disappointment can inspire.

[1] No. 8 C, rcd. 21st Jan. *Add. MSS.* 31959, f. 120 (*a*). The earliest hint of the scheme which reached England was received on 27th Aug., 1755. Ad. Intell. No. 2*c*.

[2] No. 19, rcd. 21st Jan., 1756. *Add. MSS.* 31959, f. 119 (*b*).

[3] No. 10, rcd. 7th Feb. *Add. MSS.* 31959, f. 124 (*a*) and (*b*).

. . . All Paris talks of an invasion that is to be headed by the Young Pretender.'[1]

The British defence against these preparations was based on the employment of a strong Western Squadron. Realising that the troops collected on the north coast would be unable to make good a landing from their small trading-vessels and flat-bottomed boats without the aid of a powerful battle squadron, the English Government rightly determined that the most profitable disposition for the main fleet would be off the south-west coast of England. From there the ships of the line lying in Brest and Rochefort could be watched by cruisers, and not only be prevented from entering the Channel, but also from sending assistance to America. Moreover, the protection which such a squadron afforded to British trade must be considerable, since, as the Ministry rightly claimed in defence of its conduct, 'all our trade, except that to the northward and the coasters, comes in between Cape Clear and Ushant, a station where the French cruisers and privateers might do infinite mischief if they were suffered to go out or to return in safety.' 'The experience of the last war clearly shows the importance of a western squadron, and all our great successes at sea arose entirely from it.'[2] Conversely, the occupation of one of the chief focal areas of our own trade also

[1] No. 8 C, rcd. 21st Jan. *Add. MSS.* 31959, f. 119 (*b*).

[2] Paper No. 12 in papers relating to the loss of Minorca ; see also *Add. MSS.* 35895, ff. 325–8 and 31959, f. 221. Admiral Vernon, in his pamphlet, *Some Seasonable Advice from an Honest Sailor* (London, 1746), wrote : 'It was always my opinion that a strong squadron kept at sea to the Westward, and a squadron of smaller ships in the North Seas, were the only secure Guardians to these His Majesty's Kingdoms against Invasions.'

meant a very serious menace to that of the French, which according to the Government, 'runs such risks of being intercepted by our western cruisers that the French insurance is from 25 to 30 per cent. going out and from 40 to 45 per cent. coming home, a burthen which no trade can bear, and which must destroy it.'

It was quickly realised, and had been for long known, that to maintain a squadron at sea in fighting trim it is necessary to have many extra ships to take the place of those that must come in to clean and refit, in order that a force superior to anything that the enemy can possibly send out may always be ready for action. 'Cruising in all weathers and often with tempestuous and contrary winds wears out the ships, the masts and the rigging, and ruins the health and costs lives of seamen. . . . Less than thirty of the line completed and manned will not keep twenty constantly at sea, even in the summer.'[1] This statement is an exact counterpart of the difficulties experienced by our Admiralty in keeping the Grand Fleet up to strength for cruising work,[2] while

[1] See also the Barham Papers, Vol. I., p. 304 (N.R.S., Vol. XXX., 11): 'Let us keep a stout squadron to the westward to attend the motions of the enemy.' Kempenfeldt to Middleton, 16th November, 1779.

[2] The following table shows the number of ships of the line employed on various duties from October 1755 to March 1756:

Station	*Oct.*	*Nov.*	*Dec.*	*Jan.*	*Feb.*	*Mar.*
East Indies	4	4	4	4	4	4
Boscawen (Halifax)	15	15	Arrived Spithead 14th Nov.			
Plantations	9	9	11	11	12	13
Mediterranean	1	1	3	3	3	3
Cruising and Convoys ..	24	31	14	11	22	20
In home ports	24	22	51	54	44	47*
Total	77	82	83	83	85	87

See Winston Churchill's *The World Crisis*, Vol. I., chap. ix.; Lord Jellicoe's *The Grand Fleet*, pp. 31 and 32; *Loss of Minorca*, Introduction pp. xxxi. and xxxiv.

*Including the *Princess Royal*.

the first remark means, in modern English, that we had to be prepared to meet the enemy at his 'selected' moment when at our 'average' moment.

It is interesting to see the number of ships which the Ministers thought necessary for such duty: 'Fourteen for a western squadron,' they say, 'would call for eighteen or nineteen appropriated to that service: ten for service in the Downs and Channel and to be ready upon any alarm would require twelve or thirteen, together from thirty to thirty-two. Besides the two off Cape Clear, two off Cape Finisterre and two in the fairway into the Channel would be necessary for covering the frigates and sloops, and protecting trade in their principal routes from depredations; and those six cruisers could not constantly be kept up with less than eight sail.'[1]

The Ministry rightly warned its critics against imagining that the effective and paper state of a fleet were the same. 'In times when the fleet is most effective a large proportion of it will always appear ready for service without being so: as, for example, all ships lately commissioned, all ships returned from long cruises, in dock, or waiting to go there, all ships whose men are sick or on shore absent with leave, all ships from which men have been taken and sent to others going on immediate service, all ships in want of provisions or stores—from a deficiency of which the French squadrons are often useless for months together—ships in this state

[1] Admiral Richmond, in his introduction to the papers, explains that 'cruisers' denotes ships of the line on 'cruising service,' *i.e.* the cruisers were in no sense frigates (No. 12 of the papers relating to the loss of Minorca).

may parade at Plymouth or Spithead, their true state being known to the Government only; they may create terror and respect abroad, they may produce confidence or blame at home, but they cannot sail or fight till they are what is called by the seamen "completely fitted for sea."'

These remarks are even now a very seasonable warning to temper sanguine hopes or painful disillusionment; but the distinctive rhythm of the prose and the subtlety of the phrasing, especially of the last sentence, indicate that the authorship of the composition is different from that of the usual 'official communications.'

Although it was clear that the French meant business, and though every day the intelligencers noted that the preparations at all the ports were being urged forward with 'double diligence,' the actual method by which the troops were to get across the Channel was still a matter of doubt. This was only natural, for it was quite obvious that no army could hope to slip across without a very severe mauling from our flotilla and privateers, stiffened by the squadron in the Downs. Consequently a battle fleet would have to be brought up into the narrow seas, to clear a path for the transports. This fleet would have to sail from the western ports, and either defeat our Western Squadron or else evade it. Neither course was at all easy, since Brest and Rochefort were now well watched, and the fleet capable of meeting us in action with any likelihood of success could hardly be said to exist.

The true state of the French marine was revealed

on 3rd February, when complete details arrived, showing eleven of the line at Brest and six at Rochefort. Such squadrons would be no match for our Western Squadron and the ships in the Downs, even if 'completely fitted for sea' and assisted by their thirty-seven frigates.[1] Nevertheless, the land preparation continued, flat-bottomed boats and trains of artillery appeared in great numbers, an order was issued to seize all British ships, and the Young Pretender was to lead the invasion.

'Everything now conspires,' wrote our intelligencer, 'to make it believed that an invasion would be attempted . . . as it is the only way left to France if the news of the Treaty at London between England and the King of Prussia proves true in all points.'[2] Of course, the expeditionary force would be wiped out, but even then the threat of invasion would 'alarm the nation, distress our credit, and prevent our transports being sent abroad.'[3]

Six hundred transports would convey the army, and smugglers of Kent, Sussex, and Hampshire were to act as pilots, while the Brest fleet was to be strengthened by twelve of the line and twelve frigates.

One hundred and eighteen battalions of infantry and twenty-eight squadrons of cavalry were encamped on the north-east coast,[4] and thirty thousand

[1] No. 31, Ad. 20th Jan., rcd. 3rd Feb. *Add. MSS.* 31959, ff. 122 (*b*), 123 (*a*). No. B 3, No. 13, Ad. 20th Jan., rcd. 3rd Feb. *Add. MSS.* 31959, f. 110 (*a*) and (*b*).

[2] No. 10 C, rcd. 7th Feb. *Add. MSS.* 31959, f. 124 (*a*) and (*b*).

[3] No. 8 C, rcd. 21st Jan. *Add. MSS.* 31959, f. 120 (*a*).

[4] No. B 3, rcd. 3rd Jan. *Add. MSS.* 31959, f. 118 (*b*).

troops were said to be in Provence waiting to embark for Minorca or America.[1] Should the French reach England they would only be opposed by 13,000 foot and 4,000 dragoons, and London's only defence was an additional four battalions of Foot Guards and one regiment of Horse Guards. It was true that Newcastle was praying for the arrival of the Hessians, and that even Fox was writing, 'At present if we have secur'd the metropolis it is all,'[2] but to those who understood the practical difficulties confronting the French the danger did not seem so serious. None understood these difficulties better than Marshal Belleisle. As time went on and it became necessary to translate the 'general idea' into definite 'operation orders,' the cross-Channel invasion was at last seen to be impossible. 'Few of the officers and engineers of experience that are nominated to be of the expedition like it,' wrote our intelligencer, 'but, for encouragement to them and the soldiers, it is given out by the Ministry that by the precautions taken, they are sure of landing safe.'[3] This, however, was small comfort, and the great army, assembled at so much expense, unable to carry out the practical operation of getting across the Channel, continued to eat up the land in a state of chilled expectancy.

Days went by, and our spies and intelligencers continued to report that fresh troops were arriving on the north coast. There were signs of panic in England, especially in the south-eastern counties,

[1] *Add. MSS.* 35535, f. 426; *Add. MSS.* 31959, f. 125 (*b*).
[2] 31st Jan.
[3] No. 11 C, rcd. 24th Feb.

Pitt doing his utmost to spread the alarm in order to discredit the Government. But in London the possibility of a French landing was already out of date as a method of quizzing the ladies, and it was generally agreed that we were perfectly safe. The French thought so too, and quickly arranged to keep up the supposed invasion scheme simply as a bluff and make their serious effort against Minorca.

As the centre of interest changed from the Channel ports to Toulon, our Government was able to follow every new move in the Mediterranean situation from the excellent series of advices from our naval officers and consuls, which, however, took anything from fifteen to twenty-five days to reach London. Commodore George Edgecumbe,[1] a very efficient officer and a man with considerable social influence, was in command of our small Mediterranean squadron, consisting of :

Princess Louisa	60	guns
Portland	50	,,
Deptford	50	,,
Chesterfield	40	,,
Dolphin	22	,,
Phœnix	22	,,
Experiment	22	,,
Fortune (sloop)	14	,,

The *Phœnix* was commanded by Augustus John Hervey, who later became the third Lord Bristol.

[1] The Hon. George Edgecumbe, son of the first Baron Edgecumbe, born 1721, died 1795; Rear-Admiral of the Blue, 1762; Admiral of the White, 1782; M.P. for Fowey, 1747–61; Lord-Lieutenant of Cornwall, 1761; succeeded to the barony of Edgecumbe, 1761; created Viscount Mount-Edgecumbe, 1781 and Earl of Mount-Edgecumbe, 1789; Vice-Treasurer of Ireland, 1771–3 and 1784–95; Captain of the Band of Gentlemen Pensioners, 1773-82.

At the age of twenty he had been secretly married to Elizabeth Chudleigh, the most notorious young lady of fashion at the Court of George II; but they had soon after separated, though lawsuits concerning their mutual relations continued to intrigue the polite world until 1775. The Herveys were famous for their ability and caprices, and were wittily said to form a third order of humans apart from ordinary 'men and women.' Augustus John was a good example of the family; he was the son of John Hervey, the gifted satirical memoir writer, and brother of Frederick Augustus, the 'Earl Bishop.' He had already gained distinction in the service, both as a fighter and minor diplomatist, and had been promoted to post rank in 1747. He stares out of Reynolds' canvas, a handsome, well-nourished cynic, with his left hand on a cannon and his right hand on his hip, truculently thrusting his unsheathed sword slantwise into the air. Later his distinguished service in the West Indies and under Hawke, his famous conversation with Casanova, and his prominence as an admiral, politician and administrator, combined to make him one of the most celebrated characters of the age.

Our consuls at Cartagena, Nice, Leghorn and Genoa also collected a mass of information about the Mediterranean, which was supplemented by comments from our Ministers and envoys at Madrid, Turin, Berne and the Hague.

Quite apart from the protection of Minorca and Gibraltar, Edgecumbe's tiny squadron was expected to carry out duties which would easily have absorbed

AUGUSTUS JOHN HERVEY
Afterwards third Earl of Bristol
From the picture after Sir J. Reynolds in the National Portrait Gallery

[*p.* 40

the entire strength of a considerable fleet. Although war had not been declared, the stage for it was already set, and we required to protect our overseas trade to the utmost in order to provide for the heavy strain on our finances which was bound to follow. Newfoundland, the American colonies, and even Yarmouth and Falmouth, had a very flourishing fish trade with Spain, Sardinia, Naples, Genoa and Venice, while English and colonial ships held much of the carrying trade between Tuscany and the French West Indies. Even in peace-time it required considerable address and some display of force to protect these ships from the corsairs of the Barbary States. Now, with a war imminent, Edgecumbe found himself anxiously watching for any signs of activity in the great naval harbour of Toulon, from where, if unopposed, the French might destroy our Mediterranean trade, sail out and unite with the Brest fleet, or send strong reinforcements to Canada.

These were the commitments of protection only; offensive strategy demanded something further: the cutting off of French trade with Turkey and also of the grain ships sailing to Marseilles from Italy and Sicily. In 1747 our Mediterranean fleet had numbered twenty-eight ships of forty guns and upwards, and at the end of the war had been reduced to a squadron under Forbes of one sixty, two fifties, two forties, a twenty and an eight-gun barco longo. Such a dangerous reduction might be excused in the exhaustion of the immediate first war period, but in 1756, with the French eager to begin, and after more than a year of bickerings, Edgecumbe only commanded one sixty, two fifties, one forty, three twenty-twos and a sloop.

At Toulon was concentrated the whole French Mediterranean fleet, most of the ships being laid up at the moment but capable of being fitted for sea at short notice. Throughout the wars of the Spanish and Austrian Successions all our great offensive operations had been aimed at blockading or capturing this port, from which the French could send troops to any part of the Mediterranean or the Near East. Nor was this policy abandoned after the Seven Years' War, and whenever we had enough ships, Toulon continued in importance as an objective down to the end of the Napoleonic Wars, and was actually captured and held by Hood in 1793.

Naturally, our Mediterranean intelligencers spent most of their time in trying to find out what preparations were going on inside the naval harbour. The fitting out of ships had started as early as June 1755,[1] but the French Government seemed anxious to appear as inoffensive as possible in the Mediterranean until the fishing-fleets had returned for the winter, when active preparations would be made 'for these measures which the dignity of the Crown of France will require.'[2] Consul Banks was the first to state that Minorca was included as an objective in the general offensive scheme, and that a hundred battalions were said to be marching to Marseilles.[3] Although the French worked hard all through the winter, they found it very difficult to obtain

[1] No. 3 B 2, rcd. 5th June, 1755. [2] No. 180 P., rcd. 7th Aug.
[3] No. 53 P., Banks, Cartagena, 27th Aug., rcd. 27th Sept., 1755.

guns and stores, and also cash for the dockyard workmen, whose pay was as much as a year in arrears.

Captain James Douglas, who had just come out in the *Bedford* with a convoy and was a few months senior to Edgecumbe, thought the situation serious enough to order him to concentrate his squadron at Port Mahon.[1] By the end of the year our Government knew for certain that twelve of the line were being fitted out, that M. de la Galissonnière was named commander-in-chief, and that Minorca was openly talked of as the first French objective. Clearly the French intended to send their Mediterranean fleet somewhere, and even if Minorca were only mentioned as a blind, it was just as important to prevent such a force doing damage in one place as in another. But the Government showed no wish to strengthen Edgecumbe's squadron, and for a time were rewarded for their cautiousness by news of great delay at Toulon. 'People are quite tired to hear so long that the five frigates[2] are ready to sail, whilst the English go on in the old way,' wrote Mr. Villettes,[3] and added that a bold attempt to buy 12,000 English cannon under a Portuguese name had been stopped after a partial success. 'There is no money circulating' (at Toulon), wrote Lord Bristol from Turin;[4] 'most of the manufactures in the southern provinces of France are at a stand, for no ships venture out of their ports; their trade

[1] No. 17, Ad. 15th Oct., rcd. 5th Nov. Douglas returned to England in Jan. 1786. Townsend Papers in the author's possession.

[2] These were said to be ready fitted, and there was great doubt as to their destination.

[3] Our Minister to the Swiss.

[4] 31st Jan., rcd. 24th, No. 92 P.

is declining, the merchants are breaking, as they have no vent for their goods which are impairing in their ships.' And all this internal distress was caused by the French having no ships of war actually at sea, and French trade being at the mercy of Edgecumbe's tiny squadron waiting in Mahon harbour for the French to make the first move. Such was the moral effect produced by eight ships 'in being.'

The French Government was no happier about the Toulon venture than the men on the spot, for a fierce internal rivalry existed amongst Louis XV's Ministers, and Cardinal Bernis, the Duc de Choiseul and Madame de Pompadour were trying their utmost to remove Rouillé from the Foreign Office. They eventually triumphed, and Bernis was installed, 'but meanwhile,' says Shelburne, 'the cabals ran so high against him at Court that the only struggle there was how to give the most certain intelligence to England of the design against Minorca, on purpose that it might fail, which carried them so far that he told me he was at last persuaded that we must believe that it was given out so publicly on purpose to deceive.'[1]

If Bernis really believed this in 1756, he was right in his interpretation. When our Government was solemnly told 'that the orders and counter orders, which have been given from time to time about the Toulon fleet, have been with a view to make the necessary preparations to carry the plan into execution with the greater secrecy,'[2] they naturally

[1] Lord Fitzmaurice: *Life of Shelburne*, Vol. I., p. 22.
[2] B 2 P, 17th Jan., rcd. 4th Feb.

continued to treat the whole business as an elaborate piece of strategic and diplomatic camouflage. But despite the fact that Bernis could write that at the time 'treachery and incompetence were the orders of the day,' and Villettes that 'they change their opinion so often it is impossible to fix upon anything,'[1] the French were really in earnest. General Blakeney had called the naval officers to a council of war and was making active preparations for the defence of Minorca, and Sir Benjamin Keene, from Madrid, wrote that an attack on Minorca seemed certain and that he was in correspondence with Blakeney, Edgecumbe and General Fowke at Gibraltar. The Duc de Richelieu had arrived at Toulon and was said to be in command of a large army; and Galissonnière, with twelve of the line and numerous transports, was ready to sail.

With these last advices before them, the Government could neglect Toulon no longer, and on 9th March the Secret Committee of the Council 'were humbly of opinion that as strong a squadron as can be spared from hence should be got ready to send into the Mediterranean.' From the English standpoint the situation was confused by the intrusion of an element of farce.

Naturally, the Government treated the northern invasion scheme seriously, and gave little credence to the talk about Minorca when it was first mentioned. Later, when the preparations at Brest and Le Havre seemed about to mature, they gave less credence than before to a series of rumours

[1] No. 210 P, 4th Feb., rcd. 15th Feb.

which appeared to be actuated by the frantic endeavours to call attention to themselves, though called by the proud title of 'ruses to defeat the enemy.'

In a sense, therefore, the thwarted cabals in the French Court failed; for by talking so openly of Minorca at a moment when the northern invasion appeared imminent, they appeared to be advertising it as a blind.

After the disaster, the Government was blamed for not sending ships to Minorca sooner. We can hardly censure them on those grounds. The attack on Minorca tied 15,000 troops to a barren island and kept them there at a great risk and at a great loss for many weeks. If the Government is to be censured, it must be for not realising more quickly the supreme importance of disputing the passage of the French fleet from Toulon, whatever its destination. Further, it was much to blame for leaving Minorca so weakly garrisoned, and afterwards for asserting that St. Philip's Castle, its only fortress, was an adequate protection for the naval base of Port Mahon, which could be completely destroyed by a land attack, without the attacker ever having to come within range of the castle's guns.

These are legitimate criticisms of the Government's policy, because the facts relating to them are quite clear. The blockade or capture of Toulon had been our leading strategic plan or ambition in the Mediterranean ever since the opening of the War of the Spanish Succession, and the naval base at Minorca existed for that end. The weakness of the garrison is obvious from the number of senior officers on leave in England when war had been imminent for more than a year, and the value of the guns in St. Philip's Castle for covering the naval base can be tested by looking at a map.

To draw any further conclusions from this curious story would be unwise. There is, however, a tendency, especially amongst Naval Officers, to try to make operations in past wars illustrate one or other of the 'principles of war.' Conclusions of this kind are very valuable if based on an accurate study of the data available, as they separate the wood from the trees and give coherence and purpose to what before was merely a narrative of facts. The attempt, however, to make a whole series of incidents illustrate a single principle of war is very difficult, as the least flaw in the chain of facts completely demolishes an arbitrary interpretation which attempts to go far beyond the limits of ordinary historical criticism.

CHAPTER V

ADMIRAL BYNG SETS SAIL

AFTER Byng and West had brought the western squadron home in the previous November, the ships were laid up for the winter. In February 1756 they were taken to sea by Osborne, and in March by Hawke, and on 11th March, Byng was ordered to go to Portsmouth and fit out the squadron for the Mediterranean, with West again as his second-in-command.[1]

The squadron was to consist of ten of the line, without any frigates, store or hospital ships, it being judged that when he had joined Edgecumbe he would be just superior to the French. The ships and their commanders were as follows:

	guns	
Ramillies	90	Captain Arthur Gardiner
Culloden	74	Captain Henry Ward
Buckingham	68	Captain Michael Everitt
Lancaster	66	Captain John Amherst
Intrepid	64	Captain James Young
Revenge	64	Captain Frederick Cornwall
Captain	64	Captain Charles Catford
Trident	64	Captain Philip Durell
Kingston	60	Captain William Parry
Defiance	60	Captain Thomas Andrews

[1] A copy of this order is in *Add. MSS.* 35895, f. 110.

Before leaving London, Byng received his last promotion and was made Admiral of the Blue, so that he was now ninth of the list of living flag officers, and next to Anson himself. But of these, Anson alone was capable of going to sea; while Rowley, who was also at the Admiralty, and Isaac Townshend, the governor of Greenwich Hospital, were the only others holding any official appointment. Hawke, his formidable rival, was only one year his junior, and was four below him on the list, so that at the age of fifty-two Byng might look forward to exercising the highest command in the service in the greatest naval war in which we had yet been engaged. Moreover, his appointment to the Mediterranean command seemed singularly appropriate, both on account of his great experience there and the family tradition.

Comparisons of opportunities in naval warfare are notoriously difficult, but a casual examination of the strength and circumstance of the forces opposed at the two dates will show that a repetition of Torrington's feat was extremely unlikely. In 1718 the father had defeated a weak and ill-fed Spanish fleet by an overwhelming superiority in material and *morale*; in 1756 the son was to find himself equally matched in ships and men, and opposed by a commander whose ability was the talk of two continents.

Byng reached Portsmouth on 20th March, and hoisted his flag next morning in the *Ramillies*. His ten ships were all there except the *Intrepid*, which was still at the Nore, and there were twenty-two ships besides in the harbour, mostly of the line.[1] None of his own squadron was properly manned, and naturally he expected to be able to complete his crews from all the other ships. Consequently he was very surprised to find Admiralty orders waiting him, saying that on no account were men to be taken from the *Torbay, Essex, Nassau, Prince Frederick, Colchester* or *Greyhound*, as these ships were needed for 'the most pressing service,' and in addition he was to see to the completion of the *Stirling Castle's* crew before any of his own ships.[2]

As the Government had delayed sending any ships to the Mediterranean till the last minute, this seemed very strange, especially as the Admiralty enclosed him a letter from Lord Bristol saying that the French were about to sail from Toulon, and urged him to show the 'utmost diligence' in fitting out.

Byng replied by sending a full 'state' of the squadron, showing that it was seven hundred short of its complement, and at the same time asking to be allowed a frigate to repeat signals.[3]

Next day he received details of two drafts of

[1] *Prince* (90)
Prince George (80)
Invincible (74)
Torbay (74)
Monmouth (64)
Yarmouth (64)
Royal Anne (90)
Duke (90)
Barfleur (80)
Swiftsure (68)
Bedford (64)
Elizabeth (64)
Colchester (50)
Essex (64)
Bristol (50)
Prince Frederick (64)
Firebrand (fireship)
Romney (40)
Greyhound (20)
Gibraltar (20)
Nightingale (20)
Unicorn (20)
Anson (60), arrived 25th March
Nassau (64), arrived 30th March
Princess Augusta (60), arrived 30th March

[2] Ad. Out Letters.

[3] Ad. In Letters.

soldiers to sail with the fleet. One consisted of most of the absent officers of the Minorca garrison and including Maj.-Gen. Stuart and Cols. Cornwallis and Lord Effingham. The other was only a small draft for Gibraltar.[1]

On the 24th, Byng was astonished to hear that the Admiralty wished the *Torbay, Essex, Antelope,* and the frigates *Gibraltar* and *Unicorn,* to be sent to sea at once under Captain Keppel. A French convoy of forty sail had been chased in to Cherbourg Roads, and the Admiralty could not resist the temptation to destroy or blockade them, knowing all the time that Byng's preparations must be delayed if other ships were given the preference in obtaining crews.[2] This was 'the most pressing service' previously referred to, and such was the influence of commerce upon war that the Admiralty judged it worth while to risk a few more hours' delay in getting ships to the Mediterranean in order to deny valuable supplies to the enemy.

Byng was forced to comply; he had just written to the Admiralty again asking for a frigate, of which there were four in the harbour, and now he was told to send two with Keppel into the Channel, though he himself must wait until he picked up Edgecumbe's squadron in the Mediterranean.

Byng was now finding great difficulty in completing his crews. Portsmouth and its neighbourhood had

[1] Details of the drafts:

For Minorca:	30 officers	For Gibraltar:	16 officers
	32 recruits		1 corporal
	8 deserters		2 privates
			38 recruits

[2] A copy of Keppel's instructions is in *Add. MSS.* 35895, ff. 333–5.

already been well scoured that month by Hawke, and Byng's reputation for stern discipline was unlikely to help him in collecting seafaring men, who on such occasions disappeared from the coast and camped out a few miles away in the country. Those whom the press gangs were still able to rake together were either too drunk or too physically incapable to escape. However, he received another Admiralty letter allowing him the doubtful privilege of taking men from the hospitals and from the 'tenders' which were daily expected with pressed men from Ireland and Liverpool.[1] Next day he found that the Admiralty had relented further and allowed him to take men from the *Princess Augusta* as soon as she arrived, and the *Stirling Castle*, although a few days before he had been told on no account to touch the last-named ship. He was also ordered to distribute all his Marines amongst the other ships in the harbour, and take instead Lord Robert Bertie's[2] regiment of Fusiliers.[3]

A week of strenuous preparations followed, punctuated daily by a letter to and from the Admiralty. The Marines and Fusiliers were exchanged; provisions, water and stores were taken on board; Keppel was got to sea; and except for lack of men, Byng was practically ready to start.

[1] These men were pressed by means of a special embargo on Irish shipping.

[2] Lieut.-Gen., 1777; died, 1782. See Trial, p. 112, for Ad. orders to Byng about Bertie's regiment.

[3] The Seventh Foot, now the Royal Fusiliers. *Add. MSS.* 35895, f. 109, gives Fox's letter to the Admiralty about Bertie's regiment, and a return dated the *Culloden*, 1st April, gave its strength as 35 officers; 80 N.C.O.'s; 688 effective rank and file; 12 wanting to complete establishment. Total number according to the establishment, 815.

On 1st April he received his Instructions, and was urged to put to sea at once. Doubtless the Admiralty imagined that the last word had now been said, but Byng, in a long letter of acknowledgment, gave one of those unenthusiastic appreciations of the situation which so largely contributed to his final condemnation. 'With regard to the Instructions I have received, I shall use every endeavour and means in my power to frustrate the designs of the enemy, if they should make an attempt in the island of Minorca, knowing the great importance of that island to the Crown of Great Britain.' This was quite a correct way of showing that he understood his Instructions, but he then added, with the air of a cautious and detached philosopher, 'and shall think myself the most fortunate if I am so happy to succeed in this undertaking.' He then stated that even with all those from the hospitals who could possibly be passed as fit he was still 336 men short, and requested some reply about this before he sailed, adding that as 'upwards of 100 of the recruits[1] came badly clothed and with no bedding' it might have occasioned 'a pestilential sickness,' but that happily they were now provided for. This gratuitous and unwelcome sidelight on administration was completed by the 'submission' that as he was going to command all the ships in the Mediterranean he should be given a special commission as commander-in-chief.

Next day the situation was eased by the arrival

[1] Of Bertie's regiment, presumably.

of the *Cambridge* (80), with 70 supernumeraries, and the *Ludlow Castle* (44), with over 100 'lent' men from the *Ramillies*, so by taking these, and another 70 from the *Colchester*, *Romney* and *Stirling Castle*, the deficit of men was nearly wiped out. The *Intrepid* also arrived during the day, but next morning Captain Young reported that she had made so much water coming from the Nore, although the ports were caulked in, that he would have to scuttle the lower deck, let the water down and pump it out. Moreover, as he had not been warned for foreign service he was short of water, provisions and stores.

This occasioned further delay, but Byng was determined to sail without the *Intrepid* if necessary, and had just received Admiralty orders to do so, together with his commission as commander-in-chief, and £500 for 'necessary contingent expenses.' So he unmoored and dropped down to St. Helen's ready to sail with the first favourable wind. However, the wind continued to blow 'fresh from the westward,' and it was not till the 7th April that he finally cleared the land. The delay had given time to get the *Intrepid* ready, but Byng could not resist writing a final letter to the Admiralty pointing out the inconvenience caused by their not having warned Captain Young for foreign service.

So Byng had at last got to sea. He had taken exactly a fortnight to fit out his squadron from the day he arrived at Spithead to the day he was ready to sail. In that time he had had to find 700 seamen under difficult conditions, and send Keppel to sea properly equipped with an entirely separate squadron.

The captains with whom Byng and West left England were a capable but undistinguished body of men. Henry Ward of the *Culloden* was the senior,[1] Philip Durell[2] had commanded the *Gloucester* (50) in the second battle of Finisterre and was present at the capture of Louisburg, and James Young,[3] who after the action seems to have become Byng's evil genius, had previously served under him in the Mediterranean and had been Lestock's captain at an earlier date. Charles Catford[4] had been a member of the court by which Lestock was tried; Frederick Cornwall[5] had lost an arm in the battle of Toulon, and had taken part in the capture of Louisburg; while William Parry[6] and John Amherst[7] seem to have seen little active service. Arthur Gardiner,[8] Byng's flag captain, had already served under him in the Mediterranean, and had previously been flag captain there to Rowley. Thomas Andrews[9] and Michael Everitt[10] had only reached post rank towards the end of the war. There is little to quarrel with in this recital. The most junior captain had nine years' seniority, and the majority had previous experience in the Mediterranean.

The condition of the ships and crews, however, afforded less cause for congratulation. All had been cleaned during or since December 1755; but the *Captain* and *Intrepid* were leaky, and others were

[1] Post Captain, 1741. He had distinguished himself in the same year by capturing off Jamaica the *N.S. del Rosario*, a rich Spanish vessel.
[2] Post Captain, 1742. [3] Post Captain, 1743. [4] Post Captain, 1743.
[5] Post Captain, 1744. [6] Post Captain, 1744. [7] Post Captain, 1744.
[8] Post Captain, 1745. [9] Post Captain, 1745. [10] Post Captain, 1747.

ill manned, notably the *Revenge, Trident, Intrepid* and *Defiance*. Moreover, certain of the ships were hardly up to the usual strength of the ships in their rate. The *Captain* and *Revenge* were old seventies remodelled as sixty-fours, but still weaker than the new sixty-fours then being built. The *Kingston*, an old sixty, only carried twenty-four and nine-pounder guns instead of twenty-four and twelve-pounders, according to the new establishment; and the *Trident*, a French sixty-four,[1] had had to change her lower deck thirty-twos for twenty-fours, and her upper deck eighteens for twelves, as in a heavy sea she was unable to carry the full weight of metal.

Except for the *Culloden*, which was a poor sailer, the remaining ships were well manned, in good condition, and of proper fighting strength. Nevertheless, it seems remarkable that, out of a squadron of only ten of the line, there should have been found so many defects. Naturally such facts were given the utmost publicity after the expedition by the pro-Byng writers; but as they are derived entirely from evidence given at the court martial, principally by Temple West, there seems little reason to doubt their general accuracy.

Violent criticism was levelled at the Admiralty after the disaster for having sent Byng with such a weak force, and for interfering with his manning arrangements while fitting out. It does seem strange that after more than a year of semi-war no reinforcement should have been sent to the Mediterranean and that no steps should have been taken to collect more

[1] Captured by Hawke at the second battle of Finisterre, 1747.

seamen early in the year, when it was known that many ships would have to be manned in the summer.

In the spring of 1757, when the whole question of the loss of Minorca was before Parliament, the late Ministers drew up a very elaborate defence of their conduct. According to their statement, there were forty-six ships of the line in home waters at the beginning of March 1756,[1] and between then and 1st April twenty-two of these were ordered on various services.[2] The twenty-four ships remaining were strengthened by the *Devonshire*, *Augusta* and *Colchester*,[3] thus making a total of twenty-seven in home waters on 1st April. The complement of seamen for the total of forty-six ships was 23,795, of which 17,361 were borne, and only 13,220 actually mustered on 1st March.[4] Byng's squadron required 4,245 of these, and the Ministers argued that when

[1] Excluding the *Princess Royal*, which was only fit to lie in the mouth of the Thames. See list on p. 34

[2]

Vanguard, *Somerset*	Added to Hawke off Plymouth.	2 ships.
Weymouth, *Windsor*, *Antelope*	Ordered to cruise off the French coast.	3 ships.
Grafton, *Nottingham*	Ordered to convoy transports to North America.	2 ships.
Torbay, *Essex*, *Eagle*	Under Admiral Holburne, to reinforce Hawke.	5 ships, three of which previously cruising off Batz and Cherbourg.
Squadron fitting out under Byng		10
(*Add. MSS.* 35895, f. 320.)	*Total*	22

The apparent confusion of numbers is due to the fact that the *Terrible* (70) and *Monmouth* (70) are not named as being the remaining two of the five sent to reinforce Hawke. The *Torbay*, *Essex* and *Antelope* had formed Keppel's squadron ; see p. 51.

[3] Newly commissioned, returned from Newfoundland, and returned from cruising, respectively. *Add. MSS.* 35895, f. 320.

[4] *Add. MSS.* 35895, f. 319.

all the men necessary for the twenty-two ships sent to sea had been subtracted, only 3,320 remained in the whole of England[1] to man the remaining twenty-four ships for home defence.

The argument is continued with marvellous ingenuity: 'It must be remembered that part of the above-mentioned men mustered on board of the ships of the line at home consisted of officers and officers' servants which completed soon after the ship is commissioned and remain complete till she is paid off, not being disposable of to be turned over.

'Petty officers by the custom of the Navy and Act of Parliament cannot be turned over without rating them according to their rank which cannot be done without vacancies.

'The officers, petty officers and servants on board the twenty-four ships which remained after deducting the twenty-two amount upon a moderate computation to 2,990 and ought to be subtracted from the 3,170.[2]

[1] The calculations were as follows:

Required for Byng's squadron	4,245
Required for 3 ships off French coast	1,120
Required for 2 ships for North America	920
Required for the reinforcements for Hawke	2,675
Total	9,010
Required for 2 ships joined Hawke off Plymouth	1,040
	10,000

Available men	13,220
Required as above ..	10,000
..	3,220 only left.

(*Add. MSS.* 35895, f. 321.)

The first total is 50 too many, but this is corrected in the final addition.

[2] Probably a mistake for the 3,220 of the previous calculation, as alongside is written the sum:

3,220
2,990
230 remain

'This reasoning may perhaps be by some thought to be too strict, as it proceeds upon a supposition that the 2,990 are to be all included in the number stated as only mustered; whereas part of them are probably included in the numbers borne though not mustered.'[1]

If the twenty-two, concludes the argument, had been immediately completed from the twenty-four remaining, the last-named would have had less than one quarter of their complement.[2]

A further calculation showed that on 1st April there were seventeen ships ready for sea and ten fitting out,[3] and one for harbour service.[4] The complement of these was 14,640 men, of whom 9,891 were borne and only 7,249 mustered.[5] Moreover, no mention was made of why Byng was not supplied with at least one frigate, to repeat signals, on his way out to the Mediterranean, where with good luck he would be able to find those under Edgecumbe.

[1] Therefore there would be more than 230 available for handing over to other ships. This was probably added in order not to make the claim too extravagant.

[2]

Complement of 46	23,795
Complement of 22	10,050
Complement of 24	13,645
	3,220
Wanting	10,425

(*Add. MSS.* 35895, f. 321.)

An ingenious argument, as it was stated that all the twenty-four had their destinations, and could not possibly have got ready in time if so denuded, and that no help could be expected from the frigates and other ships already cruising, as invasion was 'imminent,' and there were only 13,000 foot and 4,000 dragoons ready to take the field (ff. 322 and 323).

[3] Excluding Byng's squadron.

[4] *Princess Royal.*

[5] *Add. MSS.* 35895, f. 9.

For the seventeen frigates actually in home ports there were only 1,320 mustered out of a total complement of 2,405, of which 1,508 were borne.[1]

The object of this amazing bureaucratic jigsaw was evidently to show the extreme shortage of seamen during March, and thus explain why Byng's crews were not completed sooner.[2] Contemporary and modern critics, generally speaking, have missed the real issue. The first tended to narrow down their remarks so as to make them apply only to the delay caused by giving Keppel's squadron precedence, while the moderns incoherently catch at and expand the contemporary gibe that Anson 'minced' the Navy into convoys to protect the rich freights of the City merchants. To such stupidity the Government's defence is a sufficient answer. They were able to show a large number of ships usefully employed and placed in positions where protection for commerce would be as great as possible.

The real charge against the Admiralty is twofold. In the first place, they do not seem to have been

[1] *Add. MSS.* 35895, f. 10. Frigates, sloops and armed vessels cruising 1st April:

3 under Hawke off Brest
2 off Bass
4 off Cape Barfleur
14 under Admiral Smith
2 at Dublin
1 at Greenwich
1 at Whitehaven
2 at Liverpool
2 in Kingroad
1 at Bideford
1 at Falmouth
1 at Exmouth
1 at Yarmouth
1 at Lynn
1 in the Humber
1 at Newcastle
1 at Leith
3 going to Leith
3 convoys to Stadht
1 convoy from Ostend
1 then ordered to the Downs.

[2] A similar mode of reasoning was used to explain why no squadron could have been sent previous to March (*Add. MSS.* 35895, f. 358; 31959, f. 28).

alive to the magnitude of the war which was about to begin or to the variety of work the Navy would be called upon to perform, and therefore they did not take steps quick enough to increase the number of seamen. Secondly, no system of blockade had yet been devised that could make certain of keeping the French main fleets under restraint. The Western Squadron was supposed to intercept all sailings from Brest and Rochefort, but it was not till Hawke and Boscawen established the famous blockades of Brest and Toulon, in 1759, that our most successful method of protecting commerce was at last adopted, reaching its perfection under Nelson and Cornwallis. Until then there was no real safety along the trade routes, and unless ships of the line and frigates were scattered over most of the globe, our merchantmen were constantly open to attack by single ships of war and privateers. It would be overstepping the limits of ordinary criticism to say that Anson ought to have devised a proper system of blockades before war broke out, but it is strange that the wealth of experience we had gained in dealing with the Dutch in the Rhine delta was not utilised a little sooner in dealing with the French in the Atlantic. Matthews and others had already made the blockade of Toulon a tradition, but nothing of the kind was attempted in 1756, and Byng was sent to sea to deal with a situation which never ought to have arisen.

CHAPTER VI

GIBRALTAR

THE decision to send a squadron to the Mediterranean had been taken as a result of the Inner Committee's recommendation of 9th March, and Byng's Instructions were dated 30th March.[1] He was directed to sail at once to Gibraltar and take Edgecumbe's squadron under his command. If the French Toulon fleet had passed the straits, he was to detach West with enough ships to effect a superior concentration with the ships we already had at Halifax; it being assumed that the Toulon ships would have gone to the French North American station at Louisburg.[2] West was then to take all English ships on the

[1] The procedure followed was that the Inner Committee, consisting of:
The Secretaries of State
First Lord of the Admiralty
Secretary at War
Other members of the Cabinet
Naval and military experts
(not members of the Cabinet)
'advised' the full Cabinet, which empowered the Secretaries of State to issue orders to the Admiralty and the War Office, whence the instructions were drafted to commanders by sea and land.

[2] *French squadron at Louisburg.*

Héros (74) | *Licome* (32)
Illustre (64) | *Syren* (32)

English squadron already at Halifax.

Norwich (50) | *Kennington* (24)
Sutherland (50) | *Hornet* (14)
Nightingale (24) | *Jamaica* (14)

English ships on their way to Halifax.

Grafton (70) | *Lichfield* (50)
Stirling Castle (64) | *Centurion* (50)
Fougeux (64) | *Success* (22)
Nottingham (60) | *Vulture* (14)

station under his command and blockade Louisburg and the mouth of the St. Lawrence.

Whether French ships had passed the Straits or not, Byng was to proceed at once to Minorca and 'relieve it' if it was being attacked. If Minorca was untouched, he was to sail for Toulon and blockade it as best he could. Further, he was given the routine duties of protecting our trade, destroying or capturing all enemy ships, and keeping on good terms with the Ottoman Empire and the Barbary States.

There was never really any doubt as to the soundness of these instructions, and only the wildest of the pro-Byng pamphleteers ever attempted any criticism of them; but they required some parallel instructions with regard to the troops which would have to be used if combined operations were necessary for the 'relief' of Minorca. This side of the question did not receive quite the treatment it deserved. Lord Barrington was Secretary at War,[1] having been appointed in the previous November, and although he had had the experience of being a Lord of the Admiralty from 1746 to 1754, he seems to have been remarkably slow in picking up the duties of his new office. When told by Fox, as Secretary of State, to arrange for troops to be supplied to Byng, he attempted to settle the business without touching any of the troops then stationed in England. He wrote[2] to Lieut.-Gen. Thomas Fowke, Governor of Gibraltar, telling him that he

[1] At that time a subordinate office, ranking below that of the principal Secretaries of State.

[2] 21st March, 1756.

was to 'receive' Lord Robert Bertie's regiment into his garrison 'to do duty there,' and that if Minorca were attacked or threatened Fowke was to supply Byng with a battalion in its place, drawn from the four regiments then in the garrison. Mr. Sherwood, Lord Barrington's secretary, gave this letter to Maj.-Gen. Stuart, who left at once for Portsmouth to sail with Byng.

No sooner did the Admiralty hear of this arrangement than they objected violently. Bertie's regiment was to serve on board in place of Marines, and therefore was a part of the ships' complements. What was the use of exchanging these troops at Gibraltar for another battalion and still having no extra troops to land at Minorca ?[1] Fox realised the mistake and told Barrington to write again to Fowke, saying that Bertie's regiment would not land, but that Fowke must supply Byng with a battalion 'from the garrison of Gibraltar notwithstanding.' But as it was realised that the duty of the garrison could not be carried out properly with less than four battalions, and there were only four there, Fowke was to be told only to send the battalion 'in case the island of Minorca should be in any likelihood of being attacked.'

So Barrington again wrote to Fowke on 28th March as follows :

'I am commanded to acquaint you, that it is his Majesty's pleasure, in case you shall apprehend that the French threaten an attempt upon Minorca,

[1] *Add. MSS.* 35895, f. 366.

> that you make a detachment from the troops in your garrison equal to a battalion, commanded by a Lt.-Col. and Maj., for the relief of that place, to be put on board the fleet at the disposition of the Admiral; for such Lt.-Col. and Major to be the eldest in your garrison.'

The order was then despatched to Stuart at Portsmouth. It was a stupid letter, because it never stated clearly that Bertie's regiment was not to land. Byng and Bertie, on the other hand, were given explicit instructions that the Fusiliers were to serve on board all the time, and that Fowke would supply the extra battalion to be landed at Minorca if necessary. Barrington, however, could not resist writing one more vague letter to Fowke, saying: 'It is his Majesty's pleasure, that you receive into your garrison the women and children belonging to Lord Robert Bertie's regiment,' and this was also sent to Stuart at Portsmouth, who sailed with all three.[1]

Except that there was no definite statement in Fowke's second and third order that Bertie's regiment was not to land, the situation could be understood at once by reading the instructions issued to Byng and Bertie; in fact, Fowke's plea that his orders represented a confusion of direction was hardly worthy of his reputation, and merely acted as a counter-charge against the War Office without materially affecting the main issue.

The real fault in the drafting of the orders both

[1] 1st April, 1756.

to Fowke and Byng was the failure to state more clearly under what circumstances an extra battalion was to be taken on board the fleet from Gibraltar. A comparison of the particular phrasing of all the documents implies that a certain amount of discretion should be allowed to Fowke:

Mr. Fox's letters to the Admiralty, 30th March:

'. . . The Gov. of Gibraltar having orders in case a further reinforcement is necessary at Minorca to make a detachment equal to a battalion from his garrison, which detachment the Admiral . . . is to convey to Minorca.'

Admiralty instruction to Byng, 31st March: Idem.

Account written for the Ministry's defence, 1757:

'But as the duty of that garrison cannot be done with any convenience by less than four battalions, as it was then uncertain where the French armament at Toulon would be sent, and as a reinforcement would not be of any service at Minorca unless that island were attacked, Gen. Fowke was directed to send the detachment only in case the island of Minorca should be in any likelihood of being attacked.'

Barrington to Fowke, 28th March:

'In case you shall apprehend that the French threaten an attempt upon Minorca, that you make a detachment of troops from your garrison equal to a battalion . . . for the relief of that place.'

Was Fowke given any definite standard by which he might measure the needs of Minorca? Certainly not. But on the other hand, it was hardly possible to tie the hands of a subordinate at so great a distance, and it is easy to make out a good case for the War Office by saying that they left Fowke to decide whether the information available as to the French movements was sufficient to assume that they had embarked for Minorca. If by the time Byng arrived it was already known that the French had landed, then his duty would be perfectly clear; and it only remained to consider whether he had been given sufficient directions to enable him to act properly in the face of rumours and uncertainty.

Had Fowke been given entire control of the British troops within the Straits, it would have been permissible to send him instructions, as apart from orders, to use those troops to the best advantage for His Majesty's service. But Fowke owed a definite duty to his own command, the fortress of Gibraltar, where the Government admitted his garrison was at the minimum safety strength. Naturally, a commander of a weak garrison ordered to supply reinforcements for another would think twice before he despatched troops on a wild goose chase. Plenty of examples can be found of commanders who, when ordered to use their discretion as to whether it was safe to send away troops or not, refused to part with a single man.

But there was no room for doubt, supposing that it was known that the French had actually landed at Minorca ;[1] and, consequently, it might be argued that Fowke received adequate orders, but was left to discriminate between vague rumours of attack and definite information.

Nevertheless, there was one possibility that no one had foreseen. Supposing that before Byng reached Gibraltar the French attacked Minorca in such strength that they gained a complete ascendancy in the island, and that the fall of St. Philip's Castle was only a question of days: would there not be a strong temptation for Fowke to refuse to commit a quarter of his garrison to an enterprise which he felt already past repair? It would then be a question, not of the French having done too little to justify the despatch of a battalion, but of their having done too much, and, amazing as it may seem, this was the actual picture of the situation which Fowke had painted for himself by the time Byng arrived.

Byng made heavy weather all the way out, and only anchored in Gibraltar Bay on the second of May.[2] There he found Edgecumbe, with the *Princess Louisa, Deptford* and *Fortune*, and learnt that a French army of at least 13,000 men had sailed from Toulon on 10th April, protected by thirteen men-of-war. Later news stated that they had landed at Minorca and held everything except St. Philip's Castle.[3]

[1] The order of 28th March might have read: 'In case the island of Minorca should be in any likelihood of attack,' but was by no means necessary and would sound more like special pleading than a military order (*Add. MSS.* 35895, f. 373). So argued the Ministry, and the legal touch given to the statement is well worth noting.

[2] He was off Portland on 7th April, but met heavy weather in the Bay and did not sight Cape St. Vincent till 27th April, or Cape Trafalgar till 1st May.

[3] Consul Banks to Fowke, 19th and 21st April; see Byng's trial, p. 113.

Byng then went ashore to visit Fowke in company with Stuart, Bertie and other officers. Fowke read Barrington's three letters, and at first appeared confused, but understood what was meant by reading Byng's instructions and the special War Office orders issued to Bertie. His duty was obvious; he must supply Byng with a battalion and give him every assistance in refitting and getting to sea again. But Fowke was worried about his garrison, as his four battalions[1] only totalled 2,700, and 839 were required for each full duty complement. If he gave Byng a detachment equal to a battalion—that is to say, 700 men—he would be unable to find three reliefs, and, moreover, he chose to imagine for some obscure reason that Gibraltar was liable to attack at any moment. As he never attempted to produce any evidence to prove his assertion, even when tried by court martial, except an untrustworthy letter written from Granville on 2nd June, we must conclude that he was influenced solely by the desire to keep as many troops at Gibraltar as possible.

Now, there was a certain Major James Mace of the artillery who was one of the officers Byng was carrying to Minorca and who was apparently well acquainted with St. Philip's Castle. This man, together with Captain Alexander Leith, of the artillery, and Archibald Patoun, engineer, both of the Gibraltar garrison, were called together by Fowke and asked to give an opinion as to the possibility of landing troops at St. Philip's. Evidently Fowke

[1] They were Fowke's, Panmure's, Guise's and Pulteney's.

hoped to obtain an expert opinion from these officers which would justify him in disobeying his orders, and he was not disappointed. Whether they were tampered with or not is uncertain, but on 3rd May they produced the following extraordinary report:

> 'Having considered the question whether 'tis practicable to throw in succours into St. Philip's Castle, supposing the enemy to have erected batteries on both shores near the entrance of the harbour, an advantage scarce to be supposed they have neglected:
>
> 'We are humbly of the opinion that, unless those batteries can be silenced, 'twill be extremely dangerous if not impracticable. As the sally ports by which the succours must enter, according to the best of our recollection, are so entirely exposed, that their guns may destroy any boat employed on that attempt; and we humbly apprehend that but one boat at a time can, with difficulty, land men at the nearest sally port, and the other lying further up the harbour is more exposed.'

The amazing inaccuracies contained in this statement must be left till later for detailed discussion, it being sufficient for the moment to say that the 'opinion' was disproved by the events themselves, and no one would be surprised if it had been determined by official pressure.

Next day Fowke called a Council of War, at which were present the following officers of the garrison:

Col. Joseph Dussaux.
Lieut.-Col. J. Grey.[1]
Lieut.-Col. Charles Colville.[2]
Lieut.-Col. John Crauford.[3]
Lieut.-Col. Robert Scott.

In addition, and ostensibly to strengthen the character of the council, but in reality to implicate as many persons as possible, he invited Gen. Stuart and Cols. Cornwallis, Lord Effingham and Lord Robert Bertie. These officers were all senior to his own, and were all under orders to sail to Minorca, so that they would naturally be expected to be only too anxious to obtain as many troops from Gibraltar as possible.

Fowke laid before them the following documents: the three letters from Lord Barrington dated 21st and 28th March and 1st April; the Admiralty instructions to Admiral Byng, dated 31st March; the opinion of the artillery and engineer officers, together with the latest advices received from Minorca.

The Governor's nervousness for the safety of his command seems to have communicated itself to his advisers in a most remarkable fashion, for they produced an opinion more ridiculous and insubordinate than that of Mace's Committee.

[1] Maj.-Gen., 1759. [2] Lieut.-Gen., 1770. [3] Maj.-Gen., 1761.

'It appearing from Advice received by Admiral Byng and Lieut.-Gen. Fowke that on the 18th of April last the French forces were landed on the island of Minorca; consisting of a number of men from thirteen to fifteen thousand; and that His Majesty's troops on the said island had retired into the fortifications of St. Philip's Castle; the Council also took into consideration the situation of His Majesty's garrisons in the Mediterranean; and are humbly of opinion that the sending of a detachment equal to a battalion would be evidently weakening the garrison of Gibraltar, and be no way effectual for the relief of Minorca, for the following reasons.

'I. Because by the opinion of the chief Engineer of this garrison, who has served in that island, and that of other officers of the artillery acquainted with the situation of that harbour, it would be difficult, if not impossible, to throw in any succours, and could they be thrown in would be ineffectual; as the Council do not conceive any hopes of introducing a body of men sufficient to dislodge the French or raise the siege; and therefore though such a detachment might have been of great service in Minorca, could they have landed before the island was actually attacked, and whilst a squadron of his Majesty's ships had been there to co-operate with the troops in the defence and preservation of the island; and which seem to be the scope and meaning of the recited letters and orders; yet in the present situation of affairs, it is the opinion of the Council that the sending such a detachment from hence to Minorca at this time, instead of being useful to His Majesty's Service would be diminishing the strength of the garrison of Gibraltar, and unnecessarily risking the loss of an additional number of His Majesty's troops, without any reasonable prospect or hope of their being any assistance to Minorca.

'II. Because the Toulon squadron, by the best accounts the Council have received, is at least equal in force, if not superior to that under the command of Admiral Byng; and should the British fleet be any way weakened by an engagement or any other accident, the garrison of Gibraltar would be exposed to imminent danger; and as the garrison stands at present, it is not more than sufficient for the common duty of the garrison.

'But Admiral Byng having represented that there is a deficiency of men on board the ships late under the command of Commodore Edgecumbe, on account of his having left a number of soldiers and marines at Minorca to assist in the defence of the place, and that a detachment is absolutely necessary to render those ships useful; it is the opinion of the Council that the Governor of Gibraltar should send such a detachment on board, as shall be judged necessary to enable those ships to act in a proper manner against the enemy.'

This was a deplorable decision. In the face of the clearest intentions of the Ministry that the detachment must be sent if Minorca were in danger, Fowke took it upon himself to assume that the island was in such danger that it was not worth while.

St. Philip's was invested by a vastly superior force, but was by no means *in extremis*, while the numbers of the French must have caused them acute embarrassment. They had a large army couped up in a small island, which in the days of General Kane could not even support the wants of 3,000 English troops, and depending for the necessities of life on safe communication with Toulon.

The fact that St. Philip's was surrounded was irrelevant, for it was still perfectly easy to land a force at several points along the coast and harass the French by raiding their stores and magazines. It was for the Governor of St. Philip's to judge whether it was proper to attempt the reinforcement of the castle, not Fowke. For all he knew, the Ministry might have planned the whole business, thinking it well worth the sacrifice of one more battalion in order to discomfit an enemy numbering 15,000. Anyone with the slightest knowledge of war could grasp the effect on the French *morale* which would be caused by the arrival of a new English force operating in the interior of the island and continually preventing the active prosecution of the siege.

The council's second reason was perhaps one of the worst encroachments which military opinion has ever made on naval strategy, for it was nothing less than a curt hint to Byng to refuse an engagement at sea lest Gibraltar might 'be exposed to imminent danger.'

Richelieu was sitting before St. Philip's with an army which demanded enormous supplies, and supported by a fleet which at the most was only slightly superior to Byng's. The opportunity for guerilla operations was dazzling. What was there easier than to sail round and round the island, threatening a descent here, destroying transports there, and all the time looking out to swoop down on any convoy from Toulon, and either sinking it or forcing Galissonnière to fight for its protection at a tactical disadvantage? Yet Fowke and his council took it upon themselves to say that it was impossible to introduce troops into the castle, that the fleet could not afford to risk a defeat, and that therefore it must sail deprived of all opportunity of undertaking a vigorous combined operation.

Contemporary critics entirely failed to grasp the distinction between reinforcing St. Philip's Castle and relieving the pressure on the besieged by action against the French lines of communication by sea and land. They did not realise that, as the narrowest part of the channel at the entrance to Mahon Harbour was only 114 fathoms, and that this point was actually adjacent to the castle, no French ships could enter without being sunk, even supposing the garrison had neglected to block the entrance with a boom or by sinking a ship. Consequently all the French supplies for the siege would have to be brought overland from as far as Fornelles, since

Cala Mezquida, although nearer, was hardly suitable for a permanent base. Hence to prevent the introduction of succours into St. Philip's and at the same time protect his base, Galissonnière would have to divide his fleet, while leaving open Ciudadela, the original French landing-place.

Once tempted from his position off Mahon, the fears of the engineer and artillery men that no boats could reach the castle would be more ridiculous than before, since a couple of frigates could get close enough to the French batteries 'on both shores near the entrance of the harbour to pound them to pieces in half an hour.'

But contemporary opinion made up for its ignorance of local conditions by the vigour and acuteness of its denunciation, and in a pamphlet published next year, Fowke was severely and adroitly criticised for his failure to obey orders.[1]

'Whether a great part of the members of that Council were not under express orders to go to Mahon, and whether the eldest Lieut.-Colonel of the garrison was not of them?'

'Whether it be possible for officers who are ordered to their garrison to vote that it is not for His Majesty's Service that they should go thither?'

'If the succour of two battalions would be an ineffectual relief, whether those officers going with only one would be still less effectual?'

Again, it was urged that the primary duty of officers of a place besieged was 'to run every kind

[1] *Some Queries on the Minutes of the Council of War held at Gibraltar on the Fourth of May last* (London, 1757).

of risk in order to get into the place of their duty, and that succours were sent not to raise the siege at one blow, but to prolong resistance.' Should they not have realised that the Government knew the strength and distribution of our troops and would soon reinforce Gibraltar?

Two of the final paragraphs contain the subtlest and most biting comment on the whole of the operations which ever appeared in print:

'Whether the determinations of this Council of War had not made it impossible for them to go to Mahon? Since it could not have been kept a secret from the garrison, when they and the Fusiliers and other officers came there, that his Majesty had with great goodness ordered them another battalion, but that they would not bring it?'

'Whether when they should be obliged to give the reason of their refusal, that very reason, that the succour even of two battalions would be an ineffectual relief, would not, when heard at Mahon on their coming with one, have been an effectual declaration to the garrison that they had nothing to hope for, but ought to capitulate as soon as possible?'

But the ten army officers sitting round a table on the fourth of May appreciated the situation quite differently. They were ready to attempt the reinforcement of St. Philip's Castle if it was likely to be attacked, or if it were moderately attacked, but on hearing that it was beset so desperately they considered that they were right in refusing to commit any more troops to a forlorn hope. However, to put everything in proper order they cheerfully agreed to supply the deficiency of the 250 sailors and marines left by Edgecumbe at Minorca.

It was now Fowke's business to present the council's opinion to Byng. He had never wanted the battalion to go, and by a triumph of deliberate fraud or subconscious manipulation he had got his way and secured the agreement of nine other officers as well. The Artillery and Engineering opinion which had done so much to prejudice the issue was utterly false, and in his heart of hearts he must have known it, and now there was Byng to tackle.

Byng's face as he read the Council's opinion must have been worth watching, and as he finished Fowke said, " Well, sir, I have shown the resolutions of our council of war, and you have read them " ; and then added, either from real fear or from a satanic knowledge of Byng's character, " But notwithstanding that, I will make the detachment if you think it necessary." Whichever way he meant the remark to be taken, it was an extraordinary one to make. What could Byng say in reply? There was Fowke standing in front of him and offering to repudiate his own name at the head of the list of signatures, and go back to face the taunts of his brother officers. A great man such as Hawke or Clive would doubtless have snatched eagerly at Fowke's grudging offer, and called him a generous fellow. Quite an ordinary man would have got his own way after a time, even if it had required a little blustering ; but then Byng was not an ordinary man. Although in the '45 he had constantly co-operated with army officers, at this great crisis in his life all common sense seems to have left him. He was furious at the way in which the Admiralty had starved him of ships and men, and there stood a lunatic soldier wanting to do the same. Four weeks of bad weather had ruined his temper, and in his heart of hearts he thought that the enterprise must fail. The paramount importance of the campaign was forgotten; enthusiasm and filial aspirations shrivelled to nothing. He was ordered to relieve a 'castle,' but the Articles of War and the Fighting Instructions said nothing about castle relieving. It was a soldier's job. The Admiralty had told him that soldiers would be provided, and the senior soldier at Gibraltar stood there muttering that it was all no use. Byng agreed; he turned to Fowke and said with icy politeness that he was ready to receive the troops if General Fowke would send them, but that really it was a question for Fowke himself to decide.

Even now the situation could have been saved if Byng had possessed a second-in-command with some moral courage. Temple West was with them at the moment; he heard Fowke's wretched statement and he heard Byng's reply, and, although he must have known all that this conversation entailed, he said nothing, but sneeringly remarked afterwards that 'the manner in which this transaction passed had very little air of business in it.' And this from West, the gallant West; West who was praised for his conduct in the battle, and made a Lord of the Admiralty! He was not responsible for failing to get the troops from Fowke, but he certainly made no effort to strengthen Byng's weakening will-power by any personal protest.

Co-operation between commanders of different services, trained in different professional environments, and steeped in different warlike traditions, requires at all times great vision and great tact; vision to see the operation as a whole, and tact to appreciate the other man's methods of thought. It was vision above all things which Byng and Fowke lacked. The 'aids to command' which we now possess, such as staff systems and signal services, were then unknown, and the good relations of naval and military officers were left to chance. The only 'aid' then available was the council of war, and in the hand both of Fowke and Byng it proved a wretched failure.

The eighteenth-century council of war, far from helping to dispel that intellectual haze which is the chief impediment to vigorous action, often succeeded in increasing its density. Action taken on its advice was liable to defeat when opposed by the product of a single brain of moderate calibre, provided the opponent acted quickly and vigorously. Looking at the composition of such councils, we can easily see why this was likely to occur. They generally included all flag officers and senior captains if afloat, and all general officers and colonels when held on land. Nearly always their duty was to help the commander-in-chief to interpret his orders, or arrive at some operational decision of great importance.

Such a system was bound to lead to bad results,

as it tended to deprive the command of its responsibility by diluting its authority with that of a mass of conflicting opinions, which cancelled each other out and produced only 'a vague average opinion' devoid of all vigour and boldness. By tempting commanders fearful of disaster to shelter themselves behind its combined decision from the blame they refused to encounter alone, it could only lead to a gradual sapping of the power of initiative and activity. Moreover, being in no sense an organised body, it had no special training which would have enabled it to give the command that expert assistance which it is entitled to expect from its staff, especially in the collection and collation of data on which each decision must inevitably be based. Being a fortuitous collection of heads of departments, it confused the command when present and became useless when absent, for no sooner had it left the place of council than it resolved again into its constituent elements.

At sea the council had something to be said for it, since the difficulty of communicating by boat and signal might make it imperative for the admiral of a fleet to call together his captains in order to explain plans for ensuing operations, and to enable information with regard to the conditions of their ships to be conveniently discussed. Such councils would, in the hands of a wise admiral, partake more of the nature of an officers' conference, at which he would explain his ideas, and only encourage such comments as would tend to facilitate the practical application of his general plan.

Opinions would be asked and given, but no vote would be taken and no manifesto signed, and thus the personal responsibility of the command would remain uncompromised.

Byng now concentrated his attention on the other question—that of refitting. He had only been three days at Gibraltar, but he was already disgusted with the state of its dockyard, and hopelessly depressed about his chance of being able to be of any service at Minorca. So it was little wonder that conversation soon became general, amongst the officers in the fleet, that the whole expedition was futile.

Byng had just received a report from the storekeeper and master shipwright of the dockyard disclosing a lamentable state of affairs. Every building and shed seemed to be 'decayed and tumbling down,' while the usual stores did not exist.

Such was the measure of the Government's care for its fleet, for although the ships just out from England were in very fair condition, many of Edgecumbe's had not been cleaned or repaired for many months, and the *Portland* not for a whole year.[1] Consequently, when Byng sat down to compose a letter to the Admiralty, he determined to spare them nothing, but rather to outline with merciless accuracy the full measure of their ineptitude, regardless of the fact that this letter would be the first intimation

[1] *Princess Louisa* last cleaned December 1755.
Portland ,, ,, May 1755.
Deptford ,, ,, March 1756.
Chesterfield ,, ,, July 1755.
Dolphin ,, ,, July 1755.
Phœnix ,, ,, January 1756.
Experiment ,, ,, April 1756.
Fortune ,, ,, September 1755.

which the public would receive of what he had done since leaving Portsmouth. Unfortunately for Byng, Fowke also wrote a letter two days afterwards addressed to the War Office, and the similarity of its contents went far to involve Byng in a charge of collusion with Fowke to prevent the troops being sent from Gibraltar. Moreover, the Admiralty had no wish at this moment, of all others, to receive a detailed criticism of their administrative methods. They would have dearly liked something full of fire-eating sentiments of zeal and diligence to show to the City merchants, already on the tiptoe of expectation, together with pious remarks about Torrington and glorious traditions. Instead, they received a catalogue of exposures which would have done credit to the prosecuting counsel in a case of fraud by naval contractors.

Byng was in no hurry to cut short his disclosures, and spread out his remarks wrathfully but leisurely. Fowke's letter, on the other hand, had the merit of being short, and tactfully omitted any reference to dockyards; but it was worded in such a way as to throw the whole blame on Byng, and gave a most untruthful account of the facts. Byng wrote in anger; Fowke wrote in fear. Fowke sealed his own fate at once, and would have probably been recalled in any case. Byng was permitted to reap the full harvest of his mistakes; and then his failure served as an additional reason for recalling Fowke.

Both letters opened with news of Byng's arrival, after which their more important passages make interesting parallel reading.

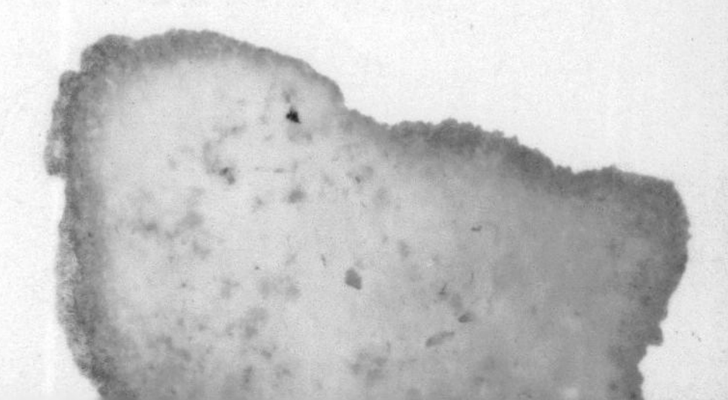

Byng's letter, 4th May.

. . . If I had been so happy as to have arrived at Mahon before the French had landed, I flatter myself, I would have been able to have prevented their getting a footing on that Island; but as it has so unfortunately turned out, I am firmly of opinion, from the great force they have landed, and the quantity of provisions, stores and ammunition of all kinds they have brought with them, that the throwing of men into the Castle will only enable it to hold out a little longer time, and add to the number that must fall into the enemies' hands; for the garrison in time will be obliged to surrender, unless a sufficient number of men could be landed to dislodge the French, or raise the siege.

However I am determined to sail up to Minorca with the squadron, where I shall be better judge of the situation of affairs there, and will give General Blakeney all the assistance he may require; though I am afraid all communication will be cut off between us, as is the opinion of the chief engineers of this garrison who have served in the Island, and that of the officers of artillery, who are acquainted with the situation of the harbour; for if the enemy has erected batteries on the two shores near the entrance of the harbour, (an advantage they would scarce be supposed to neglect), it will

Fowke's letter, 6th May.

. . . The accounts I had two days before received from Minorca giving me great reason to apprehend that the detachment required to be sent from this garrison to that Island could not (from the alteration of circumstances between the time of your Lordships' writing your letters and that of my receiving them) contribute to the relief of Minorca.

render it impossible for our boats to have a passage to the sally port of the garrison. . . .

It is to be apprehended, when they have got all the ships they possibly can ready for service, they may then think of turning their thoughts this way.

If I should fail in the relief of Port Mahon, I shall look on the security and protection of Gibraltar as my next object, and shall repair down here with my squadron.

I am sorry to find when enquiring at the naval office here that there are few or no stores in the magazines to supply any of the squadron that may want them; and it appears by a letter I received from the storekeeper and master shipwright, that the careening wharfs, storehouses, huts, etc., are entirely decayed, and I am afraid we shall find great difficulty in getting them repaired, there being no artificers to be got here; and at present we can have no assistance from the carpenters of the fleet, on account of our sailing.

It requiring a proper person to inspect into and manage this affair, I have taken upon me to give Mr. Milbourne Marsh, (His Majesty's naval officer that was at Port Mahon, who came down with Captain Edgecumbe), an order to act as master shipwright, which, I hope, their Lordships will approve; and I have given him orders to use his best endeavours to put the wharfs, etc., in the best condition he can; for very soon they will be wanted, as I apprehend this is the only place the ships of this squadron can come to refit at, and many of the ships are in want of repairs and careening, particularly the *Portland*, who has not been cleaned these twelve months, nor the *Chesterfield* ten; besides many of the ships that came out with me are foul. I fear from the inconvenience we shall meet here, there will be great difficulty in keeping the ships clean, as there is but one wharf for them to repair and careen at.

By a council of war held by General Fowke, a copy of which is transmitted, it was not thought proper to send a detachment equal to a battalion for the relief of Minorca, as it would evidently weaken the garrison of Gibraltar, and be no way effectual to the relief of that Island, for the reasons herein given; but, as I had represented there was a deficiency of men on board the ships, late under the command of Captain Edgecumbe, on account of his having left a number of sailors and marines at Minorca, to assist in the defence of that place, and that it was necessary to send a detachment on board these ships to help man them, this the General complied with, and I shall distribute some seamen from the

I assembled a council of war, to consider the situation of His Majesty's garrisons in the Mediterranean and to consult what measures to take that might be most conclusive to His Majesty's service, and after mature deliberation we were unanimously of opinion that the sending of a detachment equal to a battalion would evidently weaken this garrison and be no way effectual to the relief of Minorca. But Admiral Byng having represented that there was a deficiency of men aboard the ships late under the command of Commodore Edgecumbe, on account of his having left a number of sailors and marines at Minorca to assist in the defence of the place and that a detachment was absolutely necessary to render these ships that came out with me to complete their complement.

ships useful, it was the opinion of the Council of War that I should [send] such a detachment on board as should be judged necessary to enable those ships to act against the enemy.

The enclosed copy of the proceedings of the Council will more fully explain the motive for our opinion, and will, I hope, fully acquit me from any imputation of disobedience to His Majesty's commands.

Though it was not judged proper to send from this garrison a detachment which could not be usefully employed, yet when I acquainted Admiral Byng with the opinion of the Council of War, I at the same time told him, that if he thought it necessary, I could order a detachment equal to a battalion to be embarked, to serve on board His Majesty's fleet under his command, to which he answered that he did not think so large a detachment necessary and that he only required a sufficient number to put the ships late under Mr. Edgecumbe's command in a condition to act against an enemy.

The details contained in these letters[1] must be

[1] Byng sent two copies of his letter, one *viâ* Madrid and the other by Lieut. James O'Hara, who sailed for England in the *Lovel* packet on 7th May. O'Hara was a son of Lord Tyrawley and lieutenant on board the *Dolphin*, but on being left behind at Minorca by Edgecumbe, he afterwards persuaded Blakeney to let him slip out with twenty men, three days after Edgecumbe had sailed (*Bedford Correspondence*, Vol. II., p. 191).

left for discussion until their effect on the Government is also considered, but Byng's obtuseness and Fowke's deceit are evident throughout. Meanwhile Byng showed great energy in taking in water and wine and getting small repairs executed. The *Chesterfield*, *Portland*, *Dolphin* and *Experiment* all arrived, thus bringing every Mediterranean warship directly under his command except Captain Hervey's *Phœnix*, which had gone to Leghorn for intelligence. Edgecumbe was given command of the *Lancaster*, and Amherst of the *Deptford*.

Fowke sent the promised detachment, which consisted of seven officers and 260 other ranks,[1] and on 8th May Byng weighed and stood to the east with a fresh gale.

[1]
1 captain
6 subalterns
9 sergeants
11 corporals
5 drummers
235 privates
} Embarked 7th May.

Edgecumbe had also landed guns from his squadron as follows:

From the *Deptford*, two 24 pounders
From the *Portland*, two 24 pounders
From the *Princess Louisa*, two 24 pounders
From the *Chesterfield*, four 18 pounders

Add. MSS. 35895, f. 10.

CHAPTER VII

MINORCA

THE island of Minorca lies a hundred and thirty miles south-east of Barcelona, and is the easternmost of the Balearic group. Its prehistoric remains are extensive, but it is not till the rise of Carthage that we first hear of it being used as a naval base, Hannibal's younger brother Mago being one of its earliest patrons, and giving his name to the town of Mahon. Naturally the Romans absorbed the whole group after the third Punic War, and we hear little more of Minorca till the thirteenth century A.D., when the Aragonese kings, inspired by cupidity and crusading zeal, drove out its Moorish inhabitants and planted outposts of Catalans from the mainland. The Minorquins, as its Christian population were called, suffered continual counter-attacks from the Moorish pirates of North Africa, and by the seventeenth century were still hard put to it to hold their own.

The War of the Spanish Succession brought English squadrons permanently into the Mediterranean, operating for the most part against the French fleet at Toulon. Lisbon was too distant a base, and Gibraltar, though well placed for controlling the Straits, did not provide a safe anchorage, and was a thousand miles from Toulon. So in 1708 Sir John Leake and General Stanhope seized the opportunity to capture Minorca in the name of the 'Archduke Charles,' but kept it in English hands as a pledge for the large sums advanced to the Austrians during the war. By the Peace of Utrecht the French claimant Philip was given Spain, but our Government, feeling that Minorca was too valuable a prize to abandon, kept it.

The first act of importance under British rule was the removal of the capital from Ciudadela to Mahon. Ciudadela was a thriving and well-fortified town, but its harbour is quite unsuited for a naval base. It is deep, and well protected by steep and rocky sides, but very narrow and incapable of expansion, while the splendours of Mahon harbour were already proverbial :

> Los puertos del Mediterraneo son
> Junio, Julio, Agosto y Puerto Mahon.

Andrea Doria's couplet did bare justice to the ideal naval harbour of the eighteenth century. It consists of a land-locked bay at the eastern end of the island, which runs north-west for six thousand yards, and has an average width of five hundred yards to a thousand. The entrance is narrow, being only two hundred and fifty yards opposite St. Philip's Castle, and not being the mouth of a river, and the tide being negligible, its depth is constant, and no dredging is required to keep the passage clear. Here it is eight fathoms deep, but quickly deepens inside to sixteen, and only shallows to less than four fathoms in the last five hundred yards at the landmost end.

The town of Mahon stands on a rocky plateau overlooking the harbour from the south side. Its appearance, as you see it rising from the water's edge, is typically Mediterranean, but a closer inspection shows the steep roofs and wide windows to be of English design, its streets have English names, many local words are of English derivation, and its most prosperous traditions those of the English occupation.

In Byng's time the western end of the harbour, from the modern customs house onwards, was entirely given up to the use of the Navy. A broad quay runs all along the waterside in front of the town, and behind this stood the naval storehouses and magazine. Half way to the sea, on the Isla del Rey, is a large terra cotta coloured building in the classical style, once the naval hospital and official residence of the senior naval officer. It had been built at a cost of £3,600, largely under the influence of Admiral Sir John Jennings, and was an early sign of better times coming for the seamen, who nevertheless called the place 'Bloody Island.' On the north side the harbour entrance is sheltered by a huge peninsula of rock called La Mola, which is about three hundred feet high, facing the sea. The south side of the peninsula descends more easily to the water, and from the westward a small spit of land called Felipet protrudes into the harbour and runs parallel with it, thus helping to create the narrow entrance.

Across the water on the south side of the harbour, and facing La Mola, stood St. Philip's Castle, which

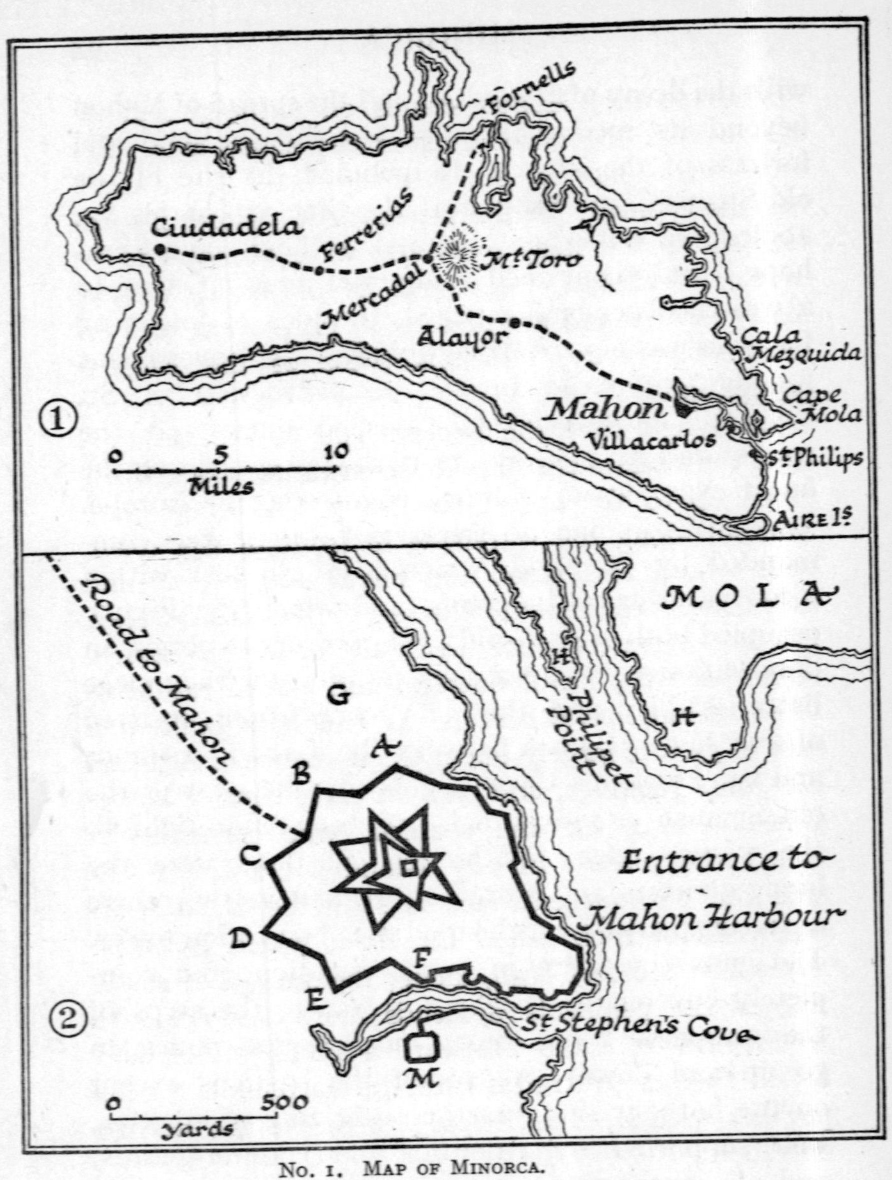

No. 1. Map of Minorca.

No. 2. Plan of St. Philip's Castle.

A. Queen's redoubt. B. Kane's lunette. C. Western lunette. D. Carolina lunette. E. South-western lunette. F. Southern lunette. G. Site of St. Philip's Town, 1756. H. Position of French batteries across the entrance to the harbour. M. Fort Marlborough, with covered passage to St. Stephen's Cove.

with the decay of Ciudadela, and the spread of Mahon beyond its mediæval walls, became the principal fortress of the island. It included the site of the old Spanish castle begun at the time of Charles V's abdication, but when captured by Leake and Stanhope it only contained a hundred guns. Owing to a wretched personal intrigue, the idea of fortifying La Mola was never carried out, and our Government weakly acquiesced in the reconstruction of St. Philip's. However, they lavished money on the works, and in a few years it ranked as one of the finest examples of military engineering in Europe. Technically it had no weak spot, but it was commanded by La Mola, which rose 150 feet within 1,200 yards from the walls, and which the French occupied both in 1756 and 1781, in order to obtain an observation post and a good position for their siege batteries. By 1756 the main fortification consisted of four huge bastions between the harbour entrance and St. Stephen's Cove, slightly to the west of the old Spanish citadel, which had been built right to the water's edge. Within the bastions were the living-quarters and store houses, and in the centre a paved square on which stood the observation tower. The guns could fire in every direction, and completely covered the harbour entrance, the steps of the ramparts being broad enough for mules to go up and down. All round the bastions except on the harbour side was the outer ring of lunettes, well supported by redoubts and counter-guards, and all contrived to give the maximum degree of enfilade fire. Finally, at the extreme perimeter there were deep ditches covering the landward side of the castle and running from the harbour to the cove. The road from Mahon is about ninety feet above sea-level, and enters the castle between what was Kane's and the Western lunette, where the ground slopes easily towards the harbour and the open sea. Thus an enemy advancing from Mahon would be able to see nothing of the works but the outer wall and the top of the observation tower five hundred yards in rear, for the castle really lies on the side of a convex slope, and the effect of fire against it could only be observed by crossing the harbour and getting up on La Mola.

Undoubtedly the castle derived its greatest strength from its wonderful system of subterranean passages and galleries, which were cut out of the solid rock, well ventilated by shafts from the surface and containing several wells. There was room in them for the whole garrison, its mules, ammunition, and stores, one of the galleries being large enough to hold sixteen four-wheeled carriages. The troops could move to their posts at the ramparts under cover, and there was no need during a siege for any man to expose himself except when on duty. Leading off from the passages under the outer walls are galleries which were used for mining, so that even if the enemy gained a footing at one particular spot, he would be quickly blown up and the rest of the castle isolated.

To-day the castle is less than a ruin, but the underground works are in excellent preservation and are a striking tribute to our early military engineers.

Entrance to subterranean rocks

Inside one of the bastions

Entrance to St. Stephen's Cove, looking out to sea from the top of the battlements

Entrance to Mahon Harbour, looking across ruins of St. Philip's
Cape Mola in the background

ST. PHILIP'S CASTLE

[p. 94

On the south side the walls rose almost from the waters of St. Stephen's Cove, even now presenting a very formidable appearance. At their base are sally ports and slipways for boats which led straight into the underground works, and so provided the castle with its own private harbour. South again on the other side of the cove the ground rises sharply to 167 feet at Penjat Tower, 600 yards from San Carlos Point. To prevent an enemy exploiting the high ground, Fort Marlborough was built south of the cove. It is a huge octagonal block of masonry, surrounded by a deep ditch and connected with the cove by an underground passage, which encircles the fort just beyond the ditch, and also has side-galleries for mines.

A few guns mounted on Felipet completed the castle's outer defences, and just beyond the walls on the Mahon road stood St. Philip's Town, the peace-time quarters of the garrison, containing barracks and private residences. After 1763 it was recognised that these buildings were too near the walls, and in case of a siege would have to be destroyed every time so as not to mask the fire of the guns or give cover to the attackers. So the suburb was rebuilt farther off and renamed George Town, and is to-day called Villacarlos.

Our occupation of Minorca is an unknown chapter in English administrative history, and one of which we may be proud.

The English Governors preserved the existing machinery of judges and jurats[1] and made no

[1] They controlled all local administration and were elected annually by the five *terminos*, or departments, of Mahon—Ciudadela, Alayor, Mercadal, and Ferrerias. A central council and supreme court sat at Mahon.

attempt to interfere with local affairs. Imports exceeded exports, but the island was saved from bankruptcy by the lavish expenditure of the garrison, and under the governorship of Sir Richard Kane it reached a degree of prosperity hitherto unknown, and still regarded to-day as one of its most fortunate periods. Kane succeeded to a remarkable degree in identifying himself with the welfare of the people; he imported sheep, cattle and poultry from Algiers, encouraged local industry, made a road from Ciudadela to Mahon, and was a constant figure at the markets.[1]

But although the Minorquins were conciliated and their prosperity made an object of official policy, little was done to create those moral and personal ties without which we could never be certain of their loyalty in case of an invasion. The priests, monks and nuns, who abounded in the island, controlled popular opinion, and were strongly opposed to our rule on religious grounds; but had our time-expired soldiers been encouraged to settle and marry there, and had the Anglican Church been represented by sincere men, a great example would have been set, and the Minorquins would have been reconciled. No attempt, however, seems to have been made to mix the races, and the army chaplains as the only representatives of their faith did little to increase its prestige in the eyes of the people, being very lazy

[1] Kane was Lieut.-Governor of Minorca from 1712–20; Governor of Gibraltar, 1720–25; and Governor of Minorca, 1725–36, when he died. One day, while at the market at Mahon, he was asked by a woman selling fruit, "What do you call this plum in England?" To which he answered, "I never saw it in England," from which arose the name of 'Never Saw Plum,' by which this particular fruit is still known.

and generally absent, as their appointments were in the gift of the colonels of the garrison.[1]

The conditions under which our troops served there were appalling. Foreign service in those days was looked upon as a punishment of indefinite duration, if not as a life-sentence, and with only too good reason, it being customary for troops sent to the West Indies and the Mediterranean to be kept abroad for as long as twenty years. Men detailed for such service deserted in large numbers before leaving England, and it was generally necessary for the homecoming regiment to leave as many as two companies behind in order to complete the strength of the battalion. No attempt was made to see that proper food was supplied, and the officers took every opportunity of getting home on the very necessary service of recruiting.[2]

The official establishment for Minorca was four battalions of infantry and one company of artillery and a squad of engineers.

This force was hardly strong enough to defend St. Philip's, regardless of operations outside, and it was recognised that in case of invasion it must retire at once into the castle, and leave Port Mahon and the naval base to their fate.[3] In April 1756 the usual scandalous conditions prevailed. Lord Tyrawley the Governor, all four of the regimental

[1] *Three Letters relating to the Navy, Gibraltar and Port Mahon* (London, 1747).

[2] See *History of the British Army*, by J. W. Fortescue, Vol. II., chap. ii., in which he discusses the whole question of foreign service in the eighteenth century.

[3] The peacetime scheme of distribution was to have one battalion at Ciudadela, one at Mahon, one at Alayor, with a detachment at the fort guarding Fornelles harbour, and the remainder at St. Philip's.

colonels and nine other officers were in England, 'being otherwise employed in His Majesty's Service,' together with nineteen ensigns gazetted between October 1755 and January 1756, who had only just received orders to join their regiments.

This meant that the command of the garrison devolved on Lieut.-Gen. William Blakeney, the Lieut.-Governor, a cheerful veteran of eighty-four, full of energy but afflicted with gout and generally to be found in bed. He dated back to Marlborough's wars, and had a high reputation as a soldier; but lacking interest, only became a colonel at the age of sixty-five. He was a brigadier-general, however, at sixty-nine and major-general at seventy-two, when he commanded the garrison of Stirling in the '45, and seeing the Highlanders about to assault, refused to make any elaborate preparations for defence, thereby luring them to a rash attack in the hopes that he did not intend to resist. At the last moment he opened fire with decisive effect, completely repulsing the attack when on the point of being arrested for treachery by his own officers. For this service he was made lieutenant-general and sent to Minorca, having reached high rank at a rather advanced age, without ever having sent or received a challenge to a duel. He was now quietly sitting in bed, waiting to be made a full general, but time was running short and, as Horace Walpole remarked of the two men on whom Minorca most depended, 'one was too late and the other was too old.'[1] Certainly they were a curious couple, and

[1] *Memoirs of the Reign of George II*, Vol. II., p. 190.

GENERAL BLAKENEY

From the mezzotint in the possession of Messrs. T. H. Parker

Showing Philipet Point on the left, and Cape Mola in the background

[*p.* 98

later on it was a great convenience to the lampoon-writers that their names both began with a ' B.'

The infantry of the garrison consisted of :

The Fourth Foot	Now the King's Own Regiment,
The Twenty-third Foot	,, Royal Welsh Fusiliers,
The Twenty-fourth Foot	,, South Wales Borderers,
The Thirty-fourth Foot	,, 1st Battalion Border Regiment.

Only seven of the field officers of these regiments were present, Lieut.-Cols. Rich,[1] Rufane,[2] and Jefferies,[3] and four majors. Major William Cunningham, late of the engineers, also arrived in time to act as a volunteer. He had resigned in disgust at not being made chief engineer at St. Philip's and was already at Nice on his way home with his family, when he heard of the intended invasion, and at once bought £1,600 worth of timber out of his own pocket to repair the gun-platforms, and by hiring a ship, just reached Mahon with his valuable cargo before the siege began. Robert Boyd, the storekeeper,[4] was another hero of the siege, and was later destined to act in happier circumstances under Heathfield at Gibraltar.

It is extraordinary that with such long warning our Government did not send the absent officers to their posts sooner, and strengthen the garrison,

[1] 1714–85 ; Lieut.-gen., 1760 ; succeeded to his father's baronetcy and dismissed the service owing to a dispute with the Government, 1768.

[2] Lieut.-gen., 1772.

[3] Lieut.-gen., 1765.

[4] The storekeeper was then equivalent to the modern quartermaster. Robert Boyd (1710–94) was promoted to lieut.-col. for his conduct at Minorca, 1758 ; col. of 39th Foot, 1766 ; Lieut.-Governor of Malta, 1768 ; lieut.-gen., 1777, greatly distinguishing himself as second in command of Gibraltar in the siege of 1779–83. Knighted and promoted general, 1793.

seeing that our whole Mediterranean strategy depended on Minorca, which was then what Malta is to us to-day. It was well placed for controlling traffic to the Levant, and also between Spain, France, Italy and North Africa, and it served as an ideal base for a fleet intended to blockade Toulon or Carthagena. Moreover, it provided a splendid jumping-off ground for more offensive measures, as the coast roads eastward along the Riviera to Genoa, and from Marseilles to Carthagena, were very vulnerable to attack from the sea, and the threat of landing a handful of troops from Minorca, to seize the lines of communication, would be enough to play havoc with the *morale* of any French army marching towards the Italian states or down the Spanish coast. Twenty of the line and ten thousand troops based on Port Mahon would have settled the Mediterranean business before it began, but of course neither were available and the French seized the initiative.

Edgecumbe was already taking precautions in case of war as far back as October 1755,[1] and from that time onwards none of the naval or military officers in the Mediterranean doubted that Minorca would be attacked, an unknown intelligencer putting the whole situation in a nutshell by saying of Gibraltar and Mahon that 'in these circumstances it will be very difficult for the English to prevent them being taken, particularly Mahon, which is not strong on the land side, and where they cannot send

[1] No. 17, Ad. 15th Oct., rcd. 5th Nov., 1755. Edgecumbe also obtained from Fowke a detachment of forty-six troops to serve in his ships.

an army capable of preventing an invasion.'[1] Yet when all was over and Minorca lost, the Admiralty complacently stated that 'in the Mediterranean our possessions were defended by fortresses and garrisons ; Minorca in particular had been strengthening at immense expense for many years, a clear evidence that it was always thought there might be periods when our fleet could not prevent an invasion of that island'[2] ; as if a fixed fortress with a garrison too weak to fight outside it was an adequate substitute for a mobile fleet.

On 10th April the French armada sailed from Toulon under the command of Roland-Michel Barin, Marquis de la Galissonnière. He was sixty-three years old, and bred up amidst great family traditions of naval and colonial service. Entering the Navy at seventeen, he slowly rose to the rank of captain at forty-five, an age at which many naval officers might be considered to have completed their career. In 1745 he was given a post ashore as '*commissaire général d'artillerie*' at Rochefort, surely a prelude to retirement, and then two years later, without any warning, he was appointed Governor of French Canada. Here he conceived the brilliant scheme for building the line of forts from Canada to New Orleans, and was about to carry it into effect when he was promoted admiral, and recalled to France to be head of the Charts Department of the Ministry of Marine. From this moment he showed extraordinary energy, sending hydrographers all over

[1] No. 216 P, enclosed by Mr. Villettes, Berne, 13th March, rcd. 22nd March, 1756.

[2] *Add. MSS.* 35895, f. 379.

the Mediterranean, reforming tactics and experimenting with flag signals, and in 1755 was raised to lieutenant-general of Marine, or admiral of the fleet. Like de la Jonquière, Montcalm and Dupleix, he showed 'toutes ces hautes vertus militaires de l'ancienne France qui doivent rester l'exemple de la France nouvelle.'[1] His vice-admiral was the Chevalier de Glandevez, whose family was intimately connected with the service, and who had been promoted to captain in 1741. De la Clue Sabran was rear-admiral, and later destined to lead the Toulon fleet to its destruction in Lagos Bay. Only six of the French captains had been promoted before the end of the last war,[2] and generally speaking, the French officers had less experience of war than those serving under Byng, but in the *Orphée* was a young *enseigne* of twenty-six who in the next war was to show himself perhaps France's greatest sailor—Suffren.

In material, however, the French had a great advantage, for though one less in numbers, their ships were better found and carried heavier metal. They came glistening with new paint to fight a fleet already battered by heavy weather, six hundred miles from its nearest base, with many of its ships foul and leaky, and with a long sick-list.[3] The *Captain* was unfit for foreign service, the *Princess Louisa* had had her masts condemned, and after all Byng's

[1] Lacon-Gayet, *La Marine militaire de la France sous le règne de Louis XV*, p. 257.

[2] 1748.

[3] See West's evidence at Byng's trial.

efforts most of his ships were undermanned, carrying a total of less than six thousand against over eight thousand carried by the French.[1]

In gun-power the difference was more remarkable. The *Foudroyant*, a magnificent eighty-four gunship, carried fifty-two pounders on her lower gun-deck, while four other ships carried forty-two pounders, and the other seven[2] carried thirty-six pounders, and all twelve carried twenty-four pounders on their upper decks. In the English fleet, the *Ramillies*, though a three-decker, carried thirty-two pounders as her heaviest, as did the *Buckingham*, *Culloden*, *Lancaster* and *Intrepid*, and the others of the line, including the *Deptford*, only carried twenty-fours. On their upper decks, the guns of the English ships varied from eighteen-pounders to nines, so that, ship for ship, they were weaker in weight of metal than French ships carrying the same number of guns. This fact had been frequently noted by our officers during the last war, but little had been done to remedy it during the peace, as Anson's policy of creating a new establishment was hardly completed by the end of the American War.

The French army of 15,000 men was carried in one hundred and sixty-three transports, and its equipment was complete in every detail. The Toulon authorities and the general officers had worked their hardest, and at Versailles the advocates of a vigorous offensive were at the moment in the

[1] The French, however, always tended to carry more men compared to English ships of the same rate or establishment.

[2] Only ships of the line are counted here.

ascendant, and the French might feel proud of the fine body of men they were sending to attack Blakeney's exiles. The Comte de Mailleboire and the Marquis du Mesnil were the lieutenant-generals, and the Prince Beauvan marshal of the camp, assisted by the Duc de Fronsac, the Marquis de Laval, de Monty, de Briqueville, de Montenard and many other noble officers. The most arresting personage, however, was the commander-in-chief, the Duc de Richelieu, 'who had early surprised the fashionable world by his adventures and imposed on it by his affectations, had dictated to it by his wit and insolent agreeableness, and had often tried to govern it by his intrigues, and who would be the hero of the age if histories were novels or women wrote history. . . . His first campaign was hiding himself at fourteen under the Duchess of Burgundy's bed. . . a genius so entertaining could not fail to captivate the ladies,' and he was recalled from Vienna 'for carrying a black lamb in his state coach at midnight, to sacrifice to the moon, in order to obtain a recruit of vigour.'[1] Galissonnière was 'petit, bossu, ne payant pas d'apparence,' while Richelieu represented 'les grâces légères, la galanterie impertinente, l'intrigue sans scrupule, tous les défauts et les travers, avec ces deux qualités qui font tout pardonner dans notre pays, le courage et l'esprit.' Unlike Galissonnière, who displayed the Catonian virtues of Montcalm and Dupleix, Richelieu was the Alcibiades of France, and 'was blessed with virtues, honours—and debts.' At Versailles, as First Lord

[1] Horace Walpole, *Memoirs of the Reign of George II*, Vol. II., p. 210.

of the Bedchamber, he was the master of etiquette; as Governor of Languedoc he was a tolerator of Protestants; and at Fontenoy he was a skilful tactician and heroic leader. Clearly Byng and Blakeney were to face men of no ordinary calibre.

Richelieu was instructed to destroy the naval base at Port Mahon, capture St. Philip's, and then return to France; only at a later stage in the operations was he told to hold the island.

Galissonnière's instruction, dated 22nd March, when the invasion was simply considered as a raid, presupposed that the whole business would be over long before an English fleet could arrive. Consequently, he was restricted entirely to covering Richelieu's landing-place with his whole fleet, and was not to leave it till St. Philip's was invested, when he might sail round and blockade Mahon harbour, by which time all the English ships in it would have escaped.

There was great excitement at Mahon and St. Philip's on 16th April, when it was known that the French had sailed, and next day part of the armada was sighted off Fornelles. Edgecumbe fixed a boom across the harbour entrance at its narrowest point and sank the *Proserpine* fireship outside it,[1] the garrison detachments in different parts of the island, already reduced in numbers as a precaution, began to straggle in, and the engineers set about destroying the gay houses of St. Philip's Town. An appeal to the Minorquins for assistance, issued eight weeks before, had only produced twenty-two volunteers,

[1] Ad. In Letters, Vol. 383.

but as Blakeney had already 'secured' all those known to be acquainted with the subterranean works 'as too dangerous to be left without,' it is not surprising that distrust was mutual.

Meanwhile, Captain Hervey was at Villa Franca, writing home an excellent appreciation of the situation.[1] He had just received the all-important news that Byng had sailed from England, and thought that the French could not make much progress 'before our fleet arrives, which must either destroy that of the enemy or else oblige them to forsake their troops as are there, and desert their transports.'

On the evening of the 18th April, Robert Boyd, Captain Noel of the *Princess Louisa,* and Lieut. O'Hara climbed up on to the great sugar-loaf hill of Mont Toro and looked down on the French dis-embarking at Ciudadela, eagerly assisted by the Minorquins—a discouraging sight. 'C'est un des plus beaux spectacles que j'aie vu de ma vie,' wrote Rochambeau, 'notre escadre mouilla en croissant, ayant derrière elle tous vaisseaux de transport. Les côtes de Majorque et Minorque étaient couvertes de peuple.[2] . . . Je distinguai avec une lunette beaucoup de femmes, ce qui ne me donna pas l'opinion de la résistance qu'on nous opposerait à la descente. . . . Les femmes et les enfants venaient au-devant de nous et nous aidaient à passer les

[1] *Add. MSS.* 31959, ff. 238–43.

[2] He could not, of course, have seen both coasts at once, but some of the French ships probably stood into Pollensa Bay and attracted many sight-seers.

crevasses de rochers ; ils étaient tous Catholiques et n'aimaient pas les Anglais.'

Edgecumbe held a naval council of war[1] and decided that it was time his squadron withdrew, otherwise it was in serious danger of being bottled up in the harbour. Feeling rather uncomfortable at deserting the garrison, he took Noel with him to explain matters to Blakeney, who agreed absolutely with this plan, as long as the French did not attack the harbour, and on Noel hinting that the garrison might become dispirited if the ships left them, cheerily replied that he would give out that they went to join Byng and would soon be back with a strong fleet. Blakeney then called a military council of war to which Edgecumbe, Noel and Baird were invited, but here opinion was equally divided on the question of withdrawing the ships. Edgecumbe was worried by this and called another naval council, but his officers refused to alter their original decision and the squadron sailed on 20th April.

However, he left Captain Scrope behind in command of the *Dolphin* and the *Proserpine*, now sunk, and in addition landed 286 sailors, marines and soldiers, ten guns and a great quantity of provisions and stores.[2]

Why did any of the land officers question this decision? And what did Blakeney mean by saying he approved of the ships going if the harbour was not attacked? Surely it was Edgecumbe's duty

[1] 19th April.

[2] Two 24-pounders each from the *Deptford*, *Portland* and *Princess Louisa* and four 18-pounders from the *Chesterfield*.

to keep his squadron in being and go to join Byng, who incidentally had no frigates. The only alternative seems to have been that some officers thought the ships would be better employed in using their guns against the French army as it advanced. The idea was certainly attractive. By standing off the west end of the harbour the ships could have brought the French under fire before they entered Mahon and thus have given temporary protection to the naval base. They could then have denied the French the use of the road from Mahon to St. Philip's and have forced them to make a detour across the rocky ground to the south, and then have enfiladed their left flank as soon as it began to deploy for the investment. They could also have made it very difficult for the French to use La Mola, as every single man would have had to march right round the west end of the harbour to get there, instead of being able to pull straight across by boat. Thus there were great possibilities for a vigorous naval defence from inside the harbour, where the French army would have been seriously embarrassed and its fleet unable to pass the boom. However, it was fairly obvious that tactics of this kind must fail in the end, as the French would bring up guns during the night to command the harbour, and the ships' ammunition would soon have been exhausted, so that they would have been compelled to sink themselves.

The garrison, meanwhile, drove in all the cattle it could find, and set about breaking up the St. Philip's-Mahon-Ciudadela road. All told, it did not number more than 3,350[1] at the most, including 'volunteers, Greeks, and Jews,' so that it could not hope to hold out long against an army more than four times its size, when defending a fortress which, though very strong, demanded a very large number to man its works.

Richelieu was received with pretty speeches and a solemn *Te Deum*; he replied affably, promised to forbid plundering and pushed out his advance guard. It reached Ferrerias easily enough and then found that the English had broken up the road. The ground is very undulating just there, and the road is at one moment in a deep ravine and the next on top of a causeway, while on each side there are small rocks covered with thick undergrowth, making a detour almost impossible, so that there was nothing for it but to order the siege train to be taken by sea and landed at Cala Mezquida. The advanced guard quickly reached Mercadal, detached a small force north to seize Fornelles, and by 21st April was on the outskirts of Mahon. Next day Richelieu, who was with the main body at Alayor, was waited on by the drum major of the 24th Regiment under a flag of truce, who came to demand a formal reason for the French landing, which was quite natural, as war had not been declared, and Blakeney had had no news from London or Paris since 1st April. Richelieu haughtily replied that the English had taught a new way of making war, without a declaration, by capturing

[1] All accounts of the number are misleading and contradictory; roughly there were 2,890 infantry, 100 artillery and engineers, 286 men under Scrope, and the 50 volunteers, Jews and Greeks.

two of the Most Christian King's ships the year before, and since then making numerous prizes. On the 24th the French marched through Mahon and camped a mile and a half from St. Philip's, and two days later Richelieu sent a drummer to Blakeney with a present of dried fruit, in return for which Blakeney sent back six bottles of English beer, after which courtesies both sides felt at liberty to begin fighting. Richelieu, however, was rather at a loss how to proceed; his plan of St. Philip's, the best the Ministry of Marine could supply, was contemporary with the English conquest of the island, and a merchant skipper had scornfully told him that it was no more like St. Philip's than the Bastille was like a good fortress. Straight ahead he could see the frowning slopes of the outer works, and the watch-tower sticking up over the top a long way in rear, and that was all. He was therefore compelled to occupy La Mola in order to find out what the castle really looked like, and then began to erect batteries in a semicircle from the harbour to the sea, in the face of such a hot fire from the garrison that it was impossible to do much work on them except at night.

Progress was very slow; the ground was so rocky that earth for the batteries had to be brought from a mile away, and it proved so gravelly that it had to be sifted, and then became so dusty that it had to be wetted. But the French were not to be discouraged, and by 6th May they had finished two of their batteries, and the artillery duel had begun.

CHAPTER VIII

THE BATTLE

BYNG slowly worked his way east in the face of a stiff head wind, and on 15th May passed between Ibiza and Majorca, steering south-east.[1] The *Experiment* was sent into Palma for news, and sighted two of Galissonnière's frigates, which at once made off, and revealed the *Phœnix*, which they had been blockading in the harbour.[2] Captain Hervey had no fresh news, so Byng, who now had his whole force with him, sailed along the south coast of Majorca, passed Cabrera, and at daybreak on the 19th was off Cala Covas, Minorca. He could not hope to take the French unawares, as the alarm must have been given by the two frigates off Palma, but he determined to try to open up communications with Blakeney as quickly as possible and find out how best to use his fleet to relieve the castle.

Captain Hervey was sent ahead with the *Phœnix*, *Chesterfield* and *Dolphin* and told to use his utmost endeavours 'to land a packet addressed to Blakeney, and if possible obtain an answer.' He was also ordered: (1) To observe any French batteries on the coast likely to interrupt communications; (2) to

[1] 14th May, Ibiza was sighted N.N.E. 15th May, Ibiza lay E.S.E. and Majorca S.S.W.

[2] 16th May, Dragonera N.N.E.

intercept any small craft seen about and send those in them to the admiral; and (3) to inform the admiral by prearranged signal:

(*a*) Whether the coast was clear of French warships.

(*b*) Whether the English colours were flying at St. Philip's.

(*c*) Whether it looked possible to send a boat to St. Philip's, or if any boat appeared to be coming out from there to the fleet.

This was all very business-like, but the letter to Blakeney was conceived in Byng's worst style. He expressed sorrow for events as they then stood, flattering himself that if he had been there sooner the French would never have landed, and wanted to know the best place for landing General Stuart and the other officers and recruits. 'The Royal Regiment of English Fusileers,' it continued, 'is likewise on board the squadron, destined, agreeable to my orders, to serve on board the fleet in the Mediterranean unless it should be thought necessary, upon consultation with you, to land the regiment for the defence of Minorca; but I must inform you should the Fusileers be landed, as they are part of the ships' complements, the marines having been ordered by the Lord Commissioners of the Admiralty on board of other ships at Portsmouth, to make room for them, that it will disable the squadron from acting against that of the enemy. However, I shall gladly embrace every opportunity of promoting His Majesty's Service in the most effectual manner, and shall assist you to distress the enemy and defeat their designs to the utmost of my power. Please to favour me with information how I can be most effectual of service to you and the garrison; and believe me to be with great truth and esteem, Sir, your most obedient humble servant.'

Obviously, he could not land the troops and fight the French properly as well, hence the dilemma; but what a discouraging letter to send to a poor old beleaguered invalid! Moreover, he made no attempt to send Stuart, Cornwallis, Effingham and the others ahead with Hervey, all in one ship and ready for an instant landing, and so he lost all chance of slipping them in by surprise. At any moment Blakeney might collapse, leaving the garrison in the hands of a lieutenant-colonel, and here was a major-general, two colonels and other officers, whose presence was worth ten times their numerical value, scattered about in different ships.

Hervey rounded the 'Laire of Mahon'[1] and stood close into the shore, signalling back that the English colours still flew over St. Philip's, and at the same time hoisted the prearranged signal by which the garrison were to recognise the *Phœnix*, and a white pennant to speak with Captain Scrope. By ten o'clock the whole squadron was round the Laire, and at once found themselves becalmed under the lee of the island. A mile ahead they could see the *Phœnix* also becalmed, and so close to the shore that Hervey was getting his boats out to tow her clear. Three miles farther was their principal objective, St. Philip's Castle, and everyone in the

[1] The Isla del Aire.

squadron could plainly see and hear the continuous exchange of fire between its guns and the enemies' batteries. It was a tantalising moment. If only they could get enough breeze to reach the castle, they would have the interior position and could bid the French defiance. But there was nothing to help them save the very slightest puffs of wind; the garrison made no attempt to acknowledge their signal or send a boat. Byng crept forward, hardly making any progress, and fired three guns to attract the garrison's attention, and then the French fleet appeared. They were first seen to the south-east, slipping along with the precious breeze that Byng, under the lee of the island, was denied. Warned by his frigates from Palma, Galissonnière was coming up as fast as he could, and Richelieu was already ordering seven hundred soldiers to be sent in tartans to reinforce him.

Any hesitation which Byng might have had as to what to do next vanished as soon as he saw the French. Up went the signal for 'general chase,' all frigates were recalled, and one hundred and fifty of their men were quickly transferred to the ships of the line. With the enemy in sight there could be no question of detaching frigates; he wanted every ship and every man. By seven in the evening the fleets were two leagues apart, but neither side wanted a night action, and Byng, who knew Minorca from old experience, stood close into the land again to get the usual off-shore breeze at daybreak.

Meanwhile what had been happening at St. Philip's? Apparently they saw nothing of the

ST. PHILIP'S CASTLE

The seamost end of the fortifications, still in good preservation, showing the entrance to St. Stephen's Cove on the near side, and the entrance to Mahon Harbour beyond. Cape Mola in the background

[p. 114

Phœnix till ten o'clock, and then Robert Boyd urged Colonel Jefferies to let him row out at once, but nothing could be done without a council of war to decide what instructions he should be given. The discussion, which presumably took place round Blakeney's bed, lasted all the morning and well into the afternoon, and when at last Boyd, fuming with impatience, was called in and given a letter for Byng, it was past three o'clock and Byng's ships were standing away to the south. This was the more regrettable as the Council eventually decided not to write anything about the conditions inside the castle for fear of capture, Boyd being authorised to explain the whole situation verbally, and having already arranged suitable signals to be made to the castle from the fleet.

At last he got away in a six-oared boat manned by ten of Scrope's sailors, but after an hour and a half's pulling they were losing distance on the fleet and it was getting dusk, so there was nothing for it but to return. Had Boyd reached the fleet, there is little doubt that he would have represented the garrison's situation so strongly that Byng would have sent the land officers ashore that night. Besides, Boyd's arrival would have disproved the Gibraltar 'opinion' and have put new life into the whole enterprise. It was obvious that in fair weather boats could land perfectly well, as the only batteries capable of firing into St. Stephen's Cove were the five-gun one on Turk's Mount, which could not see the target, and a three-gun mortar battery on Mola, a thousand yards away. In rough weather, of course, it would be different, as there are rocks at the edge of the water and the Spanish troops to-day always use a punt-shaped boat for work in the cove. Boyd was fired on from Turk's Mount on his way out, and also by some musketeers, but only one shot hit the boat and no one was hurt.

Byng was early astir on the morning of 20th May, and at 3 a.m. made the signal for the line. When the early morning haze lifted, two of the French tartans carrying troops to Galissonnière were discovered quite near the fleet, and one was captured. At six the French fleet was seen from the masthead about twelve miles south-west by south, and as St. Philip's then bore eight miles north-north-west, there was again an opportunity to open up communications, but Byng was still unwilling to detach a ship in the face of the enemy, and immediately steered towards them. Galissonnière, however, stood away to the south-east, and it was obvious that there would be a long sailing duel before they finally met.

Meanwhile, Byng hugged the wind, which was blowing on his port bow, and slowly going round to the south. This continued till after ten, when Byng, being now exactly between Minorca and the French, turned to the south-east and bore towards them, crowding sail as he went and closing up his line to half a cable distance between the ships. The French at once accepted his challenge and headed west-north-west. As the wind was blowing south-south-west, both fleets were sailing as close to it as was then possible for ships of the line—that is to say, six points off—and were rapidly approaching on opposite tacks. They were racing for the weather-gauge, as the one which first reached the point of intersection of their approaching courses would obtain the coveted windward position.

There was a great hurrying to and fro in the ships as they made final preparations for action. Byng was in his blue coat and very much at his ease, pacing the quarter-deck with Captain Gardiner and his secretary George Lawrence, and carrying a copy of the Fighting Instructions, so that he might be quite certain of fighting his first fleet action according to regulations.

Lord Robert Bertie and other Fusilier officers were looking on with great interest, while their men fingered their muskets and began to take up positions usually occupied by the marines. The able seamen—or mariners, as they were called—were distributed in little groups ready to make lightning adjustments of sail, the rest of the sailors being chiefly employed at the guns. Here they were pulling off their shirts, hitching their trousers and receiving final instructions from the lieutenants as they went along the decks; Byng ordering the *Ramillies* gunners to load with double shot. Mess tables and cabin fittings were being bundled away to make more room at the gun ports; the carpenters were getting ready to plug the holes made by wind and water shots; the surgeons looked over the terrifying armoury of their septic craft, and there was a stumbling about and quiet cursing as the 'loblolly men' shoved tables and sea-chests together in readiness for amputations.

At 12.30, when the fleets were less than a league

apart, the wind suddenly changed two points to south-west, thus blowing more astern of the English and more in the faces of the French, who at once came up in the wind with a great flapping of canvas. Byng had no wish to commit himself to a *mêlée*, and, with his own line perfectly formed, followed the wind round and steered south-south-east, thus weathering the French with his whole fleet. Galissonnière for the moment was in a very nasty position, but he quickly edged away from the wind, steering west-north-west and being quite content to resign the weather-gauge to Byng.

The fleets now began to pass each other on opposite courses and inclined at an angle of about 33 degrees, the *Ramillies*, fourth in our line, being still a long way abeam of the French rear, while the *Buckingham*, sailing tenth, was only two miles from their van.

Byng was now at liberty to tack and engage as soon as his van was level with the enemy's rear, according to Article XVII of the Fighting Instructions. At 1.20, the fleets being exactly abreast of each other, and the exact moment having arrived, Byng opened the Fighting Instructions and 'perused' Article XVII. Mr. Lawrence 'took the liberty of observing that agreeable to that Article the fleet should tack.' This would have brought both fleets on the same tack and steering converging courses, so that an ordinary ship-to-ship action would have followed.

Byng, however, was not to be tied by convention, and answered 'that he would stand rather beyond their rear before he tacked, as it would give an opportunity to every ship to lead slanting down on the one she was to engage, and they would not be so liable to be raked by the enemy's fire.' Byng knew that the French were adepts at long-range firing, and often preferred to accept the inferior tactical position to leeward in order to rake their enemies' rigging with broadsides as they bore down in line abreast. This meant that every attacking ship had its 'T' badly crossed before it could turn into line ahead again and exchange broadside for broadside with the French, and thus being crippled in its rigging at the start of the action, would find itself unable to sail properly by the end. Byng, with visions of a six hundred mile passage before he could even reach the inadequate dockyard of Gibraltar, was very anxious to suffer as little damage aloft as possible, and so meant to close the enemy on a diagonal course. This method of attack was called lasking, and dated back to Dartmouth's instructions of 1688, and differed from Anson's line of bearing in being a tactical method of bringing the enemy to action when holding the weather-gauge rather than a cruising formation.

When the *Kingston* was well past the French rear, Byng at last gave the signal to tack. As Galissonnière saw the English beginning to go about in succession, he at once divined an attack on his rear, led by the gigantic *Ramillies*, whose curious position in the line had puzzled him ever since she was sighted, it being customary for the commander-in-chief to be in the centre. Byng, having only one other flag-officer, was disinclined to appoint any of his captains commodore, and so fought in two squadrons, commanded by himself and Temple West. Galissonnière, therefore, threw all his sails aback, checking his fleet sharply and thus preventing his van sailing out of the action, as he thought that Byng intended should happen. Byng instantly countered by signalling his fleet to tack together, instead of each ship in succession, in order to prevent West's division being left out of the action when they had once got into reverse order. The French line was more extended than our own, and as Captain Andrews got the *Defiance* round he noticed that the *Orphée* was some distance ahead of him on his lee bow, and crowded on sail in order to draw up abeam of her, thinking that Byng had made a mistake in tacking so late. The *Ramillies* was now at the wrong end of the line for setting a course for the rest to steer by, and, to Byng's great disgust, he saw all the ships in the van follow the *Defiance* in a race to draw level with the French, instead of leading straight down to them on a lasking course.

Byng was furious at seeing his whole scheme about to be spoilt, remarking to Gardiner 'that he could not think what Captain Andrews was about.' However, he hoisted a striped blue and white flag at the foretopmast head and fired one gun, being the signal for the leading ship to steer one point to starboard.[1] It was useless to try to dictate the exact number of points that Andrews ought to bear away in order to get on the right course, and Byng hoped that a signal for one would send him at once to the attack. Andrews, however, was deaf to hints, and altered

[1] Additional Fighting Instructions, Article V.

course exactly one point but made no attempt to get any nearer the enemy. At two o'clock Byng repeated the signal and, seeing it technically obeyed as before, gave up trying to make any further preliminary manœuvres, and hoisted the red flag for battle at the foretopmast head. The lack of any proper signalling system such as existed in later wars had ruined his chances of controlling his fleet effectively just before making contact with the enemy.

On seeing the signal for battle, the van ships at once put before the wind, and turning nearly at right angles, rushed perpendicularly at the enemy, and soon came under a very hot fire. The *Defiance* and *Portland* were less than a mile from their opposite numbers, but the *Lancaster* was much farther and the *Buckingham* was about a mile and a half, while the *Captain* and *Intrepid* were farther still. The French ships were heading north-west and had their maintopsails to the mast, waiting for our attack with only steerage way on, the wind heeling them over slightly and giving greater elevation to the guns on their port side.

The *Orphée* opened fire at 2.30, the others as far along as the *Lion* joining in one after another at short intervals. Ten minutes later, as the *Defiance* brought to within three hundred yards and began to reply with guns and small arms, the French filled their maintopsails and stood on a few yards, nearly spoiling our deployment and forcing the *Portland* to bring to and engage at five hundred yards, and the *Buckingham* to bear away two points and begin the engagement over again. What with the French putting themselves out of range for some minutes and the great cloud of smoke overhanging all the

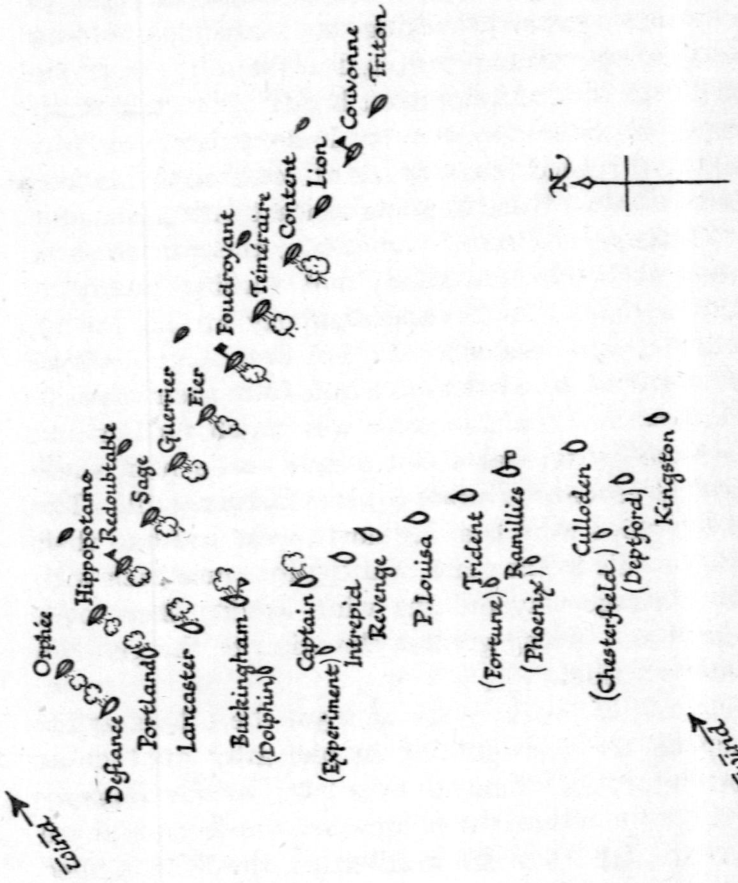

THE BATTLE, 2.45 P.M.
The English van coming into action, the rear lasking, and the *Deptford* leaving the line.

ships, it was very difficult to see what was happening, and the English ships were not doing too well.

Owing to the sharp inclination of the two lines of

battle, the English van in the new order after tacking was straggling into action one ship at a time, and the centre and rear ships, being still at a slant to each other, were in great danger of causing a hold-up astern of them if anything went wrong. Temple West had hoisted the signal for closer action and, seeing the *Sage* run out the line to leeward, was convinced that his division was defeating the enemy single-handed, but this was only the beginning of a prearranged retirement which was to take place as soon as the French van had inflicted enough damage on our rigging, and was beginning to get hotly engaged. The *Redoubtable* shot ahead to close the *Hippopotame*, pursued by the *Lancaster* and *Buckingham*, upon which the *Guerrier* also left the line.

At 3.20 the *Redoubtable* retired, and was soon followed by the *Orphée* and the *Hippopotame*, thus leaving the first five ships of West's division to enjoy their rapid victory. They were, however, badly knocked about aloft. Edgecumbe pushed the *Lancaster* to the head of the line minus her mizen-top-mast, just as M. de Glandevez brought his ships into line again some distance to leeward. The *Portland* came next, with her mainyard and bowsprit smashed and her foremast shot through in several places. The *Buckingham* and *Captain* followed some distance astern, and to windward lay the *Defiance*, with Captain Andrews and his boatswain killed, four gun-ports smashed, all her masts shot through and her boats useless.

Pursuit was out of the question, but as they went slowly ahead waiting for the rear to close them, the French centre loomed out of the smoke. Where was Byng? The explanation was simple. Captain Young had put the *Intrepid* before the wind and gone down to engage the *Fier*, who, being over-eager fired her first broadside when out of range, and was closed by the *Intrepid* before she could reload. A few minutes later, however, she brought down the *Intrepid's* foretopmast and sent her staggering into the wind and quite unmanageable, the smoke being so thick that the *Experiment* and *Chesterfield* huzza'd loudly, thinking a Frenchman had been hit.

Captain Young had the *Intrepid's* damaged rigging cut away, and got her on to the port tack again, but incapable of making any headway. Galissonnière, being scarcely engaged at all, came up with his two seconds[1] and gave her a frightful pounding, the three French ships dropping their aim from the rigging and hulling her time after time. Just when the *Intrepid's* position was becoming quite desperate, the *Revenge* fetched up alongside and Captain Cornwall politely sent a boat to enquire if Young thought it was 'for the King's service' that the *Revenge* should stand to leeward and so cover the *Intrepid* from the enemy's fire. Young, thinking that enough homage had been paid to the doctrine of the unbroken line,[2] agreed, and the *Revenge* passed between him and the enemy. This was the first hold-up in the English line, and one which Hervey, in the *Phœnix*, lying to windward of the fleet, had been afraid would

[1] The ships immediately ahead and astern.

[2] 'No ship in the fleet shall leave his station under any pretence whatsoever till he has acquainted his flag or the next flag officer to him with the condition of his ship and received his direction herein.'—Fighting Instructions, Article XXIV.

THE BATTLE, 3 P.M.

A. The French Fleet: the *Sage*, *Guerrier* and *Couronne* turning away. B. The English Van.

C. The *Intrepid* disabled. D, E, F, G. The *Revenge*, *P. Louisa*, *Trident*, and *Ramillies* all shown with their sails aback. *From the engravings published with the Trial.*

Note.—The rears of the two fleets are shown too close together

[p. 124

happen. Next in the fight came the *Princess Louisa,* who received heavy damages aloft as she neared the French, while Captain Noel had a leg shot off and died of his wound a few days after. In the general confusion the ship 'flung up in the wind with her topsails shaking,' but Captain Durell, astern in the *Trident,* ignored the Fighting Instructions, and ran to leeward of her without much hesitation, and also passing the *Intrepid,* fetched up astern of the *Revenge.* Thus, by making an attack when our leading ships were nearer to the enemy than our rear, Byng allowed his fleet to be engaged in detail as it bore down. Moreover, his own division was still on a lasking course and not running before the wind, so that when the *Intrepid* and *Princess Louisa* became unmanageable, the ships astern of them were bound to be held up too, supposing they insisted on keeping in a line with those ahead, and thus a dangerous gap soon opened between the *Captain* and those astern of her.

The *Ramillies* had been just over two miles from the French when the action began, and at 2.43 Byng had signalled the *Deptford,* his weakest ship, to quit the line and join the frigates, thus equalising his numbers with the French.[1] Byng soon saw that he was getting ahead of the *Trident* and *Princess Louisa,* who were being held up by the *Intrepid* and *Revenge,* so he shortened sail to let them get into station and bore away three points to starboard, whereupon Captain Gardiner suggested that, by setting more sail himself, Byng would give these ships an example

[1] As directed by the First Article of the Additional Fighting Instructions.

and reach the enemy with less damage. Byng was quite willing to attempt an unusual form of attack by arranging the angle which our line should make with that of the enemy, but to break the line itself when once formed seemed tactical sacrilege, and turning to Gardiner, he reminded him of the 'misfortune' of 'Mr. Matthews,' and asked in mingled tones of pomp and pity if he really thought it was fitting for the admiral of the fleet to go down alone as if to engage a single ship.

Only five minutes, however, were wasted in waiting for the ships ahead, and soon after the French centre began to send random shots high over the *Ramillies'* masts. Owing to her lasking course, some of her starboard guns would bear, although the French were quite half a mile away, and at 2.50 a gun was suddenly fired without orders from the upper deck. All the rest followed, thinking there must have been an order, and Byng saw no reason to stop them, as they were now well within range, although he was at that moment telling Gardiner and the Fusilier officers that he intended to reserve his fire for close quarters. The *Ramillies* was too far abaft the beam of her opposite number, the *Lion*, so concentrated on the *Couronne*, whom she presently drove out of the line with her maintopsail yard broken. The smoke was now so thick that the gunners could only get occasional glimpses of their target, and suddenly someone shouted that there was a ship under the *Ramillies'* lee bow. Byng dashed on to the poop to stop the gunners firing until they found out if the ship was French, and

Captain Gardiner and Lord Robert Bertie did the same for the upper, lower and middle decks. The

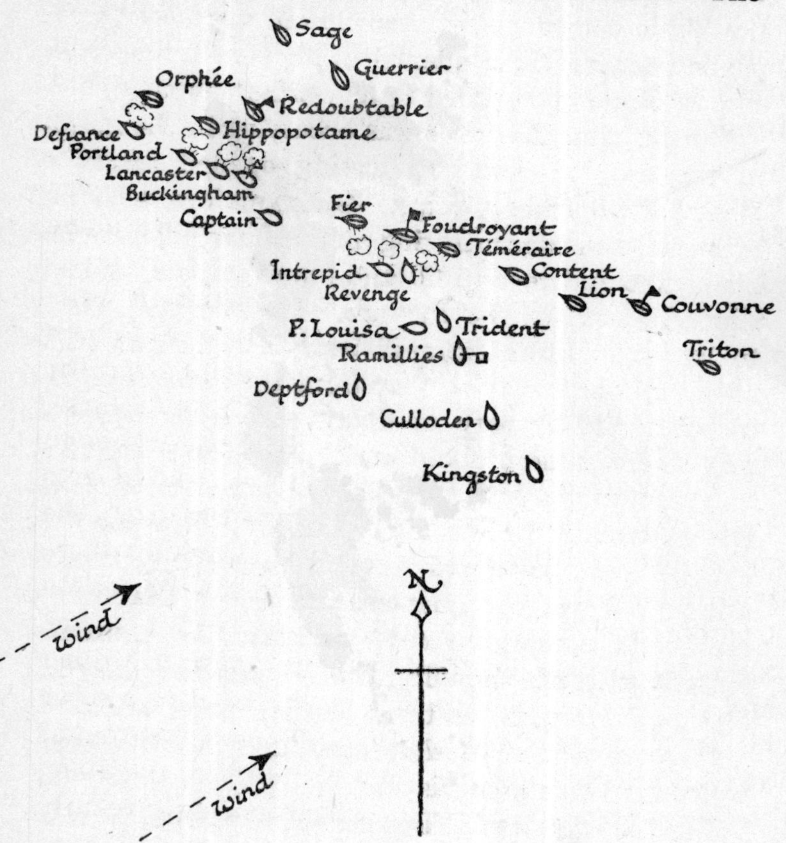

THE BATTLE, 3.20 P.M.

The French van withdrawing. The *Revenge* passing the *Intrepid*, and the *Trident* passing the *P. Louisa*. The *Fier* and *Foudroyant* trying to cut through the English line. N.B.—Frigates omitted.

Ramillies was brought up short by laying her top-sails aback, and the strange sail was found to be the *Trident* just getting clear of the *Princess Louisa*. Byng then signalled the fleet to brace to, and five minutes afterwards to fill and stand on, a signal intended only for the ships astern of him, so as not to hold up the whole fleet, and in a quarter of an hour he managed to pay clear, and passed to leeward at about 3.30.

By this time the crisis was occurring in the middle of the line, a wide gap having opened astern of West's five leading ships. Galissonnière, who had hitherto been concentrating on the *Intrepid*, signalled his centre and rear to fill and stand on, and quickly slipped ahead of the *Revenge*, who had just passed to leeward of the *Intrepid* but was still two miles astern of the *Captain*, four from the *Lancaster*, and to windward of both of them. Once through this gap, Galissonnière could easily crush our shattered van from to windward, and at the same time prevent Byng coming to its aid. Luckily, however, the English rear appeared at this moment, crowding sail on his weather quarter, and seeing that it was useless to attempt a *coup de main*, he contented himself with cannonading the *Buckingham*, *Captain* and *Defiance* with his three leading ships, and firing his bow chasers at the *Lancaster*, and then bore away to leeward to rejoin his van.

The *Culloden* and *Kingston* followed the *Ramillies* without firing a shot, and Byng soon closed his van in good order, sending the *Chesterfield* to lie by the *Intrepid*, and the *Deptford* to take her place in the line. By five o'clock all firing had ceased, and the French could be seen heading north-north-west more than two miles to leeward. Both fleets stood on till 6 p.m., when Byng tacked in succession,

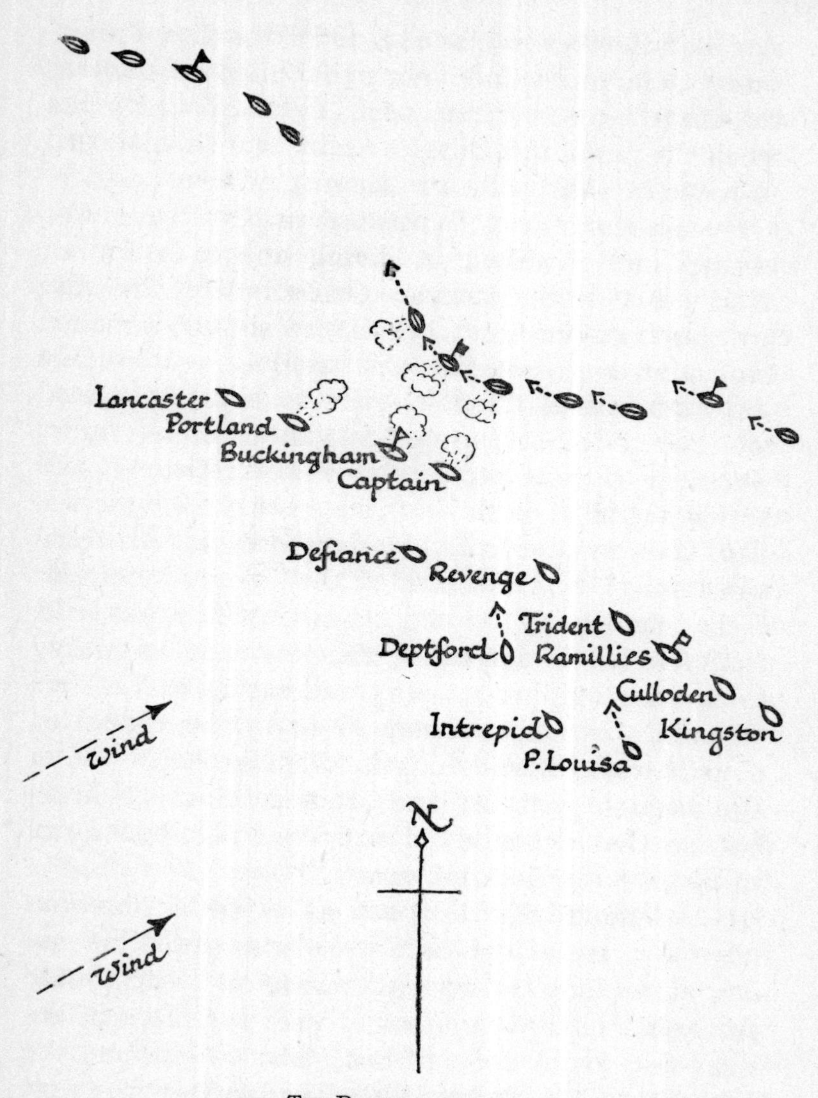

THE BATTLE, 4.50 P.M.
French centre and rear turning away to join their van. Gap in the English line closed. *Defiance* and *Intrepid* lying to windward disabled. *Deptford* and *P. Louisa* trying to take and recover station in the line.

West's division leading, so as to bring the *Ramillies* in rear again, and therefore nearer to the French in case they wished to renew the action, but they were soon lost in the dusk, and Byng brought to for the night.

So ended the battle of Minorca. By attacking the enemy's van first, Byng allowed his ships to be engaged and punished in detail, and because he combined it with a lasking course the crippling of two ships' rigging held up all the ships astern of them, and a serious disaster was only averted by good seamanship. Galissonnière fought the action with fine judgment, using his van to cripple and disorganise their opposite numbers and retiring them as soon as the English ships began to develop their full fire power. Clerk of Eldin rightly emphasises that Galissonnière was the first of the French admirals of the eighteenth century to accept the leeward position in battle, and aim at destroying the mobility of our ships by long-range accurate gun-fire. They had even shown a tendency to do this as far back as the battle of Bantry Bay in 1689, but it was only fully developed during and after the Seven Years' War, so that Byng was the first of a long list of distinguished victims, including Keppel and Rodney. But Galissonnière's instructions forbade him to undertake any of the risks usually accepted by an admiral wishing to exploit minor successes, and consequently, although his ships showed superior sailing powers, he only made a half-hearted attempt to cut through the English line and crush our damaged van, and the battle ended without any definite advantage to either side.

CHAPTER IX

THE COUNCIL OF WAR

'I AM to thank you a thousand and a thousand times for your fine and gallant behaviour this day,' wrote Byng to West as soon as the action was over. 'I wish you had been better supported . . . your behaviour was like an angel to-day. God bless you.' West at once went on board the Admiral to return thanks, and found Byng very uneasy about the damage done to the rigging of the van ships, and doubtful if it were wise to make sail and so risk losing the *Intrepid*. He also seemed much dissatisfied with the behaviour of some of the ships in his own division.

Next morning Cape Mola bore about twenty-five miles north-west, but the French fleet could be seen from the masthead exactly between us and St. Philip's, and there seemed no chance of opening up communications. Meanwhile, the crews of the damaged ships worked hard to carry out such repairs as were possible at sea, and the frigates were sent to look for the *Intrepid* and the *Chesterfield*, which had parted company during the night. The first-named was known to have been badly hit, and the *Defiance*, *Portland*, *Captain*, and *Buckingham* were reported unfit for action. Had the French attacked on the 21st, and forced Byng to fight at a tactical disadvantage in order to protect his injured ships,

there is no doubt that he would have been severely defeated. The French fleet had suffered little damage aloft, and could always retire to Ciudadela, where, however, there were no naval stores. On the other hand, they could, if compelled, get back to Toulon in half the time that it would take Byng to reach the inadequate resources of Gibraltar.

Byng now realised that, had he occupied the orthodox position in the centre of his fleet during the battle, he might have controlled its movements more successfully, and he conferred with West as to the propriety of forming the line in three divisions. After some discussion they decided that this was impossible, as Byng 'did not know whom to trust with the third division.' He appointed Hervey to command the *Defiance* in place of Andrews, and Lloyd to command the *Princess Louisa* in place of Noel. On the 22nd the missing ships were sighted to the south-west, and were soon recovered without being threatened by the French fleet. On the 23rd, Byng gave out a new order of battle, taking the *Captain* and *Defiance* into his own division in exchange for the *Kingston* and *Revenge*, and after consulting with West, decided to hold a council of war next morning. West arrived very early, and represented that those captains whom Byng thought had not done their duty ought not to be allowed to take part. Byng, however, was disinclined 'to stigmatise gentlemen's little failings in their duty,' and said that he would reprimand them later, and at seven o'clock the signal was made for all captains. Few realised, as they climbed up the side of the

Ramillies from their boats and filed into the great cabin, that they were about to endorse one of the most disastrous expressions of opinion ever made in the annals of our Navy, and one which was to result in the execution of their commander-in-chief.

The following attended:

Admiral Byng.	Captain Henry Ward.
Rear-Admiral West.	Captain Philip Durell.
Maj.-Gen. Stuart.	Captain James Young.
Col. Edward Cornwallis.	Captain Charles Catford.
Col. Lord Effingham.	Captain Frederick Cornwall.
Col. Lord Robert Bertie.	Captain George Edgecumbe.
	Captain William Parry.
	Captain John Amherst.
	Captain Arthur Gardiner.
	Captain Augustus Hervey.
	Captain Michael Everitt.
	Captain William Lloyd.

Patrick Baird of the *Portland* was left out for some unexplained reason, possibly sickness, but no reference was made to the fact afterwards. The land officers were summoned, as the operation was a combined one, and they considered themselves under Byng's command, and therefore 'bound to co-operate' with him, although three of them were only 'passengers.'

Byng laid before them:

(1) His Instructions of 30th March.

(2) Orders with regard to Lord Robert Bertie's Regiment of Fusiliers.

(3) The opinion of the artillery and engineer officers of Gibraltar on the practicability of landing troops at St. Philip's.

(4) The opinion of council of war held at Gibraltar on 4th May.

(5) The sick and wounded state for 24th May, which was: sick, 389 on board and 71 left at Gibraltar; wounded, 168; killed, 43. Total, killed or incapacitated, 671.

(6) The latest report on the damaged ships, which was:

The *Defiance* would have her foretopmast up by nightfall.

The *Captain* had had her foremast repaired and was fit to sail.

The *Portland* could sail, but the knees of her head were quite loose and she would have to go into dock at Gibraltar.

The *Intrepid* was under jury topmasts and would have to be towed to Gibraltar.

The *Buckingham*, *Revenge* and *Princess Louisa* fit for action.

The council was invited, in the light of this information, to advise Byng how best to carry out his instructions.

Speaking after the event and in terms of twentieth-century strategy, we would now say that the French army besieging St. Philip's was the real object of attack, and that everything should have been done to make their situation as uncomfortable as possible. There were several ways of doing this, of which the boldest would be to draw Galissonnière a few miles south by a feint of action, and then land a party of sailors and fusiliers at Cala Mezquida, from where they could advance on Mahon and destroy the

French stores parked in rear of their camp. An easier task would be to drive them off Cape Mola and spike their guns, retiring again at once, while even the feint of landing by showing boats full of troops at various points along the coast would have disturbed the French *morale* and have forced them to detach large bodies from the siege to cover the threatened spots.

But, after all, the most obvious and safest plan was to attack the army's lines of communication with Toulon, since it had increased the population of Minorca by half, and Byng knew that the garrison had driven all the cattle that it could lay hands on into St. Philip's. This meant that the French army depended for supplies entirely on what could be brought from the mainland. Byng could, therefore, sail straight to Toulon and blockade it, or else destroy such transports as were still lying in Ciudadela harbour and Fornelles. The only reply the French could make would be for Galissonnière to abandon his watch off Mahon, and go at once to protect his lines of communication. If he divided his fleet and left a few ships to prevent Byng landing Stuart and the officers and recruits, Byng might return in superior numbers and drive them away, and if he took all his ships away, the soldiers could be rowed into St. Stephen's Cove under the guns of a single frigate.

But this was not the way Byng looked at the situation. He thought his force too weak to interrupt the French communication with Toulon, and that St. Philip's could only be relieved by defeating the French fleet, and that at the moment he was not even capable of fighting it. The *Intrepid* would have to go back to Gibraltar for refitting, escorted by one of the frigates, and his other ships, which were originally slower than the French, were less mobile than ever since the damage done to their rigging during the action. Then there was his heavy sick-list, increasing every day, and no hospital ship, whereas Galissonnière was at liberty to land his sick and casualties, and would be supplied by Richelieu with any number of soldiers in their place. Most of the ships of the line still had over a hundred tons of water, and bread and provisions enough for another ten weeks, but lacked boatswain's, gunner's and carpenter's stores. It was a very difficult situation, and one in which the advice given by the land officers might easily have been decisive, but they preferred to play the same inglorious part that they had done at Gibraltar, and fully demonstrated that in the eighteenth century co-operation between the two services was a matter of chance.

At that moment Blakeney's garrison was suffering acutely from being cooped up underground during a Mediterranean summer, unable to get any sleep through the perpetual noise of gunfire, and with not enough officers for the usual duty complements. General Stuart and his colleagues could probably have explained this to Byng if they had wanted to, and they certainly must have known how difficult it was for the French to construct their siege batteries, and how demoralised they would become if their lines of communication were attacked. On the other hand, they could not know that at that moment Richelieu had hundreds of men incapacitated by dysentery and wounds, and that he was already despairing of success. But the officers who surrounded Byng, both naval and military, had no conception of the strategic value of their fleet as a menace to the French army; they appreciated the situation much as he did, and were only too willing to agree with his wretched ideas. These he proposed to them in the form of five questions, on which he asked them to advise and vote. The first was:

> I. 'Whether an attack upon the French fleet, gives any prospect of relieving Minorca?'

This was unanimously decided in the negative, and with very good reason, regardless of the fact that although the French fleet was in an unassailable position, the French army was not.

The next question was the most important one, and the resolution upon it the most discreditable that any body of naval officers has ever made.

> II. 'Whether, if there were no French fleet cruising off Minorca, the English fleet could raise the siege?'
>
> *Answer:* 'Unanimously of the opinion that the fleet could not.'

Not only was the question purely academic, and therefore quite out of place, as the French fleet could be seen at that moment off St. Philip's, but it assumed that our fleet was incapable of disturbing the enemy because he was on land, and that it was impossible to throw any succours into St. Philip's. Nearly every officer present knew that St. Stephen's Cove offered a safe entry to the castle, and the land officers at any rate could have shown the incalculable moral effect on the garrison of giving it a major-general, two colonels, many other officers and a strong force of sailors and fusiliers, even at the risk of leaving some of the ships undermanned. The pamphleteer who suggested that these officers already appointed to serve in the garrison never meant to land at all, seems to have been fairly near the mark. Again, to imagine that our fleet could do no damage to Richelieu's army was the wildest folly. Without ships to guard their supplies of food and ammunition, the French must have been starved out in a few weeks after seeing the English fleet surging like leviathans through the ranks of their helpless transports. Had Galissonnière withdrawn from his position, Richelieu, marooned on a barren island, would have surrendered to a force a fifth of the strength of his own, and the English public, applauding rapturously, would have been convinced that Newcastle had planned the whole business.

The last three questions dealt with the future conduct of the fleet, and were all framed with the object of producing an opinion in favour of retiring to Gibraltar.

III. 'Whether Gibraltar would not be in danger by any accident that might befall the fleet?'

Answer: 'Unanimously agree that it would be in danger.'

IV. 'Whether an attack with our fleet in the present state of it, upon that of the French, will not endanger the safety of Gibraltar?'

Answer: 'Unanimously agree that it would.'

V. 'Whether it is not for His Majesty's Service, that the fleet should immediately proceed for Gibraltar?'

Answer: 'We are unanimously of opinion that the fleet should immediately proceed for Gibraltar.'

All five questions were framed in such a way that no one could doubt for a moment the answers looked for by the person who proposed them. That person was Byng, and though he persuaded seventeen others to agree with his view, he was in no way compelled to ask their opinion, and he alone must be held responsible for the final decision. Far from allowing a general debate on the situation, he carefully framed the questions so that the same kind of answer was suggested each time, and then stopped all discussion and took a vote. He cannot be accused of allowing the council to usurp his function as commander-in-chief, but he must be considered guilty of using the council as a screen for the execution of his own plans. The resolutions 'would have been more numerous,' he wrote to Anson, 'but I put a stop to the reasons being expressed for these resolutions, which were only inflaming people at our being so weak with regard to the French fleet and left without stores, or hospital ship, or any visible manner of being of service to Minorca when arrived there, where the French had been above a month landed, much more on this subject; but I cut all short by saying we had no business with these reflections, I only wanted the opinion of the gentlemen for our future motions to be a government to my judgment in the execution of my instructions.'

So Byng determined to sail away to protect Gibraltar, regardless of the fact that the only one French army capable of attacking it was that moment tied to Minorca, and that the only transports capable of carrying it were busily engaged in fetching it supplies from Toulon.

Minorca might have been 'covered' by the destruction of these transports.

Next day Byng wrote to Anson to explain the reasons for his retirement. 'When I sailed from Gibraltar,' he wrote, 'I found it was the general opinion not to leave that place, when there was so little, if any hopes of relieving Minorca, and (? not) much more of hoping for the success we have had against a fleet superior to ours; but the many advantages they have of being reinforced from their camp, and landing their sick and wounded ashore, and the weight of their ships made it evident to me, after a trial which I was determined to make, that no further risks should be (?) of His Majesty's fleet, lest by any irreparable accident Gibraltar should become exposed.'

Then followed his view of the battle, which might be called a victory since some of the French ships were driven out of the line, but they could have attacked again had they chosen. After making the comment on the council of war previously quoted, he expressed great hopes that reinforcements would be sent to enable him to defeat the French and recover from them the command 'of that part of the Mediterranean, which now exposes all our commerce, as I am not able to send any ship to support it.'

'As to Minorca, the enemy have 17,000 men there, and I fear the castle will shortly be obliged to surrender; it was invested in such a manner that it would be impossible to have thrown in this regiment on board the squadron, could we have spared them. I wish it may ever be practical to starve their army by cruisers about the island when we have the superiority of these seas without endangering Gibraltar. I hope your Lordship enjoys perfect health, and am with the greatest respect,' etc.

It was singularly tragic that of all his contemporaries, Byng was the one man who stated that the French army might have been starved out, and yet denied himself the heaven-sent opportunity of doing it for fear of 'endangering Gibraltar.' Moreover, by writing such a sentence he showed that he must be in disagreement with Resolution No. II. of the council of war, which stated that our fleet could not do anything to raise the siege if there was no French fleet there. To Anson and the Ministers it must have looked as if Byng were sheltering himself behind the council's opinion, because he was afraid to do what he knew in his heart of hearts to be right. Actually he was no coward, but thought the correct strategic move impracticable at the moment, and so never attempted it, while sending back a resolution which seemed to mean that the correct move could never be practicable under any circumstances. If the French army could not be starved out by seventeen ships unopposed, then it could not be starved out at all, yet Byng admitted to Anson that with superior numbers the thing could be done even with opposition.

After this unfortunate display of sound and bad judgment, he went on to write a public letter to the Admiralty in the shape of a formal despatch. Regardless of all feelings but his own, he again produced a luminous and impartial appreciation of the situation, and this was the last of a series of acts which had already laid up for him dishonour and death.

'*Ramillies*, off Minorca,
'25th *May*, 1756.

'Sir,—I have the pleasure to desire you will acquaint their Lordships, that having sailed from Gibraltar the 8th, I got off Mahon the 19th, having been joined by his Majesty's ship *Phœnix* off Majorca two days before, *by whom I had confirmed the intelligence I had received at Gibraltar, of the strength of the French fleet, and of their being off Mahon. His Majesty's colours were still flying at the castle of St. Philip; and I could perceive several bomb-batteries playing upon it from different parts. French colours I saw flying on the west part of St. Philip's. I despatched the 'Phœnix,' 'Chesterfield,' and 'Dolphin' ahead, to reconnoitre the harbour's mouth; and Captain Hervey to endeavour to land a letter for General Blakeney, to let him know the fleet was here to his assistance; though everyone was of opinion we could be of no use to him; as by all accounts, no place was secured for covering a landing, could we have spared the people. The 'Phœnix' was also to make the private signal between Captain Hervey and Captain Scroop, as this latter would undoubtedly come off, if it were practicable, having kept the 'Dolphin's' barge with him: but the enemy's fleet appearing to the south-east, and the wind at the same time coming strong off the land, obliged me to call these ships in, before they could get quite so near the entrance of the harbour, as to make sure what batteries or guns might be placed, to prevent our having any communication with the castle.* Falling little wind, it was five before I could form my line, or distinguish any of the enemy's motions; and could not at all judge of their force, more than by their numbers, which were seventeen, and thirteen appeared large. They at first stood towards us in a regular line; and tacked about seven, which I judged was to endeavour to gain the wind of us in the night; so that being late, I tacked in order to keep the weather-gauge of them, as well as to make sure of the land wind in the morning, being very hazy, and not above five leagues from Cape Mola. We tacked off towards the enemy at eleven; and at daylight had no sight of them. But two tartans, with the French private signal, being close in with the rear of our fleet, I sent the *Princess*

Louisa to chase one, and made the signal for the Rear-Admiral, who was nearest the other, to send ships to chase her. The *Princess Louisa, Defiance,* and *Captain,* became at a great distance; but the *Defiance* took hers, which had two Captains, two Lieutenants, and one hundred and two private soldiers, who were sent out the day before with six hundred men, on board tartans, to reinforce the French fleet on our appearing off that place. The *Phœnix,* on Captain Hervey's offer, prepared to serve as a fire-ship, but without damaging her as a frigate; till the signal was made to prime, when she was then to scuttle her decks, everything else prepared, as the time and place allowed of.

'The enemy now began to appear from the mast-head. I called in the cruisers; and when they had joined me, I tacked towards the enemy, and formed the line ahead. I found the French were preparing theirs to leeward, having unsuccessfully endeavoured to weather me. They were twelve large ships of the line, and five frigates.

'As soon as I judged the rear of our fleet the length of their van, we tacked altogether, and immediately made the signal for the ships that led, to lead large, and for the *Deptford* to quit the line, that ours might become equal to theirs. At two, I made the signal to engage: I found it was the surest method of ordering every ship to close down on the one that fell to their lot. And here I must express my great satisfaction at the very gallant manner in which the Rear-Admiral set the van the example, by instantly bearing down on the ships he was to engage, with his second, and who occasioned one of the French ships to begin the engagement, which they did, by raking ours as they went down. The *Intrepid* unfortunately, in the very beginning, had her fore-top-mast shot away; and as that hung on her fore-top sail, and backed it, he had no command of his ship, his fore-tack and all his braces being cut at the same time; so that he drove on the next ship to him, and obliged that and the ships ahead of me to throw all back. This obliged me to do so also for some minutes, to avoid their falling on board me, though not before we had drove our adversary out of the line, who put before the wind, and had several shot fired at him from his own Admiral. This not only caused the enemy's centre to be unattacked, but the Rear-Admiral's division rather uncovered for some little time. I sent and called to the ships ahead of me to make sail, and go down on the enemy; and ordered the *Chesterfield* to lay by the *Intrepid*, and the *Deptford* to supply the *Intrepid's* place. I found the enemy edged away constantly; and as they went three feet to our one, they would never permit our closing with them, but took the advantage of destroying our rigging; for though I closed the Rear-Admiral fast, I found that I could not gain close to the enemy, whose van was fairly drove from their line; but their Admiral was joining them, by bearing away.

'By this time it was past six, and enemy's van and ours were at too great a distance to engage. I perceived some of their ships stretching to the northward; and I imagined they were going to form a new line. I made the signal for the head-most ships to tack, and those that led before with the larboard tacks, to lead with starboard, that I might by the first, keep, (if possible), the wind of the enemy, and, by the second, be between the Rear-Admiral's division and the enemy, as his had suffered most; as also to cover the *Intrepid*, which I perceived to be in a very bad condition, and whose loss would give the balance very greatly against us, if they attacked us next morning, as I expected. I brought to about eight that night to join the *Intrepid*, and to refit our ships as fast as possible, and continued doing so all night. The next morning we saw nothing of the enemy, though we were still lying to. Mahon was N.N.W. about ten or twelve leagues. I sent cruisers to look out for the *Intrepid* and *Chesterfield*, who joined me next day. And having, from a state and condition of the squadron brought me in, found, that the *Captain*, *Intrepid*, and *Defiance* (which latter has lost her Captain), were much damaged in their masts, *so that they were in danger of not being able to secure their masts properly at sea; and also, that the squadron in general were very sickly, many killed and wounded, and nowhere to put a third of their number, if I made an hospital of the forty-gun ship, which was not easy at sea:* I thought it proper, in this situation, to call a council of war, before I went again to look for the enemy. I desired the attendance of General Stuart, Lord Effingham, and Lord Robert Bertie, and Colonel Cornwallis, that

I might collect their opinions upon the present situation *of Minorca and Gibraltar, and make sure of protecting the latter, since it was found impracticable either to succour or relieve the former with the force we had. So, though we may justly claim the victory, yet we are much inferior to the weight of their ships, though the numbers are equal; and they have the advantage of sending to Minorca their wounded, and getting reinforcements of seamen from their transports, and soldiers from their camp; all which undoubtedly has been done in this time that we have been lying-to to refit, and often in sight of Minorca; and their ships have more than once appeared in a line from our mast-heads.*

'I send their Lordships the resolutions of the council of war, in which there was not the least contention or doubt arose. I hope, indeed, we shall find stores to refit us at Gibraltar; and, if I have any reinforcement, will not lose a moment of time to seek the enemy again, and once more give them battle, though they have a great advantage in being clean ships, that go three feet to our one, and therefore have their choice how they will engage us, or if they will at all; and will never let us close them, as their sole view is the disabling our ships, in which they have but too well succeeded, though we obliged them to bear up.

'I do not send their Lordships the particulars of our losses and damages by this, as it would take me much time; and I am willing none should be lost, in letting them know an event of such consequence.

'I cannot help urging their Lordships for a reinforcement, if none are yet sailed, on their knowledge of the enemy's strength in those seas, and which, by very good intelligence, will in a few days be strengthened by four more large ships from Toulon, almost ready to sail, if not sailed, to join these.

'I despatch this to Sir Benjamin Keene, by way of Barcelona; and am making the best of my way to *cover* Gibraltar, from which place I propose sending their Lordships a more particular account.

'I am,
'Sir,
Your most humble servant,
'J. BYNG.[1]

'Hon. John Cleveland, Esq.'

[1] *Note.*—The words in italics (except names of ships in other places), were omitted by order of the ministers when the despatch was published in the *Gazette*.

CHAPTER X

THE NEWS

No sooner had Byng left England than interest in his venture momentarily subsided. The public were convinced that the son of Lord Torrington would relieve Minorca and give the French fleet a severe drubbing if it dared to oppose him, but knowing that several weeks must elapse before news of his success could reach home, there was a general disposition to wait in patience. The Ministers were deeply involved in the intricacies of the Prussian Alliance and in trying to regain the ascendancy in North America, and though some of them had private doubts of saving Minorca they generally agreed with Newcastle's remark to Fox " that the heart must be secured first."

Mr. Pitt was alone in asserting from his place in the House as a private member that the Ministers designed the loss of Minorca on purpose, " in order to justify a bad peace." [1] Few people took this tirade seriously, but it at once set Newcastle quivering with alarm, especially as what little news had trickled through from the Mediterranean was none too good.

An account of Richelieu's landing and the beginning of the siege was received through the Spanish Ambassador during the first week in May, [2] and was

[1] 7th May, 1756. *Add. MSS.* 32864, f. 486.

[2] Dodington's Diary, p. 380.

confirmed in detail a few days after by a letter from Col. Joseph Yorke, our Minister at the Hague.[1] 'It will be indeed a great reproach to our conduct,' he wrote, 'if we lose Minorca and are beat at sea by an enemy we despise because of our superiority on that element. I am afraid the Admiralty has been deceived in its intelligence about the Toulon squadron.' 'What have our fleets been lying in harbour for so long? Not for fear of invasion, for that has never yet been probable and I have always asserted it, because I did not care sixpence for a 100,000 men upon the coast opposite to you, when I did not see ten ships to convey them. I am afraid the Administration will have brought a storm upon itself which will not be easily laid, and how they will satisfy the public is a secret I should be glad to know, for I live amongst people we have been abusing these fifteen years for neglect, and I don't see we are a bit better.' This was strong language even from an ordinary diplomat, but from a son of Lord Hardwicke it was a bitter indictment. Several people were now beginning to ask the same question as Joseph Yorke, and Newcastle, fearing a personal attack in Parliament, hurriedly explained to Dodington that 'he had not the direction of the sea,' and tried to shift the blame upon Anson. Fox, with his eye on the political barometer, began to recall that he had always been in favour of sending out a strong squadron as far back as Christmas, and behind him loomed the figure of his patron Cumberland; while Lord George Sackville made the 'abominable'

[1] *Add. MSS.* 35364, f. 91.

assertion 'that the danger Minorca was in, was a proof of our not being sufficiently, or early enough, armed at home.' For the first time the public realised that St. Philip's was in serious danger, and the Ministers that it was likely to fall. Every item of news emphasised the great progress made by the French, and that their fleet was equal, if not superior, to Byng's. Pitt saw that the only way to obtain control of the direction of the war for himself was to ruin the prestige of the Government, regardless of the effect it would have on the national *morale*. He described Newcastle as a child driving a go-cart on the brink of a precipice, with an old king and his family as its precious freight, and earnestly prayed that His Majesty might not die with Minorca engraved upon his heart. Such words were bound to have an effect, and it was soon noised about that 'the City were extremely displeased with the leaving Minorca exposed,' and Newcastle kept on repeating 'that the City imputed nothing to him, as the sea was not his province.' Fox, wishing to exculpate himself, anxiously asked Dodington, "was it not true the chief in an Administration would always be the most obnoxious?" To which that wily cynic replied, "Yes, unless they had one to make scapegoat"; at which Fox grew very alarmed, and asked if Dodington thought that he was likely to be a scapegoat.

The Ministers, at last convinced that there was no hope of preventing an extensive European war, issued a belated declaration of war against France on 18th May, and sent out Commodore Thomas

Broderick with instructions to reinforce Byng with the following squadron and a battalion of infantry:

Prince George	80 guns
Hampton Court	64 "
Ipswich	64 "
Nassau	64 "
Isis	50 "

This was a very useful force and, had it accompanied Byng originally, would undoubtedly have turned the scale on 20th May, but unfortunately it did not reach Gibraltar till 15th June.

The situation, however, was rather nicely balanced, as a despatch from Richelieu dated 28th April and a private letter of 2nd May showed that Edgecumbe had made good his escape from Mahon, and that owing to the difficulty of bringing up heavy artillery the progress of the besiegers was very slow.[1]

The suspense, meanwhile, was exasperating, and there was not a word from Byng. He must have left Gibraltar long ago, and have brought the French to action. If only he would write announcing a great victory, or at least the successful relief of St. Philip's! It was difficult work in the eighteenth century to conduct a war when news took a fortnight to arrive even from the Mediterranean, and in this case every scrap of it had come either from an enemy or a neutral source.

At last, on 31st May, when the nerves of the Ministers were already showing a rough edge, a despatch reached the Admiralty, being the first that

[1] News contained in a letter from Joseph Yorke 18th May. *Add. MSS.* 35364, f. 93.

had come in since Hervey's appreciation written from Villa Franca on 18th April. Needless to say, it was Byng's Gibraltar letter of 4th May, which to the enraged and disappointed Ministers seemed to contain nothing but complaints of present inconvenience and excuses for future disaster. One outstanding fact, however, was clear—Byng had not succeeded in getting the battalion from Gibraltar, and therefore St. Philip's could not be reinforced, even if it were relieved. By this extraordinary act of moral weakness Byng had practically sealed his fate before a shot was fired, as only news of a decisive victory could now save him from severe censure, and the king voiced the general feeling of his Ministers when he threw the letter on the ground, exclaiming, " This man will not fight."

Meanwhile, what should the public be told? To publish the letter in full was quite out of the question, and to make excerpts from it was equally distasteful. Byng's dispassionate phrases would rouse the whole country against the Government, astonish the neutrals, and set the Court of Versailles rocking with laughter. Better let him commit himself still further, it was argued, and then recall him in disgrace, thereby ridding the Administration of every atom of blame. So later on in the day a notice was published in the *Gazette* as follows: 'Admiralty Office, 31st May. This morning Lieut. O'Hara, of His Majesty's ship the *Dolphin*, arrived here with despatches from Admiral Byng, dated the 7th of this month[1] at Gibraltar, giving an account of what

[1] The original of 4th May, sent viâ Madrid, had not yet arrived.

happened there on the 2nd, after a tedious passage occasioned by contrary winds, and that he should depart from thence for Minorca on the 8th; and Lieut. O'Hara gives an account, that the Admiral having been joined by Commodore Edgecumbe, sailed accordingly on that day, with 13 of the line and three frigates, and had a fair and fresh gale of wind for three days from the time of sailing.'

This bulletin was a triumph of ingenious editing, for, set side by side with Hervey's despatch, published on 8th May, it showed Byng to have a superiority of three of the line over the French, as Hervey had estimated them at only ten of the line and five frigates. Though this piece of temporary camouflage might be enough to gull the public, those connected with political life knew that something was very much amiss, and there was an ominous stirring amongst the various groups at present in a state of independent opposition or passive acquiescence, but capable at any moment of uniting to overthrow the Newcastle régime should a great crisis arise. Richard Rigby, the jackal of the 'Bloomsbury Gang,' was writing to his chief, the Duke of Bedford, that the opinion of the council of war was thought 'very extraordinary,' and everyone with a knowledge of the inner workings of politics was on the *qui vive* for the next piece of news.

On 2nd June it came, in the shape of Galissonnière's despatch to the French Ministry of Marine, written on 22nd May and giving an account of the battle. Machault had given a copy of it to the Spanish

Ambassador at Paris, who had sent it to D'Abreu, the Spanish Ambassador at London. 'The action,' it ran, 'lasted three hours and a half to four hours, but was not general all the time. The English ships that suffered most from our broadsides withdrew to windward out of gunshot. They all along preserved this advantage, that they might keep clear of us as they pleased. After having made their greatest effort on our rear division, which they found so close and from which they were so furiously cannonaded that they could not break in upon it, they resolved to sheer off, and did not appear all the next day. In general, none of their ships stood the fire of ours for long. The ships of our squadron received little damage; they were completely repaired during the night, and were fit to fight next day.'

This was enough for the Ministers. They had no despatch from Byng to place side by side with it, but they had all that they required; Byng had not won a decisive victory, thereby discounting his gross conduct at Gibraltar, and therefore he must be recalled, even on the uncertain information received through a neutral source from the enemy.

Next day the Inner Cabinet met in the Duke of Cumberland's apartments and considered the letters from Fowke and Byng and the opinion of the council of war. It seemed clear to the Ministers present that both officers were guilty of disobedience to orders, and from what they had just heard they were convinced that the King had been right in his prophecy that Byng would not fight. They judged, however, that a rapid change of command might still save the situation if Blakeney could only hold out for another month, and so decided to make the following drastic recommendations to the full Cabinet:

(1) Lieut.-Gen. Lord Tyrawley to supersede Lieut.-Gen. Fowke as Governor of Gibraltar.

(2) Maj.-Gen. Lord Panmure to supersede Maj.-Gen. Stuart as second in command to Gen. Blakeney, and to be landed at St. Philip's if possible.

(3) Major Mace to be dismissed the service.

(4) Vice-Admiral Sir Edward Hawke to supersede Admiral Byng.

(5) Captain Charles Saunders to be rear-admiral and to supersede Rear-Admiral West.

No one could accuse the Ministers of lacking vigour, but the question was, had they given way to panic and superseded tried officers on the strength of unconfirmed news from an enemy source? The changes certainly looked well on paper, but closer inspection showed the recommendations to be a little ambiguous. To begin with, Lord Tyrawley already held the post of Governor of Minorca, so that, despite his great military and diplomatic reputation,[1] his presence in England at the moment demanded some explanation, and hardly seemed to justify his appointment to an additional command. As far as could be judged, Stuart, the senior of the officers detailed for St. Philip's, had made little

[1] James O'Hara, Lord Tyrawley, 1690–1773. Served with distinction in Spain and Flanders in the War of the Spanish Succession; Ambassador to Portugal, 1728–41, and to Russia, 1743–45; general, 1761; field marshal, 1763.

attempt to reach his post, and was clearly compromised by signing the council of war's opinion, so that he could be superseded with comparative safety, and the wretched Mace, being only a major and holding no special appointment, could be brushed aside with an easy conscience. Hawke was obviously the man to succeed Byng, if supersession was necessary, and his appointment was taken as a matter of course, but the promotion of Saunders to be his second in command was a stroke of real genius, and worthy of Anson's unerring eye for talent. Wolfe's future colleague in the capture of Quebec was one of the heroes of Anson's voyage round the world, had greatly distinguished himself at Hawke's victory off Finisterre, and had since become Comptroller of the Navy and a Member of Parliament; nevertheless he was still some way down the list of captains, and was junior to both Broderick and Ward amongst the Mediterranean officers. There were no valid grounds, however, for superseding West except on the assumption that a clean sweep was necessary. 'It is by no means clear,' wrote Fox next day to the Duke of Bedford, 'whether or to what degree Byng or West are blameable, but I hope your Grace will think (as I confess I do) that there was no staying for enquiries, and that nothing but an immediate change of command could maintain the spirit of the fleet, which must be sufficiently dispirited if they have any sense of honour left. The consternation, shame and anger of everybody here on receiving these accounts, has been extreme. His Majesty and the Duke are struck to the greatest degree. But H.R. Highness still thinks we may save Minorca, and Lord Tyrawley (who at a minute's warning was ready to set out with great and commendable spirit) thinks so too. I heartily wish I did.'[1]

To the Ministers, overwrought by the long delay and irritated by political and commercial pressure, Fox's view seemed the only possible one, but other people not living in the same state of nervous tension were apt to take the whole business more calmly and to be rather cautious in endorsing Fox's praise of Tyrawley, who had every reason for being 'ready to set out' ever since Christmas. George Grenville characteristically refused to form any opinion on the matter till he heard Byng's account, 'who is not reckoned backward in point of personal courage.[2] Joseph Yorke, enclosing another copy of Galissonnière's despatch, described the action as a 'brush,' and said it was clear that the French were 'too strong' for Byng and 'he seems to have conducted himself perfectly well; for he kept the advantage of the wind and retired when he saw proper, without risking anything with too great a disadvantage. The French had four 74 gun ships and, from all I have ever heard from our seamen, they are fit to fight our 90's as long as their masts can stand, and consequently superior by many hundreds of tons to all our 70 gun ships, of which Mr. Byng had four and one 74, which is a new one. What I lament is the fate of Minorca and the brave garrison of

[1] Correspondence of the fourth Duke of Bedford, Vol. II., p. 195.
[2] Grenville to Pitt, 7th June, 1756.

Fort St. Philip's, which I fear will be disheartened not knowing the reasons; but still I think had Mr. Byng been beat, the Italian powers would have done more than waver, which is of as much consequence as Minorca. To say the truth, I don't know why the French account is so modest, and that makes me want another from our people, for there are circumstances in this relation which I don't comprehend. I think in England there will be a great outcry upon this affair, and people will complain that a greater force was not sent there, which I confess I don't comprehend neither.'[1] This was sound common sense and a pretty accurate forecast for the future, but it left the harassed Ministers quite cold. It was all very well, they argued, to sit philosophising at the Hague, but it was the duty of the Government, as it has been countless times since, to make a rapid decision on very meagre information, and the decision had now been made for better or for worse.

Although the public was very concerned about the whole business, it was for the moment bewildered rather than angry, and while St. Philip's still held out, the 'great outcry' was unheard, so that Horace Walpole accurately expressed the general feeling when he wrote at the beginning of a letter[2]: 'By all one learns, Byng, Fowke and all the officers at Gibraltar were infatuated . . . all, all signed the Council of War, and are in as bad odour as possible';

[1] Joseph Yorke to Lord Royston (Hardwicke's eldest son), 4th June, 1756. *Add. MSS.* 35364, f. 97.

[2] To John Chute, 8th June, 1756.

and then at the end: 'The world condemns extremely the rashness of superseding admirals on no information but from our enemies.' To the public everyone in authority seemed to have lost their heads, from the principal Ministers to the sailors and soldiers on the spot, while there was a widespread belief, hinted at by Walpole and Rigby, that Byng and possibly West had signed the opinion of the Gibraltar council of war. On 8th June the Admiralty sent Hawke letters and instructions, ordering him to sail at once for Gibraltar in the *Antelope*, taking with him Saunders, Tyrawley and Panmure. Arrived there, he was to assume command of all ships in the Mediterranean, and send home Byng and West, and all officers of the *Ramillies* and any captains whom he had reason to believe had been 'tardy, and not to have acted with due spirit and vigour for the honour and service of the King and nation.' Next he was 'to use the utmost despatch' in getting to St. Philip's and to do everything in his power for its relief, and 'to take, burn, or sink, or otherwise destroy any squadron of the enemy's ships, that may be employed to favour and assist in their attack upon that Fort.' If St. Philip's were captured, he was 'to endeavour by all means to destroy the French fleet in the Mediterranean,' and in case of illness Saunders was to assume supreme command.

Hawke sailed on 16th June, with his 'little cargo of courage'; there was a few days' lull in the general excitement, and Joseph Yorke continued to bombard his family with sensible platitudes. 'I am convinced from the force of La Galissonnière's 74 gun ships,' he wrote on 15th June, 'that he was much an overmatch for Byng. . . . I am confident we have had bad intelligence, and as confident that if Mr. Byng had had another 90 gun ship, he would have beat the French fleet out of the sea. . . . Without all dispute you must keep your superiority in the Mediterranean. . . . It would be hard indeed if the French should be masters of the sea, with only 12 men of war of the line riding in it, which is the case at present. . . . You must not be too easily alarmed, for that will be destruction to you. If I were First Minister, I would support the navy with all my might and defy all continent schemes. . . . If you will only keep your superiority at sea, which you must do if you will be a power, you need not be afraid of any system Austria and Versailles can form. . . .'

Advice of this kind, if it were ever seriously considered by the Ministers, must have been extremely provoking. Newcastle was at a loss how to proceed, as St. Philip's still held out, though news of its fall was hourly expected, and it was doubtful to what extent the public would consider Minorca a serious loss, and therefore to what extent the blame could be put upon Byng. Meanwhile he feared the votes of the 'Bloomsbury Gang,' the eloquence of Mr. Pitt and the possible desertion of the paid henchman, Henry Fox.

Byng's despatch arrived on 23rd June, together with his private letter to Lord Anson, and while they were still being deciphered Fox wrote to Dodington in great excitement, 'He [Byng] says he beat the French fleet, or rather that it was a drawn battle. But he says they are too strong for us, and that the fort is invested with 17,000 men (in buckram I suppose), so that a letter cannot be conveyed into the place ; and that by the advice of a Council of War he is going back to Gibraltar to refit, wait for reinforcement and return. He hopes to make a more complete victory. *Hélas ! Adieu.*'[1] Late that day he wrote again, 'You will observe how like Galissonnière's account was to this of Byng's, *mutato nomine.* I own I cannot but suppose this as far as it goes authentic, as all the accounts from France agree that the siege of Fort St. Philip's is not at all advanced. What if we should at last save it ? This is the first time I have divulged myself in such a superstition.'

Fox well knew that he was master of the situation, as he could always point to his previous advocacy of strong measures, but it was difficult to decide whether it would be best for him to resign now as a disgusted patriot, in case the Ministry should fall, or to demand a peerage in return for keeping it in power. At present he preferred not to commit himself, as the fate of St. Philip's was still in the balance, and with it that of the Ministry.

Newcastle's immediate problem was how to publish Byng's despatch so that the public might receive as much information as possible, the French as little information as possible, and Byng as much blame as possible. This was quickly solved by publishing

[1] Fox to Dodington, 23rd June. *Hist. MSS. Com.* New series MSS. in various collections, Vol. VI., p. 33.

about half of it in the *Gazette*, without anything to show that it was not the whole. The paragraph about Hervey's efforts to open communications was suppressed, and the despatch was made to start with the appearance of the French fleet on 19th May. The account of the battle was allowed to stand, but nearly all the last part, describing the damage to the ships and the opinion of the council of war, was also suppressed, though enough remained to show that a council of war had been called together. In the last sentence of all, the word '*cover*' with reference to Gibraltar was omitted, so that it read as if Byng was seeking refuge there, instead of going to protect it. It was not a despatch that any Government would wish to receive, still less to publish, but to do so in a way calculated to make Byng appear cowardly as well as unenlightened was the height of meanness and folly. As a final stroke they omitted all mention of sickness in the fleet, but added the list of casualties, showing the *Ramillies* to have:

Officers killed	0
Officers wounded	0
Men killed	0
Men wounded	0

Apparently the flagship had kept out of the battle.

As a piece of thoroughly unscrupulous editing it achieved its immediate purpose, and the Ministers breathed freely again as they listened to the wolfish howl which proclaimed that the public had at last discovered a scapegoat, and which redoubled in fury when it became known on 14th July that St. Philip's had fallen.

On 27th June the French had assaulted the castle by land and in boats from every side, regardless of casualties. Blakeney and the garrison had resisted with extraordinary gallantry; Major Cunningham, Major Godfrey and Captain Sir Hugh Williams were wounded, and Lieut.-Col. Jeffries was captured in leading a party to dislodge the French from the outer works where they had gained a footing. Soon after midnight the fighting died down, but the garrison could hold out no longer. It had had no sleep for weeks; it had been cooped underground during a hot Mediterranean summer, and wasted by sickness and casualties; and when Blakeney found at 2 a.m. that the French were established in the outer lunettes and that he had not enough men to man the guns, he asked for an armistice to prevent useless slaughter. Had the Ministers personally devised it they could not have created a better foil for Byng than 'honest Blakeney,' in whom, wrote Joseph Yorke, 'all Europe interests itself, and even our enemies wish him good luck, so much has he gained upon their minds.'[1] The floodgates of popular hate now gave way, the mob attacked Byng's seat in Hertfordshire, he was burnt in effigy, and the shops were filled with acrostics and lampoons proclaiming his cowardice and Blakeney's heroism, the following even appearing in the *Gentleman's Magazine*.

[1] *Add. MSS.* 35364, f. 108.

T——R————————N'S GHOST

Could not my honours fire thy heart,
Nor Glory's powerful charms?
But must thou act the Coward's part
And fly from Gallic arms?

EPIGRAM

Cries Blakeney to Byng, as he kept at a distance,
" You'll be hanged, you poltroon, if you don't bring assistance."
" Why, Age," replied Byng, " what you say may be true,
But then I may chance to be shot if I do.
Sudden death I abhor; while there's life there is hope;
Let me 'scape but the gun, I can buy off the rope."

AN ACROSTIC

Beloved by all the good, to Britain dear,
Long may'st thou shine, a bright example here;
And may thy action on the roll of fame
Kindle in times to come the patriot's shame.
Ease, peace and honour crown thy future days,
Nor let this land be silent in thy praise.
Exalted as thy deeds be thy renown;
Yonder awaits thy bright immortal crown.

These were only the first bright sparks struck off the anvil, the advanced line of skirmishers sent out by ' Grub Street ' to try the popular taste, but when they were accepted with acclamation, and the wretch Byng was at last brought to England, the tried pamphleteers, the many verse ballad-mongers, the bad writers and the good writers, all took a hand, till England rang with the words of the attackers and defenders. The Ministers, too, were active in preparing for the great political struggle which must open on Byng's return, and it was advertised in the *Gazette* that strict orders had been issued to arrest him wherever he landed. When it had looked as if the Ministers would be to blame for losing Minorca, its strategic and commercial importance had been purposely minimised, 'but no sooner did the Ministry find the public odium removed from themselves and fixed on Admiral Byng, than Minorca was cried up for its importance, possessing the best port in the Mediterranean, its happy situation for protecting our trade there, capable of vast improvements.'[1] Newcastle is popularly supposed to have behaved like a child on hearing of the fall of St. Philip's, wailing, "We are undone! Sea and land are cowards!" It is quite probable that he did so, as his letter to Hardwicke on 19th July, outlining the steps to be taken by the Ministry, is one of the grossest examples of timidity and spite ever penned by a Cabinet Minister. After comparing Minorca to Ireland in value (hardly in conformity with the latest public ministerial pronouncement upon it), he at once begins excusing himself for any share in its loss. 'I dread to think of the Attorney-General being out of the House of Commons (as he must be) when this question comes on. I hope your Lordship will talk seriously to my Lord Anson to prepare materials for defence, and also (which is still of more consequence) for the immediate trial and condemnation of Admiral Byng, if, as I think, there can be no doubt he deserves it. The sea officers should be learnt to talk in this manner, and not to think to fling the blame upon civil Ministers. Your Lordship knows the little share we have in the choice of

[1] Beatson, *Naval and Military Memoirs*, Vol. I., p. 485.

THE DUKE OF NEWCASTLE

From the crayon drawing by W. Hoare in the National Portrait Gallery

[*p.* 166

military men, either at sea or land. . . . Could any object of attack, either in the Mediterranean, the West Indies or North America be agreed upon, that would keep up people's spirits and divert their resentment? Without it we must expect everything that is bad. I know your Lordship feels for me as much as I can do for myself.'

The head of the Government ready to condemn unheard one of his foremost admirals, suggesting that pressure should be put on the admiral's brother officers to this end, and advocating a hectic offensive in any quarter of the globe if only to 'keep up people's spirits'; it is not a pleasant picture.

CHAPTER XI

THE ARREST

SATISFIED that it was useless, if not dangerous, to remain off Minorca any longer, Byng made the best of his way to Gibraltar, which he reached on 19th June. There he found Broderick, who had arrived on the 15th with his five ships. Evidently this was a sign of contrition on the part of the Ministers, and, encouraged by such a welcome addition to his force, Byng exerted himself to be ready for action again as quickly as possible. The thousand sick were landed, the carpenters and sail-makers were set hard at work; wine was ordered for ten weeks, dry provisions for three months, and beef and pork for four, Broderick's men helping in refitting the damaged ships and in loading the provisions. Everything seemed to be going on well, and Byng wrote quite a cheerful despatch to the Admiralty on 23rd June,[1] expressing his wish to be off again as soon as possible, which, however, would not be before 6th July; but he could not resist enclosing the full text of the report of the storekeeper and master shipwright on the disgraceful state of the Gibraltar dockyard. Captain Cornwell meanwhile asked for a court martial as a result of certain insinuations about his behaviour in the battle. Byng wisely gave him two or three days in which

[1] Ad. In Letters, 383.

to reflect, but as he still insisted, a court was formed with West as president, at which, no accusers appearing, 'the affair dropped much as it began.'

Preparations for a fresh start were nearly complete, and everyone was looking forward to meeting the enemy with superior numbers, when on 3rd July, the *Antelope* dropped anchor in the bay and discharged 'the little cargo of courage'—a new admiral to be commander-in-chief, a new admiral to be second-in-command, a new governor for Gibraltar, and a new second-in-command for Blakeney. The sailors of the fleet and the soldiers of the garrison were utterly dumbfounded, and thought the Ministers must have gone mad. Byng's surprise was increased when he opened the Admiralty letter brought for him by Hawke, and saw that it was dated 8th June, long before his own account of the battle could possibly have reached London. When he read it his surprise turned to bewilderment.

> 'His Majesty, having received an account that the squadron under your command and that of the French under M. de Galissonnière, came to an action off the harbour of Mahon the 20th of last month; and that the French (though inferior to you in force) kept before the harbour, and obliged you to retreat; I am commanded to send you an extract of M. de Galissonnière's letter to his Court, giving an account of the action; and to acquaint you that His Majesty is so much dissatisfied with your conduct that he has ordered their Lordships to recall you and Mr. West, and

to send out Sir Edward Hawke and Rear-Admiral Saunders to command the squadron.

'I am extremely sorry to be obliged to inform you of such a disagreeable event; being with regard, etc.

'J. CLEVELAND.'

He then read the extract from Galissonnière's despatch and, thinking that he was being superseded on that alone, and not for his conduct at Gibraltar, became furiously angry, and stripping off his great blue coat, threw it in the sea. Next day he replied in tones made violent by pent-up anger, and quite unlike his usual colourless prose:

'My surprise at being so ignominiously dismissed from my employment, in the sight of the fleet I had commanded, in sight of the garrison, in sight of Spain; at such a time, in such a manner and after such conduct as I hope shall shortly appear to the whole world . . . I flatter myself that Mr. West and I shall make evident the injury done to our characters, which I know of nothing in the power of any living being whatever can atone for; so high an opinion I have of that which was ever unsullied before, and which I hope to make to appear has been most injuriously and wrongfully attacked now, on the grounds of a false gasconade of an open enemy of our king and country and which would have evidently appeared had the proper time been allowed for my expresses' arrival, in which there is nothing false, nothing vaunting, nothing shameful nor nothing which could have hindered our receiving His Majesty's royal approbation, for having with a much inferior force, fought, met, attacked and beat the enemy. . . .'

Having slightly relieved his feelings in this way, he went through the formalities of handing over the command to Hawke, and then went on board the *Antelope*, which sailed for England on 9th July. This time her cargo was equally remarkable, consisting of Byng and West, Captain Gardiner and Captain Everitt, all the officers of the *Ramillies*, including those promoted to command other ships, also the gunner, purser, master, surgeon and several officers of the *Buckingham*, and General Fowke.

The voyage home was a fairly quick one, Spithead being reached on 26th July, by which time Byng expected that his own despatch would have been published in full, and that the Admiralty would be ready with a handsome apology. Of course, he would demand an enquiry, but the idea would be obsequiously rejected, and his conduct would be enthusiastically approved. But imagine his surprise when his brother-in-law, Vice-Admiral Henry Osborne, and his brother, Colonel Edward Byng, came on board and informed him with some embarrassment that he was under arrest till further notice. On writing[1] to ask the reason for this, he was told that it was 'in pursuance of the King's pleasure, in order to your being brought to a trial,

[1] 27th July. Ad. In Letters.

for your late conduct and behaviour in the Mediterranean.'[1] So there was to be an enquiry after all, and for the first time Byng realised his danger. Something must be wrong, he must have been cruelly misrepresented at Court; doubtless some political faction was at the bottom of it; the affair might be very tedious, and even uncomfortable; he must be careful. Another event also depressed him deeply. Edward Byng had come to see him, though in a bad state of health, anxious to be of what service he could, but on arriving at Portsmouth he was so overcome by the fatigue of the journey and violent demonstrations in the town against his brother that he was seized with a sudden illness, and died next morning on board the *Antelope*. Although profoundly grieved by this tragic event, Byng never faltered in his public attitude, but wrote a long letter to the Admiralty trusting that his conduct would soon 'be impartially represented' to his 'Royal Master' and asking for a copy of the charge against him. Citing the cases of Admirals Matthews, Lestock, Griffin and Knowles as precedents, he also asked to be allowed to go ashore to regulate his affairs, adding with some dignity that this was the more necessary as his only surviving brother was now lying dead beside him in the cabin. He also wrote to his sister-in-law, Lady Torrington, asking permission for his brother's body to be buired in the family vault at Southill, where his own was so soon to follow, and adding that he had not the least doubt that he would be able

[1] 28th July. Ad. Out Letters.

to show that he had 'acted in every respect like an officer.'

But the Admiralty were taking no risks. They knew the temper of the mob, and feared that Byng might be lynched if allowed on shore; while Anson even stooped to consider the chance of his trying to escape, and agreed that the Tower of London would be the best place to put him.[1] They therefore told him that orders would be given next week for bringing him to town, and the same day they applied to Barrington to provide 'a very strong guard.'[2] A copy of the charge to the Marshal of the Admiralty was enclosed, based on the wording of the Twelfth Article of War, the punishment for breach of which was death, and adding 'that the said John Byng did not do his utmost to relieve St. Philip's Castle, but acted contrary to and in breach of his Instructions.'[3] He was now transferred to the *Royal Anne*, and seeing that his conduct was considered sufficiently bad to justify the charge being in what was practically capital form, he immediately sent in a list of thirty-six officers whom he would like called as witnesses, including most of the captains, Lord Robert Bertie, and all the officers of the *Ramillies*.[4] The same day he was

[1] Burrow's *Life of Anson*, pp. 256–7.

[2] Ad. Out Letters, 31st July.

[3] The Twelfth Article runs as follows: 'Every person in the fleet who through cowardice, negligence or disaffection, shall in time of action withdraw or keep back, or not come into the fight or engagement, or shall not do his utmost to take or destroy every ship, which it shall be his duty to engage, and to assist and relieve all and every of His Majesty's ships or those of his allies which it shall be his duty to assist and relieve; every such person so offending and being convicted thereof by the sentence of a court martial shall suffer death.'

[4] 4th August. Ad. In Letters.

told that he was to start for London next morning by coach, with an escort of a captain and fifty dragoons, but the cavalcade only got three miles out of Portsmouth when it was met by an express cancelling the order. Byng protested angrily at being 'exposed and tossed from one prison to another; then on shore, and now back again to the *Royal Anne,* I believe a treatment the meanest subject seldom or ever met with.'[1] At last, however, arrangements were properly made for his journey, and setting out on 9th August, he reached Greenwich Hospital the same night.

While Byng was suffering this undignified treatment, especially galling to a man of his aloof and sensitive temperament, the loss of Minorca was becoming the sole topic of political discussion. In the eighteenth century 'His Majesty's Opposition' did not exist as an organised constitutional group, the Ministers being actively supported by their friends and dependants, while their opponents consisted of small and loosely associated groups, whose action was spasmodic and generally unconcerted, perpetual resistance to all Government measures then being looked upon as unnecessary and factious. No hard and fast line was drawn between those who supported the Government and those who did not, so that although in ordinary times the passive acquiescence of a large majority of Members enabled the Ministers to carry through the 'King's business' fairly easily, a great crisis might unite all the waverers against them, and produce a sudden collapse. It

[1] 5th August. Ad. In Letters.

was this that Newcastle feared, and consequently he took the lead in trying to saddle Byng with the whole blame for the failure of the expedition. The Opposition, or potential Opposition groups, on the other hand, at once began to lay the blame on the Government, but in so doing they made no attempt to justify Byng ; on the contrary, they were just as eager to prove him a poltroon as Newcastle was, in order to discredit the Ministers for making him their choice.

> 'Whatever was the cause,' wrote Lord Lyttelton on 8th August, 'the effect has been fatal, and should he die by the sentence of the Court Martial, which is going to sit upon him, (as he probably will, or by the hands of the mob if he should be acquitted) his death will make a poor satisfaction to his country for the mischief he has done it. You know the temper of the nation too well to suppose that their anger for the loss of Minorca will be confined to Admiral Byng. All arts are used to inflame them against the Administration and particularly against the Duke of Newcastle.'

Fresh news, too, began to appear from the scene of action. Captain James Young wrote a most virulent account of the expedition to some unknown correspondent.

> 'You will, to be sure, all be surprised that by the express Mr. Byng sent, there was not a line from anybody in the fleet but his own ship. It

was, I think, not only unkind but cruel in him not to give some notice of it at a Council of War that was held on the 24th, the resolutions of which he stole away in the night, with a small vessel in which he sent an officer to Barcelona. He might well think some of us had friends and families that would be uneasy, at hearing of an engagement and not having a line.'

A long description of the battle followed, in the course of which he remarked :

'Only us six engaged, that is the Red Division. You'll naturally ask why? It's what I can't answer. The wind that carried us down still continued and never failed the whole time ; could we have made a day it was impossible to have a finer. All the advantage that a fleet could have, we had, except in force, where they were a trifle superior. However, there astern of us he [Byng] lay with his division, and to windward, by which means the poor *Intrepid* was cut to pieces. . . . This I suppose will make fine work in England. I really believe as does everybody else that had we all engaged, by the behaviour of the French, the 20th May, 1756, might have been recorded with as much glory to the British Fleet as the 19th May, 1692, was,[1] or more so, as they were rather superior to us. . . . All the Fleet are open-mouthed against Byng ; his own division more than ours, as well as all the land officers that were on board to be

[1] Defeat of the French off Cape Barfleur.

landed at Minorca. Mr. West is greatly displeased. I suppose this affair will come to enquiry. . . . What is next to be done I know not.'

To Lord Lyttelton, now Chancellor of the Exchequer and perhaps the recipient, the letter appeared rather indiscreet in its comprehensive abuse, and he felt bound to minute it with the following note :

'When Captain Young says the French were a trifle superior a force to our Fleet, I presume he means by the weight of their metal, for we had more ships and more guns ; our Fleet also was much better manned. All our seamen expressed the greatest alacrity at the sight of the enemy, and would have done their duty well if Byng had done his.'

From the *Revenge* came an equally virulent letter, dated 3rd July, claiming that the *Foudroyant* was set on fire twice and would have struck if she had been pressed harder ; 'we broke our line to run through the French and pick her up, but were immediately ordered to keep it.'

These criticisms might be unjust, but they were certainly rational, and not to be compared to the flood of wild nonsense which poured from the pens of 'Grub Street' during the next few weeks. Byng was accused of loitering away his time at Portsmouth before setting sail, of soliciting the appointment of commander-in-chief out of gross vanity ; a satire appeared describing his condemnation by a court martial held at the 'Lion and Anchor,' Wapping, and he was burnt in effigy in the street every few days. West, on the other hand, received nothing but praise, and it was publicly announced that at a drawing-room at Kensington of 28th July, at which he had been presented by Anson, the King had said, "Admiral West, I am glad to see you. I return you my thanks for your gallant behaviour, and I wish every admiral had followed your example."

Popular excitement was increased more than ever by the court martial held on Fowke, which lasted from 10th August to the 14th. Having written several letters, which were liable to be produced at the trial, showing that there was never any question of misunderstanding his orders, he was persuaded at the last moment to put forward the wretched plea that they were contradictory and ambiguous, in addition to the one that his garrison was too weak for a full battalion to be spared. After an equal division of opinion amongst his judges, the president of the court gave his casting vote against, and Fowke was suspended from his rank for one year. His sentence was not severe, and to some extent it was deserved, but it was a bad omen for Byng.

Worse followed, for not only was Minorca the talk of all London, but addresses to the King, carefully contrived by various political magnates, began to pour in from every quarter of England, all demanding stringent enquiry and punishment. They came from the counties of Dorset, Hampshire, Buckingham, Bedford, Suffolk, Salop, Surrey, Somerset and Lancashire, and from Bristol, Chester and Southwark. By far the most important, however, was the one presented by the Lord Mayor on behalf of the Corporation of London, for it contained a very severe threat.

> 'The loss of the important fortress of St. Philip's, and the island of Minorca (possessions of the utmost consequence to the commerce and naval strength of Great Britain) without any attempt, by timely and effectual succours, to prevent or defeat an attack, after such early notice of the enemy's intentions, when your Majesty's Navy was so evidently superior to theirs, will, we fear, be an indelible reproach on the honour of the British Nation. . . . We cannot doubt of Your Majesty's directing the authors of our late losses and disappointments to be enquired into and punished, that your Majesty's known intentions of protecting and defending your subjects in their rights and possessions may be faithfully and vigorously carried into execution, and that the large supplies so necessarily called for, and so cheerfully granted, may be religiously applied to the defence of these kingdoms and colonies and their commerce.'

This was the bombshell which Newcastle had all along been dreading; his beloved City, the source of all supplies, the treasure-house from which he financed his bribes, was threatening to shut its doors to him unless 'the authors of our late losses' were punished. Thankful that they made no attempt to brand him personally as one of the criminals, he fairly blubbered with expressions of zeal. "Oh, indeed, he shall be tried immediately," he exclaimed, carefully making Byng the sole 'author,' and then, as if that was hardly enough, he added, "He shall be hanged directly."

The official reply from the King was equally severe. "I will not fail to do justice," he declared, "upon any persons who shall be wanting in their duty to me and my country, to enforce obedience and discipline in my fleets and armies, and to support the authority and respect due to my Government."

It was well for the King that he answered with such firmness, and he knew it, for without the support of the merchants no Government of any kind could hope to carry out its duties. Only Sir John Barnard, the well-known alderman and Member of Parliament, made any attempt 'to stem the torrent,' said Horace Walpole, and 'is grown almost as unpopular as Byng. That poor simpleton, confined at Greenwich, is ridiculously easy and secure' and has even summoned on his behalf a Captain Young, his warmest accuser. Pamphlets and satirical prints teem; the courts are divided; the ministers quarrel—indeed if they agreed one should have much more to expect from them.'[1]

Byng's immediate situation, however, was less

[1] Walpole to Mann, 29th August, 1786. The 'courts' refers to the King's Court, and the Princess of Wales' Court at Leicester House and Kew, where the future George III was living.

'easy and secure' than Horace Walpole supposed. He had made no complaint about his confinement at Portsmouth except the uncertainty of its duration and the indignity and inconvenience of not being allowed on shore, and Henry Osborne seems to have done his best to make things tolerable for him in the *Royal Anne*. But, on coming to Greenwich, he quickly exchanged detention for gaol, and though a Member of Parliament and the son of a peer, he was treated like a common criminal. Admiral Isaac Townshend, the Governor of the Hospital, seems to have taken every opportunity to treat him severely, hoping thereby to curry favour with the Ministers, and fearful of what they might do to him if by any chance his prisoner should escape. Accordingly, when Byng arrived on 9th August, after spending a whole day in a coach, he was shown up to an uninviting room at the very top of the Queen Anne block, where there was not even a bedstead, and in consequence of which he had to sleep on his portmanteau. His door was never left unguarded, and Townshend seems to have taken a fiendish delight in joining in the general baiting which he was suffering by spreading alarms that he was trying to escape, perhaps in his sister's clothes, and thus making an excuse to bring in smiths and bricklayers to bar the windows and chimney, and to wall up suspected doors. Outside, the temper of the mob was very uncertain, and Newcastle was attacked and pelted while passing through Greenwich on 11th September, and was forced to take refuge in the Observatory.

Meanwhile, Byng discovered that it was useless to

protest to the Admiralty at the way he was being treated, and therefore set about putting his case before the public in printed form, as a counterblast to the infamous attacks being made on him by the agents of nearly every party. For this he obtained the assistance of Mr. Paul Whitehead, the disreputable political satirist and secretary of the Hell Fire Club at Medmenham Abbey. Whitehead had been politically associated with the late Frederick, Prince of Wales, being counted as a satellite of the Leicester House Party, and therefore opposed to the Yorkes and Pelhams. He was the author of several party squibs, had some acquaintance with law, had spent several years in the Fleet prison, and was known to be a first-class publicist. Downman's portrait gives him a sharp-cut face, with thin lips, and an expression of kind-hearted cunning, which his actions hardly belie. Under his direction, Byng's case was at once put on a proper professional basis, and Samuel Johnson was briefed to write two pamphlets, one for those with intelligence, and the other for the credulous.

The first was called: *A Letter to a Member of Parliament in the Country, from his Friend in London, relative to the Case of Admiral Byng: with some Original Papers and Letters which passed during the Expedition.*

It was given the motto 'Audi alteram partem,' and was published by Mr. J. Cooke of Holborn, being evidently intended to give the Members of Parliament material for consideration before the next sitting in November. No one, says the author,

PAUL WHITEHEAD

From the picture by J. Downman in the National Portrait Gallery

[*p*. 182

was at first more clamorous against the admiral than himself, or 'exulted more in the flames of his effigy,' but on observing that it was those who should have been most scrupulously impartial who urged on the attack, he at once grew suspicious, and finally 'the very mob discovered the name of Byng to be bandied round the kingdom, only as a bubble to their proper indignation.' The suppressed paragraphs of Byng's despatch after the battle were printed in full, together with the Gibraltar despatch of 4th May, with the remark that 'the receipt of this letter may be fixed as the era of Mr. Byng's destined disgrace.

'How must his formidable account of the enemy's Force and preparations falsify the predictions of those, who represented them as the mere phantom of our imagination?

'May not the complaint of the ruinous condition of the wharfs, pits and storehouses at Gibraltar, together with the almost total want of necessary stores for the security of the fleet, prejudice in his disfavour those to whose province the care of these affairs more particularly belong?

'May not the foulness of his ships be deemed a secret improper to be divulged after so much boasted excellency of his equipment?'

A full list of the English and French fleets and their guns followed, to prove that the Admiralty had no right to send Byng a 'death warrant' to his reputation, solely on the evidence of a French 'romance.' Finally came Byng's spirited reply to his letter of recall, and a striking peroration appealing for a suspension of personal judgment, 'till upon a fair and candid trial, the admiral shall be found (what at present I have great reason to believe him very invidiously misrepresented to be) a son unworthy of his father, a native unworthy of his country, and an officer unworthy of his command.'

It was only a moderate piece of literature, but as a means of putting Byng's case before the public it was excellent, since the suppressed paragraphs in the battle despatch were now published for the first time, and the pamphlet was therefore an important contribution to the political situation at that moment.

The second pamphlet was designed to be more popular in style ; it was called : *An Appeal to the People,* and was said to contain Byng's 'genuine and entire letter' to the Admiralty, and the reasons for the omissions.

It opened with a very prolix introduction, condemning Ministers who 'throw the whole blame and disgrace of the ill success on the visible object who presided in the scene of action,' and afterwards 'skulk behind the resentment which their adherents and abettors have craftily raised against the commander in the day of battle.

'What profligate and abandoned hearts must such men possess, who by omissions of whole paragraphs of a commander's own letter, and additions of others, can lessen the force of his justification in an affair of life and death? . . . Is it not a crime equal to that of forgery . . . ?'

After further invective, it vehemently pleads for 'a calm and dispassionate examination of the whole affair.' The despatch and the lists of the fleets follows, together with a fantastic numerical comparison of their fighting qualities. All ships are ignored but the *Ramillies* and *Foudroyant*, which are estimated as throwing a total of 1,696 lbs. and 2,268 lbs. respectively, supposing all their guns on both sides were fired at once—an unlikely event if they fought in line. The ships are also shown to carry 730 men and 950 men respectively, and the argument continues in nightmare fashion :

> Allow 8 men to one gun on board the *Foudroyant*
> (as her metal is heavier)
> And allow 6 men to one gun on board the *Ramillies*.
> This will make 672 at the great guns } on board the *Foudroyant*.
> 278 at the small arms }
> And 540 at the great guns } on board the *Ramillies*.
> 190 at the small arms }

Therefore the French guns' fire exceeds the English by 572 lbs. in each discharge, and the French small-arms' fire exceeds the English by 88 shots in each volley.

If each gun is fired once a minute, the fire of the *Foudroyant* in one hour will exceed the *Ramillies* by 34,320 lbs. of shot—' a most amazing superiority.'

If each small arm is fired four times a minute, the excess of small arms' fire in one hour will be 21,120 lbs.

' The advantage drawn from the small arms is then exactly in proportion to the number in which one ship exceeds the other, and the advantage of the heavier shot discharged from the cannon is as the diameter of each exceeds the other. Let me suppose a thirty-two-pound ball to be ten inches in diameter ;

such a shot can pass between two objects eleven inches distant from each other and touch neither of them; whereas, allowing a ball of fifty-two pounds to be twelve inches diameter, and to pass in the same direction with the former, this last ball may destroy, but must inevitably wound, both objects. Again, if you suppose a ball of ten inches diameter, to pass within half an inch of any single object, that of twelve passing in the same line by the increased diameter, must destroy or injure it.'

Having accepted everything up to this point, the credulous reader is probably not surprised to find that the foregoing argument proves 'the *Foudroyant* is superior to the *Ramillies*, almost as three to two.' But if, as might be objected, the rate of fire was slower, 'the superiority is not so often exerted and the proportion of four to three still remains.' It is only a short step after this to prove that the twelve English ships were really faced by a French force equivalent to sixteen, 'a superiority not to be attacked by a prudent man.'

After these droll and fantastic calculations, which were apparently quite suited to the popular taste, the omissions in Byng's despatch are dealt with in sound style. Emphasis is laid on the wish to hide the fact that he had no hospital ship, tender or store ship, and therefore his losses during the action and through sickness are omitted. Also the Ministers wish it to appear that he was never in sight of St. Philip's, and therefore Hervey's reconnaissance is left out. But a few pages farther, the ludicrous element again appears, and Feuquieres and Santa

Cruz are quoted to support the doctrine that no commander should risk a battle unless there is more to be gained by a victory than there is to be lost by a defeat, and therefore Byng was right to refuse battle a second time, even if he was 'not a little culpable' in accepting it on 20th May. After comparing his return to Gibraltar to a masterly retreat by a land force in the face of superior numbers, 'one of the most distinguishing, difficult and meritorious exploits of a general,' the pamphlet returns to pithy comments on the omissions in the despatch. A specious effort is made to defend Byng's retirement after the action by saying that if he saw the French from the masthead, the French must have seen him, and that if they made no attempt to attack him with a superior and undamaged force, why should he be criticised for not attacking them? This again is an argument for a popular audience, as it ignores the dissimilar objects of the two fleets, and does not mention that Galissonnière, by covering the siege from an interior position, was actually doing all that his instructions required, whereas Byng, although justified in not fighting a second time, had no business to neglect striking at the French lines of communication. Impartial critics, too, might be inclined to agree that, in leaving out the absurd remark that the French sailed three feet to our one, Byng's reputation was protected rather than injured, though the pamphlet stoutly denies it. The omission of the word 'cover,' however, in relation to Gibraltar is dealt with very well, and the pamphlet ends with ten pages of splendid invective.

All aspersions are denied, and counter-charges are hurled at the Ministers of spreading infamous rumours. 'One day it was given out that he had sold out of the stocks, forty-four thousand pounds, before he sailed, which was to insinuate that he left England with a design never to return.' 'At one time he is represented as mad, and then as killing himself with drinking; then that it is to be feared he may attempt suicide.

'Are not such proceedings in men of rank below the behaviour of the meanest beggar? What an insult on your understanding, to conceive the absurd idea of screening themselves from your enquiry, and seeking preservation by drawing, hanging and burning a man in effigy, who, however culpable in this action, must be as white as snow compared with them, whose sins are red as scarlet.

'. . . To you I appeal; be Englishmen, and I fear no injustice to him who is thus unjustifiably pursued, him whom you have already been deceived to condemn, you now be resolved to see treated according to the laws, rights and privileges of a fellow-subject and free Briton.'

Both pamphlets show Johnson at his worst; he spoilt an excellent opportunity to explain to the public the real difference in fighting powers of the French and English ships, and wrote pages of pseudo-scientific nonsense when it would have been enough to say that the French big guns fired farther and hit harder than ours. Nor could he plead entire ignorance of sea affairs, as, the year before, he had prepared a tract on the attempt to determine longitude at sea, and later posed as an authority on naval strategy and foreign trade. This melancholy picture of one of our master writers selling his genius for a mess of pottage, and then doing the job badly, is, however, a less melancholy one than that of one of our master lawyers, Edward Coke, wantonly perverting justice at the trial of Walter Raleigh. Johnson, doubtless, believed in Byng's innocence, and honestly tried to save his life as well as to earn a pittance.

The pamphlets, however, immediately produced an effect, which they could hardly help doing, seeing the important and original matter that they contained, which, though poorly handled, at least convinced the public that there really was a Byng point of view. Hitherto he had been a shuttlecock used by the Ministers and their opponents for strokes and counter-strokes, but the appearance of the pamphlets opened a breach amongst the Ministers themselves. Fox, who realised that his position as Secretary of State marked him out for special criticism, became more nervous than ever lest Newcastle should dissolve their recent alliance and offer him up as scapegoat to the City and the public. He again sought comfort from his crony, Dodington, but that worthy time-server only increased his depression by writing, 'Remember how you were misled into a belief that Byng's squadron was too strong for all they could put out, which it certainly was not; for those who affirmed that to you could have no certainty of his being joined by Edgecumbe—but this is between ourselves.'[1]

[1] Dodington to Fox, 6th September, 1756.

The contest had now become three-cornered, the Ministers attacking Byng, Byng attacking the Ministers, and the opposition attacking both. A further batch of pamphlets appeared in answer to Byng's, endeavouring to identify his failure with that of the Ministers by proving that they must be held entirely responsible for the acts of their incompetent servant. The support of the City was canvassed by *The Conduct of the English Ministry impartially examined, in a Letter to the Merchants of London*, and the old *Three Letters relating to the Navy, Gibraltar and Port Mahon,* originally published in 1747, was reprinted, with a special preface on *New Reflections on the Conduct of the War and the Present State of Public Affairs, particularly the Loss of Minorca and the Behaviour of Mr. Byng.* This was an able piece of work, and showed a sound appreciation of strategy in saying that a few ships well placed in Hyères Bay could have watched Toulon and been cleaned at Mahon. It also repeated Dodington's assertion that Byng could not be certain of meeting Edgecumbe, and then went on to suggest alternative questions for Byng's council of war, such as:

'Will not Minorca fall unless succours reach St. Philip's?'

'Is this possible without beating the French fleet?'

'Even if the English fleet is beaten at last, will not half the French fleet be equally damaged and have to retire to Toulon?'

'Is it possible for the French to attack Gibraltar before taking St. Philip's, seeing that they have no more transports?'

'Will not help arrive from England before then?'

'Ought not some risk to be run to preserve St. Philip's?'

This was very good criticism after the event, and, at any rate, showed that the author knew how Byng might have acted if he had been in a happier state of mind.

On the lighter side, a number of fresh ballads appeared, which were soon published in a collected edition of 'Bungiana.' One day Mr. Potter heard 'the whole city of Westminster disturbed by the song of a hundred ballad-singers chanting':

> Draw nigh, my good folks, whilst to you I sing,
> Great Blakeney betrayed by Newcastle and Byng.
> Before, such a story ne'er has been told;
> We're bought all, my friends, by shining French gold.
> *Chorus:*
> To the block with Newcastle, and the yardarm with Byng.
> Tara ra ra ra ra ra ra ra ring.

The savage mob was as quick to follow the lead of the ballad-mongers as the half-educated mob is to follow that of the newspapers to-day. Regardless of dissimilar conditions and of the fact that half of them had never seen the sea in their lives, they eagerly snatched at the ridiculous comparison between Torrington and his son, and were soon gabbling:

> It was in the very same sea, Sir,
> His father's fleet did swim:
> His father fought well, we agree, Sir,
> But his father was nothing like him.
> Sing, sing, O great Admiral Byng.
> . . . .

At length he descried the foe, Sir,
Whom he bravely determined to beat.
If he could without striking a blow, Sir,
Or hurting His Majesty's fleet.
Sing, sing, O brave Admiral Byng.

. . . .

And when the engagement begun, Sir,
The Admiral stuck to his plan,
For he fought without firing a gun, Sir,
Or losing a single man.
Sing, sing, O rare Admiral Byng.

. . . .

West gallantly charged in the van, Sir,
Without dismay or fear ;
But Byng who would not risk a man Sir,
Kept cautiously snug in the rear.
Sing, sing, great Rear-Admiral Byng.

. . . .

For behaving so well in the ocean,
At least he deserves well a string ;
And if he would sue for promotion,
I hope they will give him his swing.
Swing, swing, O rare Admiral Byng.

So far the Ministers had made no attempt to defend themselves formally, but were content to inflame the public against Byng by indirect methods. It was they who had published in the newspapers the order that he was to be arrested wherever he landed, and that the King had complimented West on his conduct in the battle. They now encouraged the mob by hints to enact mock trials of Byng in London and the seaports, and ' to haul along a log of wood in a lace coat,' and burn it after first submitting it to many coarse and undignified rites. Mock sentences, epitaphs and dying speeches followed, and so the mob was worked up to a pitch of muddled indignation and passionate desire for revenge, which made it willing to believe Byng the author of every calamity, from Lake Ontario to the Black Hole of Calcutta. The Ministers even went so far as to circulate the following infamous libel in the Press :

'Though he solicited the command, he deferred sailing from England till very pressing letters were sent him from authority ; many strange delays happened in the course of the voyage ; he lost seven days at Gibraltar when the utmost expedition was necessary for the public service ; he was twelve days upon his passage from Gibraltar to the distance of twelve leagues off Minorca, where the French fleet happened to find him ; he called a council as to the prudence of venturing an engagement ; the bad condition of the enemy's fleet occasioned their only maintaining a running fight ; night, and the cautiousness of our admiral, put an entire end to the skirmish ; after staying four days without seeing or seeking for the enemy, a council was called to determine on the expediency of relieving port St. Philip's—the errand they were sent out upon ; when off Mahon harbour another council was called in which it was resolved that the endeavouring to throw in the designed reinforcements was too dangerous, and that the preservation of the fort was impossible ; (against this Lord Effingham of the land forces nobly protested ;) another point determined was that the van appearance of the enemy's fleet made it possible they were sailed against Gibraltar, and therefore that it was prudent to get there as fast as possible: where the British admiral has since remained in perfect security and freedom from them.'

Byng's friends had now been able to collect a large number of papers and orders connected with the expedition; and it was determined to publish them at once and at the same time deal with the latest attacks on him, and his treatment by Townshend at Greenwich. Samuel Johnson was again employed, and produced *Some Further Particulars in Relation to the Case of Admiral Byng*. The pamphlet was given the motto 'Fiat Justitia,' and was said to be written 'By a Gentleman of Oxford,' and was to be sold 'at all the Pamphlet shops and Booksellers in London and Westminster, Price one shilling.' This time a complete narrative of events was given from 17th March, the day when Byng received his commission, by using the letters he had received and the copies of those he had sent.

A very full and accurate account was given of his preparations at Portsmouth, which easily disposed of the charge that he had wasted time. The failure to get the troops at Gibraltar was cleverly masked by a counter-attack on Barrington for writing confusing orders, and the council of war's opinion was given without comment. Hervey's reconnaissance off Mahon on 19th May was well explained, and Byng's orders to him printed in full—a useful stroke of propaganda. The battle was not described, but the council of war's opinion of 24th May was printed in full, and emphasis was laid on the damage to the ships, and Byng's efforts to get them quickly repaired at Gibraltar, and great indignation was expressed at his supersession on the strength of an enemy's dispatch.

All the recent libels against him, and the methods used by the Ministers to prejudice his trial, were vigorously exposed. The petty brutalities of Townshend were denounced with great spirit, and the pamphlet ends by asking if the conduct of the Ministers will not ruin the service 'by discouraging men of character and parts from engaging in it, and thereby throwing it wholly into the hands of fools and madmen; since none but such will accept a commission on the ignominious terms of serving with a halter about their necks, that a knot of domineering grandees may be exempt not only from punishment but imputation?'

At the same time another important pamphlet appeared, entitled *Impartial Reflections on the Case of Mr. Byng, as stated in An Appeal to the People and a Letter to a Member of Parliament.* As an example of literature and advocacy it is far in advance of any of Johnson's efforts, and quite fulfils its claim to be impartial. Its theme is that Byng's case is still *sub judice* and that the Ministers cannot seriously injure him by persecutions which must eventually recoil on themselves, by making him appear a martyr. All that really matters is whether Byng is guilty under the Twelfth Article of War, and that question will be decided shortly by a fair trial, in which only his delay at Gibraltar and his conduct during and after the battle will be discussed.

'Circumstances of comparison with others, whose guilt being greater than his, is certainly an unanswerable reason for ulterior justice upon them, but can never serve to acquit him. It is in quality of Admiral he will be judged, and not as Minister.'

The omissions in publishing Byng's letters, whether to protect the Ministers, to incriminate Byng, or out of tenderness to his reputation, are such as 'can by no plea or evasion be defended,' justice demanding that they should have been published entire. The 'appeal' is then criticised in detail with great ability. Byng's opinion that it was impossible to open communications with St. Philip's after the action owing to the French covering the position is ably condemned as justifying 'the consequences of his attempt, but can hardly acquit him of not doing everything humanly possible to carry it. . . . It is certain that it is one thing to have an ill opinion of the service one is sent upon, and another thing to have an ill-will to it.'

Johnson's absurd comparison of the strength of the two fleets is lightly satirised as a 'nice canvass of weights and numbers,' and the conclusion reached that Byng's failure to engage them a second time 'depended on this yet unreceived doctrine in the Navy that twelve English ships are excusable to quitting the field to sixteen at any time. . . . Mr. Byng, however, to do him justice, ventured so far as to disobey those authoritative injunctions of the two Marquis of Feuquieres and Santa Cruz . . . in his engaging at all.' His sins are characterised as those of omission rather than commission, 'a charge which he has in common with others, whose duty it was to have provided earlier and better for the saving of Minorca,' though he is stoutly upheld in the complaint that the passage referring to sickness and casualties and lack of a hospital ship was entirely suppressed. The omission of the word 'cover' in connection with Gibraltar is also condemned, as it imputes flight instead of strategy, but Johnson's pamphlets are cleverly ridiculed for trying to read more into this than was really intended by saying that Byng's phrasing showed too clearly what the Government's ultimate intentions were. A fair trial, the writer concludes, is all that is required; 'the orders, the signals, the management provincial to our admiral in such an engagement, must be facts of a nature too manifest, too evident not to defy any evasive subtilties of Mr. Byng's, or any malicious aggravations of self-interested persecutors.'

In the handling of the material, in powers of expression, and above all in its great sense of restraint, this was by far the ablest piece of writing which appeared on the subject. Its authorship is uncertain, but it was obviously both aimed at the Ministers and Byng, and artfully contrived to draw together all popular opinions and centre them on the interest which must be aroused by the trial.

Meanwhile, Byng still lacked solid political support, since the opposition were less than ever inclined to saddle themselves with the defence of the Ministry's incompetent admiral. A few independent men in the Navy, Parliament and the City rallied to his support, but those who hoped either to obtain or retain office carefully avoided espousing the cause of the scapegoat.

Byng, too, began to realise that his trial would be a serious affair, and decided to ask for additional witnesses to those included in his original list. He, therefore, wrote to the Admiralty on 6th September, asking for the officers of the *Captain*, *Trident*, *Revenge*, *Princess Louisa* and *Deptford*, and all the midshipmen of the *Ramillies*. Only eighteen of them were mentioned by name, Byng apologising for being 'obliged to distinguish many by their offices and the spheres they acted in.' But again a good letter was spoilt by tactless remarks, as he insisted on referring to 'the industry of some as yet invisible persons who are indefatigable in propagating falsehoods to my dishonour' as an excuse for this delay of his trial and inconvenience to the service. Moreover, he had challenged the Admiralty to show that there was no special bias against him, but it was a charge they were at no pains to deny, and in their reply three days later they treated him as a guilty criminal attempting to escape justice by illegally wasting time. They even went further, and suggested that many of the witnesses then in England were wrongfully biased in his favour. Byng's letter was certainly provocative, but the Admiralty's reply was the work of bullies, who knew that unless they crushed Byng they might themselves become the scapegoats.

'Their Lordships,' Mr. Cleveland wrote, 'were desirous, in justice to the public as well as tenderness to yourself, to give you the earliest opportunity of acquitting yourself, if possible, from so heavy a charge.' They considered that the twenty officers in England on 31st July alone sufficient, 'as amongst them there were several who must be presumed under a particular bias (as far as truth will permit) in your favour.' Nevertheless, when they received a demand for thirty-seven witnesses, written on 4th August, of whom twenty-three[1] were in the Mediterranean, they ordered them home without hesitation. Now, therefore, they profess the utmost astonishment at this further demand, and 'look upon it merely as a scheme suggested to you to delay your being brought to trial. . . . By the same means you may put off your trial for ever, it is but by applying for a new list every month or six weeks, and at last concluding with a desire that the whole fleet may be brought home.' They, therefore, see no reason to delay his trial any longer, and refuse to grant a request 'very dangerous to the service and discipline of the Navy.' The list was certainly a long one, and Byng's pompous complaints had been met with well-bred insolence reminiscent of the Court of Versailles. He replied at once,[2] fastening on the two most objectionable phrases in their lordships' letter—that of acquitting himself 'if possible,' and the presumption that certain witnesses were biased in his favour. He then protested angrily at 'being kept moving backward and forward from one place of confinement to another for near three weeks after my

[1] According to the original list, twenty-three were in the Mediterranean and thirteen at home, but this was because Byng did not include West in his list.

[2] 14th September.

arrival in England,' and thus preventing him preparing his defence. At Greenwich, too, the false report of his intended escape had resulted in precautions being taken as if it were true, and the Governor of the Hospital, in whose name he is now confined, 'seems diligent in distinguishing himself in the service of his country by imposing on me all the indignities and inconveniences that power can enable him to do.' Had their lordships wished for speedy trial, why had they not informed him of it when he struck his flag to Hawke, 'for surely no person was to suppose that I was to look upon an extract of an enemy's letter and that extract (if from a genuine letter) a mere gasconade and absolute falsehood, as sufficient to ground a charge against me?' Besides, the Admiralty had ordered home their own witnesses with him in the *Antelope* at a time when no one knew for what purpose they had been recalled.

He then repeats his demand for all his witnesses, expressing himself 'eager and solicitous' for trial, 'but a trial without the necessary witnesses cannot be considered any trial at all; rather an act of power than an act of justice.'

This letter received no answer, and the correspondence was closed for a month, because the Admiralty, for all their blustering, knew that a 'speedy trial' was quite impossible. Horace Walpole thought that the Ministers were waiting till the effect of Byng's pamphlets had worn off, and that nothing was likely to happen till Parliament met in November. But the real reason for this extraordinary delay was that the Ministry was tottering to its fall, and had no wish to run the risk of staging a legal drama which might reproduce in miniature the effects of the Trial of the Seven Bishops.

Not only was Henry Fox growing more anxious about his position every day, but William Murray, the Attorney-General, who after Fox and Pitt, was the best debater in the House, was clamouring for a peerage, and promotion to the late Sir Dudley Ryder's office of Lord Chief Justice. Newcastle became more depressed and nervous than usual. 'The army is absolutely under other direction,' he wrote to Hardwicke; 'the sea does not love to be controlled, or even advised; and yet I am to answer for any miscarriage in either. . . . My dear Lord, pity me, alone as I am in my present distress.' It was not till 6th October that Mr. Charles Fearne, Judge-Advocate of the Fleet, was ordered to take the depositions of the witnesses then in England, and it was obvious by that time that the loss of Minorca had wrecked the Ministry. Byng was told by a letter of 14th October that the *Colchester* was returning with his first batch of witnesses, and he at once wrote to protest that his last letter, insisting on the second list, had been ignored. He again talked of 'persons too powerful for me to contend with,' and submitted that he ought to be given every possible assistance for making his defence, declaring that all he desired was justice. But their lordships were 'much surprised,' and again refused his request.

Realising that if they did not have to resign they would at least be seriously shaken, Newcastle and

Hardwicke now employed David Mallet to put the Ministry's case in pamphlet form. Johnson speaks very disparagingly of this poet, though Gibbon admired him as a playwright, and he had lately been connected with Lord Bolingbroke and Frederick, Prince of Wales. His work, which dealt chiefly with the reasons for the omissions in Byng's despatches, was written under the title of *A Plain Man*, but Hardwicke was 'not much enamoured with it.' He made several suggestions for altering it, but was cunning enough, as he explained to Anson, to arrange it so that he was not 'named as joint author.'

Although we had regained the initiative in India and America, and Frederick the Great had seized Dresden and defeated the Austrians at Lobositz, Fox was determined to resign. He knew too well the loose ties which bound him to the Newcastle Whigs, and that they would not scruple to sacrifice him along with Byng. As Secretary of State, he was a marked man, and had acted as bailiff for the Ministry all the last session, while his colleague Holderness sat sheltered from criticism in the Lords. Besides, he hoped, by provoking a crisis now, to bring about a reconstruction in the Ministry which would give him extensive patronage as well as high office.

On 13th October he told Newcastle that he wished to resign, and presented a memorial to the King, through Lady Yarmouth, the King's mistress, explaining that he lacked support in the House 'to carry on His Majesty's affairs there, as they ought to be carried on.' Newcastle and Hardwicke were utterly nonplussed, and there seemed no solution but to offer Fox more power to stay, or let him go and bring in Pitt, for whom, wrote Newcastle, 'I am hand and heart.'

He approached the King next day, and the following humorous conversation took place:

"What is to be done?" said the King.

NEWCASTLE: "Sir . . . either to gratify Mr. Fox . . . or take in Mr. Pitt."

KING: "But Mr. Pitt won't come."

NEWCASTLE: "If that was done we should have a quiet session."

KING: "But Mr. Pitt won't do my German business."

NEWCASTLE: "If he comes into your service, sir, he must be told he must do your Majesty's business."

KING: "But I don't like Pitt; he won't do my business."

NEWCASTLE: "But unfortunately, sir, he is the only one in the Opposition who has ability to do the business."

At last the King was won over, and Hardwicke asked Pitt for an interview. They met on 19th October and again on the 24th, but Pitt refused to be made responsible for the Ministry's past actions, and haughtily demanded its complete reconstruction. The result, therefore, was 'totally negative.' Pitt then took the unusual step of going straight to Lady Yarmouth and explaining his devotion to the King and his desire to serve him in every way. The

King then tried to unite Pitt and Fox, but without success, and found that, whether he liked it or not, Pitt would have to come in alone. So the one man who was capable of directing the war with spirit and success was at last called to the task; but he was a commoner, and without votes or money, being only supported by the 'Cousinhood,' Legge and half of Leicester House. The Duke of Devonshire, therefore, consented to be titular head of the new Ministry as first Lord of the Treasury, his wealth, influence and talent, and his complete freedom from political intrigue, being an indispensable supplement to Pitt's vigour and oratory.

The delicate negotiations which brought this about took seventeen days, Newcastle resigning on 11th November, and being followed by Hardwicke, Anson and Fox. Pitt became Secretary of State for the south, and the Great Seal was put in commission. Although only a part of the Ministry resigned, the Board of Admiralty was reconstructed as follows:

	Old Board	*New Board*
First Lord:	Lord Anson.	Lord Temple.
Lords:	Lord Duncannon.	John Pitt.
	Admiral Rowley.	George Hay.
	Admiral Boscawen.	Admiral Boscawen.
	Lord Bateman.	Admiral West.
	Rich. Edgecumbe.	Gilbert Elliot.
	Lord Hyde.	Thomas Hunter.

This complete change in the Board seemed to augur very well for Byng. Lord Temple, a vigorous but saturnine character and of uncertain temper, was Pitt's brother-in-law, and a strong opponent of

Newcastle. Temple West was still much attached to Byng, and anxious to see him treated fairly, and, with John Pitt, was a remoter member of the famous Cousinhood. On the other hand, Admiral Boscawen was bitterly opposed to Byng on professional grounds. Like many other naval officers, he was disgusted at his display of intellectual weakness in returning to Gibraltar, and openly stated that he expected him to be condemned. His partisanship, however, may have had a more sinister origin, for as the only surviving member of the late Board, he had every reason to justify the policy of his patron Anson, and like Barrington, who also remained in office as Secretary at War, he helped to give the policy of the new Ministers an unfortunate and embarrassing continuity.

CHAPTER XII

THE TRIAL

THE new Ministers are so little provided with interest in boroughs, that it is almost an administration out of Parliament. . . . The Duke of Newcastle is already hanging out a white flag to Pitt; but there is so little disposition in that quarter to treat, that they have employed one Evans, a lawyer, to draw up articles of impeachment against Lord Anson. On the other hand, they show great tenderness to Byng, who has certainly been most inhumanly and spitefully treated by Anson. Byng's trial is not yet appointed.'

Horace Walpole was right in assuming that the new Ministers would be weak, but that was one of the chief reasons why they could not afford to treat Byng with too much 'tenderness.' Lord Barrington was still Secretary at War, and there were so many friends of Newcastle still left in office, that it would have been fatal for Pitt to release Byng and saddle the late Ministers with the whole blame. Besides, to attack Byng would be a popular act, and with so little weight in Parliament they did not dare forfeit the support of the public. On the other hand, they had no special reason for wishing his death, and would be quite content if he were cashiered.

Meanwhile, days and weeks passed and Byng heard nothing further about his trial, except that

Charles Fearne, the judge-advocate, had been taking the evidence of some of the witnesses. Actually, it was Byng's right to question them before anyone else, and he had left letters for them at Portsmouth explaining this, and urging them to say nothing whatever about the campaign until they had consulted him at Greenwich. Hoping, therefore, to get better treatment from the new Board, he wrote on 27th November to complain of his flagrant disregard of the prisoner's rights, 'which I presume is tending illegally to discover my defence, and expose me to the malicious and virulent attacks of my enemies.' He then asks the Admiralty to order the witnesses to visit him, as in the case of Matthews and Lestock, 'as I have seen very few of these gentlemen as yet, owing to their not knowing of my right and the fear of doing what might be deemed improper.'

The new Board was too busy to attend to him for the moment, and meanwhile public interest centred round the arrival in England of the Minorca garrison. Blakeney was at once created a Baron and made a Knight of the Bath at the instigation of the retiring Ministers, so as to reinflame the public against Byng. The two men, says Hume, 'were viewed at different ends of a false perspective through the medium of passion and prejudice; of a perspective artfully contrived, and applied by certain Ministers for the purpose of self-interest and deceit.'

'These honours are a little ridiculed,' writes Horace Walpole; 'we have too many governors that will expect titles, if losses are pretensions.'

Lieut.-Cols. Jefferies and Rufane were promoted

full colonels, and Jefferies was given Fowke's regiment; Robert Boyd and Major Cunningham were made lieutenant-colonels, and Captain Sir Hugh Williams was promoted to major. In contrast to these rewards, Maj.-Gen. Stuart and Cols. Cornwallis and Lord Effingham had to appear before a special board of general officers to explain their failure to join their regiments sooner, their failure to get into St. Philip's during the campaign, and their reasons for taking part in a sea council of war.

Three days before the enquiry, Newcastle wrote to Hardwicke in great excitement to say that Barrington had just told him 'a circumstance' which justified 'all that was done here more than any one which I have heard yet. Gen. Blakeney assured my Lord Barrington: first, that the communication was open and that they might have flung in succours at any time, even in daytime, whilst he was master of St. Philip's; secondly, that he surrendered the place because the garrison was worn out with continual duty; thirdly, that had our fleet been successful and the reinforcement been flung in, Marshal Richelieu and his army must have capitulated.' Newcastle suggests that Anson should be told of this at once, 'that Mr. Byng's trial should be carried on effectually or the partiality appear to all the world.'

'P.S.—Admiral Boscawen was, and I believe, is, as violent against Byng as anybody.'[1]

Hardwicke at once replied that the information 'is very material and I have communicated it to my

[1] Newcastle to Hardwicke, 5th December, 1756. *Add. MSS.* 32869, f. 249.

Lord Anson, who will make the best use of it he can in his private situation. I have gone a little further, and as Lord Barrington called upon me last night, I desired his Lordship to give a hint to Sir John Ligonier[1] that General Blakeney should be very particularly examined before the general officers upon those points, and that they should take care to have his examination very correctly taken down, and inserted in the report to be made by the general officers to the King; that his Majesty should be advised to order a copy of that report to be transmitted to the Admiralty, that they be ordered to summon General Blakeney to attend as a witness upon Mr. Byng's trial. This will be a regular method of proceeding.'[2] Considering that Hardwicke was out of office, his conduct in suggesting what advice should be given the King was quite unconstitutional, and he can hardly be acquitted on this occasion of the charge of labouring 'like a little attorney' to compass Byng's destruction. With dependents of the old Ministers such as Barrington in his Cabinet, Pitt could do nothing to stop malpractices of this kind, as he had no means of finding them out, and Hardwicke 'in his private situation' was at liberty to stage an execution for which he need not take the blame.

On 8th December Barrington obsequiously reported to Newcastle that the officers had cleared themselves of any suggestion of disobedience or neglect of duty, and three days after that they were

[1] President of the court of enquiry on Stuart, Cornwallis and Effingham.

[2] Hardwicke to Newcastle, 6th December, 1756. *Add. MSS.* 32867, f. 253.

'well received at Court.' He enclosed Blakeney's evidence and also that of Robert Boyd, together with the court of enquiry's report, which justified the officers having taken part in a sea council of war in a manner 'perhaps not altogether regular,' because they looked upon Byng as their commanding officer. The date of Byng's trial, said Barrington, was not yet fixed, but it was to be at Portsmouth and under the presidency of Vice-Admiral Thomas Smith.

This extraordinary creature was a true product of the eighteenth century. He was the son of Sir Thomas Lyttelton and a Wapping lodging-house keeper, and entered the Navy under his father's auspices, where he quickly distinguished himself by compelling a French warship to salute his own ship when leaving Plymouth. The affair made a great diplomatic stir at the time, and Smith was dismissed the service, but reinstated as post-captain immediately afterwards, by which he acquired the nickname 'Tom of Ten Thousand,' and continued his useful but undistinguished career. He was very generous to his brother officers and to Richard Wilson, the painter, whom he patronised, and seems to have been genuinely liked by everyone with whom he was connected, including Byng. He was appointed president of the court martial to try Byng because he was at that time commander-in-chief in the Downs and the senior officer employed in home waters; but the public, knowing his close relations with the 'Cousinhood' and his warm friendship for Byng, interpreted it as a sign that the new Ministers wished to be as lenient as possible.

'THE COUSINHOOD'

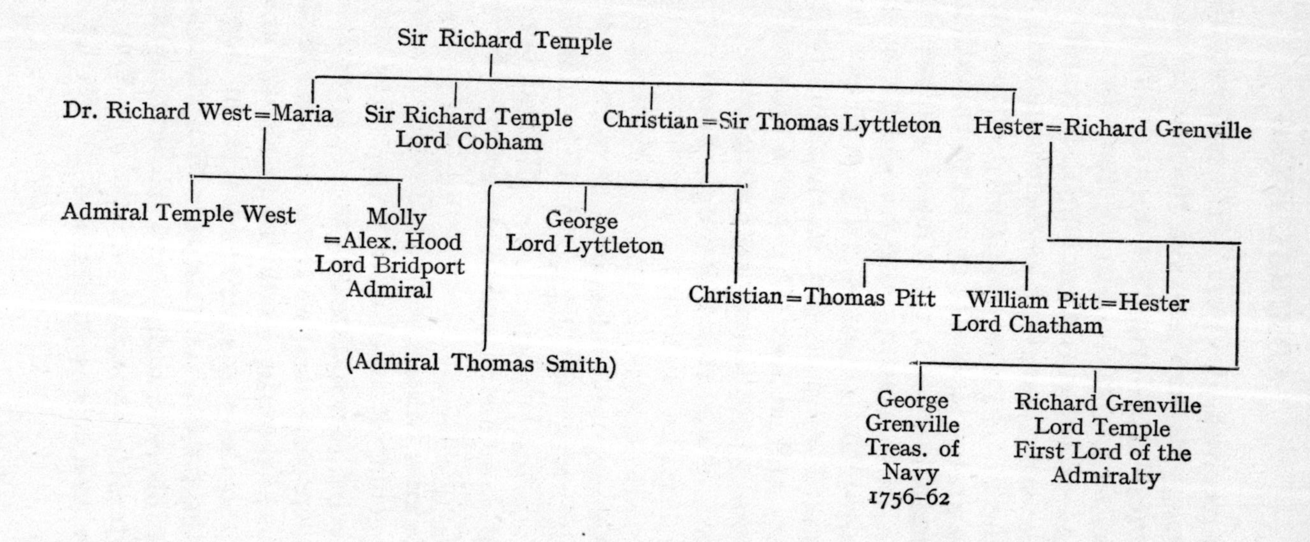

It is doubtful if they had any settled opinion on his case at the moment, and they hardly wasted any more time about it, but on 14th December the Admiralty issued an order for the trial. It took the form of an order to Admiral Smith quoting the two warrants to the marshal under which Byng had been arrested on reaching England, 'whereas it appears highly fitting, as well in regard to the public and the party accused, as to the officers who have been sent home as witnesses upon this occasion, that a court-martial should be assembled as soon as conveniently may be . . . to proceed to an enquiry into the before-recited conduct and behaviour of the said Admiral John Byng, and to try him for the same.'

Smith chose the following officers to form his court :

Rear-Admiral Francis Holbourne.
Rear-Admiral Harry Norris.
Rear-Admiral Thomas Broderick.
Captain Charles Holmes.
Captain William Boys.
Captain John Simcoe.
Captain John Bentley.
Captain Peter Dennis.
Captain Francis Geary.
Captain John Moore.
Captain James Douglas.
Captain Augustus Keppel.

There does not appear to be any special significance in the appointment of these officers. Most of them had been recently employed in the Channel and off Brest, or in the squadrons sent to America, and happened to be at Portsmouth during the winter, when many cruising and blockading ships were withdrawn to harbour.

The court was to be held in the *St. George* in

ADMIRAL THOMAS SMITH

From the picture by Richard Wilson in the Painted Hall, Greenwich

By permission of the Lords Commissioners of the Admiralty

[*p*. 212

Portsmouth harbour, and was to meet every morning at nine o'clock and sit till about four in the afternoon, none of its members being allowed to go ashore till the trial was finished. The witnesses could please themselves as to their movements, and were at liberty to leave Portsmouth as soon as their evidence was finished. Byng was told that he might have lodgings in the dockyard at the discretion of Commissioner Hughes, and need only attend on board when the court was sitting. This was a great convenience to him, as it meant that he could have Paul Whitehead and Mr. Cooke, his shorthand man, constantly working for him at his lodgings.

All the officers on the first list desired as witnesses had come home in the *Culloden* except Charles Catford, who had died on the way. The Admiralty were also calling West, Blakeney, Boyd, Captain Everitt and the lieutenants of the *Buckingham*. They made no attempt to bring home any of those on Byng's second list, but Captain Durell, Captain Cornwall and Lieut. Boyle, also of the *Revenge*, and John Scott and Harry Harwood of the *Deptford*, happened to be in England, and of these the Admiralty allowed the first three to attend.

Byng was brought down from Greenwich on 23rd December, and at nine o'clock on the morning of 28th December a gun was fired on board the *St. George* to signal the start of the trial. Proceedings began with the swearing in of the court and the judge-advocate, and the reading of Byng's instructions, Barrington's letters to Fowke, the opinions of the two councils of war and other documents, after which the court had to decide what dates should limit the scope of their enquiry.

The form of the charges showed that they would have to devote most of their time to considering Byng's conduct during the battle, and his failure to open up communications with St. Philip's; but to make quite certain, it was decided to enquire into everything which took place since the fleet left England. A paper from Byng was then read, expressing his happiness at being able 'to evince the falsehood of all the malicious aspersions' of his enemies, and asking to be allowed one of his officers to take short-hand notes for him during the trial, as his eyes were inflamed by a 'severe cold' caught during his confinement. This was agreed to, but on Lieut. Edward Clarke, late of the *Ramillies*, being named, he was found to be on the list of witnesses, and the court adjourned to give Byng time to find a substitute.

Next morning, Temple West was called as first witness, and his evidence lasted for more than a day and a half. He talked vaguely of the voyage out, inferring that he knew nothing of Byng's intentions and was not favoured with his confidence, but on coming to the battle he described the doing of his own division with evident pleasure and a wealth of detail. They had apparently attacked 'agreeable' to the signals received, no mention being made of Captain Andrews' misunderstanding, and had thoroughly trounced the French van. Galissonnière had then approached with his centre and rear, but 'declined coming to a closer engagement,' presumably out of respect for the *Buckingham*.

In contrast to this lavish praise of the conduct of his own ships, his answers to questions dealing with Byng were curiously constrained, as if he strongly resented not being better supported, but was trying to appear impartial by saying that the smoke and his own immediate difficulties prevented him noticing what was happening in the rear. Asked if the wind and weather were such as to have enabled Byng to have come to close quarters if he chose, he replied, "Yes, it appeared to me so ; I saw no impediment. I beg leave to observe that I don't say there was none, but that none appeared to me."

He was then asked straight out, "Did you during the action, or at any time afterwards, express your opinion or sentiments of the behaviour or proceedings of any officer or ship, particularly of the behaviour or proceedings of the admiral, and if so, what was it ?"

To this he promptly objected, and the question was eventually withdrawn, the court returning to what prevented the rear coming to close action, and were told, "I know of nothing to prevent their doing so."

Obviously, there was no more to get out of him on this topic, and the court went on to the business of St. Philip's. Here West adopted a far more favourable tone, which was only natural, seeing that he had signed the council of war opinion. He approved of the first stop at Gibraltar, said that Byng consulted no one on the voyage out "in any manner so as to divert him from pursuing his orders," and that the day before the battle everyone seemed "in great spirits" aboard the *Ramillies*.

Byng now began his cross-examination, and at once raised the question of Fowke and the battalion of infantry which he was unwilling to embark. This was a mistake, as West became quietly sarcastic, and repeated his remarks made at Fowke's trial that the conversation between the admiral and the general "had very little air of business about it"; but Byng cleverly changed his tactics and began to press all the previous points in West's evidence which were in his favour, and received most agreeable answers to fifty consecutive questions. West made it quite clear that he thought the delay at Gibraltar inevitable, and that Byng was right not to detach a single ship to communicate with St. Philip's when faced by the enemy's fleet, and that to have tried to land any troops would have been imprudent and impracticable. He was next closely questioned on the individual condition of many of the ships, and again returned satisfactory answers from Byng's point of view, instancing many defects in balance of metal, seaworthiness and manning. This led up to Byng's final point in getting him to admit that, owing to the French being superior in sailing power, pursuit after the action was impossible. Here Byng should have stopped, but with amazing stupidity he reverted to the action itself, and tried to make West say that if the French had lain to longer our rear would have come to close action. This again touched a sore point, and West would not bear him out, and said that the French lay to quite long enough, and that he had seen the *Ramillies* and other ships lying to with their maintopsails aback. The court here asked how it was, if our ships were in such bad condition, that those in the van managed to repulse the French, to which he gave a very long answer in general terms, implying that it was chiefly due to the *Buckingham* and the *Lancaster*, "both very fine men-of-war."

As a Lord of the Admiralty, West's evidence was very important, and except for a difference of opinion with regard to the battle, it was much in favour of Byng's conduct, especially in regard to the condition of the ships, for which the late Ministers were responsible.

Blakeney was called next, his entrance naturally creating a great sensation. It was already dark, and they were lighting the lanterns in the great cabin as the closely packed spectators strove to get a sight of the old man for whom Byng was such a foil. They addressed him as "your lordship," treating him with great respect, and as he gave his quiet, decisive answers, he seemed to convey a sense of reproach to the Navy for not having done more to help his garrison. He was very emphatic about the possibility of landing at St. Philip's by boat, and pointed out the strain placed upon his officers during the siege on account of the great number of absentees from the garrison, many of whom were aboard the fleet.

Byng then tried his hand at cross-examination.

Q.: "Do you apprehend that troops could have been landed, from the landing-place most advanced towards the town, safely from the fire of the enemy?"

A.: "I have served sixty-three years, and I never knew any enterprise undertaken without some danger, and this might have been effected with as little as ever I knew."

Byng, however, was quite unperturbed by this withering reply, and pressed for further details about the enemy's batteries. Blakeney explained that those on Mola could not have harmed approaching boats, as they would have had to depress their guns so much that hits would have been almost impossible. St. Stephen's Cove was also safe, as the French batteries to the south could not see over its steep banks into the water below, and boats could easily get in and out without receiving a shot if they chose "a proper time of night for it."

"Is the night a proper time to land a body of men?" enquired Byng.

"I know that I have landed in the night with men," retorted Blakeney.

These answers produced a great effect on those present in the court, as, unlike West, Blakeney gave his answers decisively, and never prefaced them with the hesitating formulæ "I believe so" or "I apprehend so." Byng, however, had the last word, asking if Boyd would not have reached the fleet if he had started at ten o'clock instead of four, to which Blakeney had to agree, but begged leave to state that Captain Scrope was as expeditious as a man could be in getting the boat ready; which, however, was not a very convincing statement.

Nevertheless, when the onlookers went ashore that night they spread it about, and wrote it to their

THE TRIAL
General Blakeney giving evidence
Admiral Smith presiding and Rear-Admirals Holburne, Norris, and Broderick wearing their hats

[p. 218

friends in town, that the trial was going very badly for Byng.

Next day Robert Boyd gave a frank account of his attempt to reach the fleet in the boat, and of how easy it was to get backwards and forwards. Byng now had his chance to convict the garrison of gross delay in ordering the boat to be got ready, and he made the most of it.

" What time in the morning of the 19th did the fleet appear ? " he asked.

A.: " About noon."

Q.: " What time did you make the proposal to Col. Jefferies to go off ? "

A.: " As soon as I believed them to be the English fleet."

Q.: " What time of the day was that ? "

A.: " I cannot be very certain as to the hour."

Q.: " Do you think it was an hour or two hours after you saw the fleet ? "

A.: " I have already said that as soon as I thought they were the English I made my proposal."

Boyd was now obviously rattled and trying to hedge, and Byng pressed his advantage, asking, " Was it one or two hours ? Or five hours, do you think ? " with a concluding sneer ; but Boyd had lost count of the hours.

Having shown that no attempt was made to get the boat ready as soon as the fleet was sighted, on the chance that it might be our own, Byng went on to make Boyd acknowledge that he had had to wait some time for it even after he had received his orders from Blakeney late in the afternoon, and that when he did row out there was no chance of coming up with the fleet or of being seen by it.

All this was excellent from Byng's point of view, as it tended to destroy the pathetic picture conjured up by the thought of the beleaguered garrison straining its eyes in vain for the sight of the relieving forces. Moreover, it convicted Blakeney of wasting precious hours, and undermined his prestige as a witness.

Captain Everitt of the *Buckingham*, who followed, was closely questioned about the whole campaign, and said that he saw no reason why the rear of our fleet could not have set more sail, and so have got to close quarters with the enemy, but that this was only an expression of opinion.

Byng was now sufficiently elated to recall Blakeney and ask him if it were true that he had stated that Minorca could not have been held, even if Fowke had sent the battalion from Gibraltar. Evidently Byng had just received private information about this statement, and Blakeney wavered; Byng repeated his question, and Blakeney attempted to bluster. "By the oath I have taken," he fumed, "I believe I could have held out till Sir Edward Hawke came, if that detachment had been landed."

But Byng was not to be denied, and again demanded an answer to his question, had Blakeney made the statement that he could not have held out, or had he not?

"I did declare it," he answered at last, and then excused himself on the grounds that, as it was his duty to remain in one place all the time, he had had to rely on reports in order to form his opinions.

Robert Boyd was also recalled, and bombarded with questions by Byng and the court as to the French batteries; but here his evidence told rather against Byng, as it proved that they could do very little to prevent boats reaching St. Philip's.

The lieutenants of the *Buckingham* had nothing material to contribute, but agreed that in their opinion there was nothing to prevent the rear setting more sail and at once running to leeward of the *Intrepid*.

Byng recalled Captain Everitt, and cross-examined him on the propriety of landing troops at St. Philip's, and he agreed with West that it would have been improper to have weakened the fleet in any way when in the face of the enemy, and that if the officers and recruits belonging to the garrison had been landed they would have made little difference to its powers of resistance.

Captain Augustus Hervey was the first witness called from those on Byng's list, and, owing to his ship having been immediately to windward of the *Ramillies* to repeat signals, and therefore out of the line, he was able to give such a clear account of what passed that his evidence formed the basis for the court's resolutions. He would not admit that Byng ought to have set his topgallant-sails, as, being out of the line, he was not in a position to judge, but agreed that, irrespective of the danger of fouling other ships, the weather was quite suitable. He attributed the French van retiring to a signal which he saw flying from the *Foudroyant,* especially as none of their ships was disabled, and noted that their centre and rear outsailed us under their top-sails and foresails alone, while Byng was crowding on his jib and staysails. He saw the hold-up in our line caused by the *Intrepid* going down before the wind and being badly raked and disabled, but held that whether the rear could have run to leeward of her at once was a question of opinion and not of fact, and one of which the court could judge better than he. From this attitude he refused to budge, and after several futile attempts to make him commit himself to opinions, which were quite inadmissible according to the strict rules of evidence, they gave it up and dismissed him.

Captain Lloyd, of the *Chesterfield,* had seen most of the action from the rear, as he was stationed abreast of the *Culloden,* and later took the *Intrepid* in tow. After incautiously stating that our rear could have reached the French if it had set more sail, he was forced by Byng to admit that it was the slowness of the *Revenge* in running to leeward of the *Intrepid* which really caused all the trouble, and that the Admiral was impeded by the *Trident* trying to clear the *Princess Louisa.* Most witnesses who had been in the van ships thought that they had driven their opposite numbers away by sheer hard hitting, but Captain Baird, of the *Portland,* acknowledged that the French never looked like waiting for a general action, and were simply concerned with covering the siege of St. Philip's. Nobody denied that the rear could have set more sail, but there was great hesitation in saying that it ought to have done.

So far the trial had gone in Byng's favour. All the sailors supported him in having refused to land even the officers and recruits of the garrison, let alone any of Bertie's men, and Blakeney himself had been forced to admit that in the end they would have made very little difference.

It was clear that Byng's method of attack was poor, as it had exposed his leading ships to being raked in detail, but as at that date concentration on the enemy's van was still in favour, this naturally passed unnoticed. Instead, the court were trying to discover if he had acted timorously in not setting more sail himself, and so carrying down his whole division at once to close action. Admittedly, they would have got down after the van, but could they have got down at all? Byng said no; the *Intrepid* had held up the rear, the ships being at half a cable distance, and the court had to discover what that hold-up really meant.

Much, therefore, depended on the evidence of Captain Young, and it is almost certain that he would have been called as a witness by the Admiralty, but Byng had already put him on his own list, regardless of the fact that he was 'his warmest accuser.' He appeared on 7th January and refused to give a narrative of the action, but said he was ready to answer questions, and did so with a great show of unrewarded heroism. He denied any injury to the *Intrepid* before she turned broadside on to engage, and was entirely ignorant of having caused any 'impediment' to Byng's division, but talked vaguely of seeing ships on his weather quarter with their topsails aback, as if they were there from sheer caprice. Apparently the ships astern of him made no attempt to get past till the French had themselves made sail and shot ahead.

Q.: "How long was it after you had lost your foretopmast that the Admiral and rear passed to leeward of you?"

A.: "Not much above three-quarters of an hour, or an hour, I believe"; and then sarcastically, "It can't be much above."

He was quite sure that the rear could have got to close action if all sail had been set, and that as it was they were never closely engaged.

Q.: "Did you see them engaged at all?"

A.: "Yes; some of the ships; they fired."

There seemed 'no objection' to the rear crowding all sail, and as the enemy were lying to, and the *Intrepid* got to close quarters with them, presumably the rear could have done the same. "To be sure the two rears were at the greatest distance from each other," he remarked, "because our rear was to windward of our van," as if Byng had held his rear to windward on purpose to refuse action with it; and further questioning about signals produced the would-be heroic answer, "I took no notice of any signals after the signal for battle was made."

He had no idea how or when the *Revenge* came alongside to relieve him, and thought every ship astern might have passed at once if the Admiral had set an example by crowding sail and putting before the wind. Thus he would not have had to withstand the fire of three French ships, including the *Foudroyant,* for they filled and stood on when our rear began to come up. Under cross-examination, he again denied that his foretopmast went before he began to fire, thus implying that it was the result of hard fighting and not of a bad approach.

"I did not see the ship next astern," he said on being asked for the distance, adding, "I did not look for her," as if looking behind suggested cowardice.

Byng asked, in that case, how he was in a position to judge whether he impeded the attack or not, especially as the signal was for the line at half a cable, and he had just admitted being a whole cable astern of the *Captain,* the ship ahead of him, presumably in order to magnify the manner of his gallant resistance to the three French ships. This was quite a neat point, and he could only reply sulkily, "I answer for my own ship, that I made no impediment to any other ship's closing, no impediment appeared to me." Having successfully shown him up as being grossly prejudiced, Byng led him on by easy stages to descant on the deficiencies of his own and other ships and the unharmed state of the French at the end of the action. This was a congenial topic, and he gave no further trouble.

Captain Cornwall vividly described how he closed the *Intrepid,* and at the same time nearly had the *Princess Louisa* and *Trident* aboard him from astern, and that, looking out of the stern windows, "great was my surprise to see the Admiral, with the other ships, at a considerable distance astern." Seeing no signal for the *Intrepid* to quit the line, he sent a boat to ask Young's permission to go past him to leeward, and so rejoined the van, denying that he was in the least obstructed by the *Intrepid*, or that he in turn obstructed any other ship. As he mentioned being afraid of the *Intrepid* becalming him, Byng asked why he did not pass her to windward, Captain Young having already stated that it would have been quite easy. "I could not think of withdrawing from the enemy," replied Cornwall, as if he were a reincarnation of the Chevalier Bayard instead of an unimaginative stickler for the letter of the law, and "as to going to leeward, I believe I might, if I had thought myself authorised." Byng again demanded why he lay by the *Intrepid* at all, and was told because there was no signal for the *Intrepid* to leave the line. "What does the twenty-fourth article of the Fighting Instructions direct a captain to do?" asked Byng very pompously.[1] "I'll read it," said Cornwall with great eagerness, "for I read it in the day of action"; and without more ado, this extraordinary pedant naïvely pulled out a copy of the Instructions and read aloud, convinced that he had done the right thing in not passing the *Intrepid* sooner. As, however, he had just acknowledged that he was "never very near the enemy" himself, he might easily have passed the *Intrepid* to leeward so as to have got near enough, without appearing to disobey or to withdraw. This

[1] See page 124, note 2.

must have been sufficiently obvious to the court, and Byng soon let him go.

Captain Durell, of the *Trident*, showed that, had the rear put before the wind in the same manner as the van, they would have passed astern of the French, who were not quite abreast of them. Consequently they had to steer obliquely with the wind four points abaft the beam in order to cover the distance of three and a half miles which separated them from their opposite numbers. There seemed nothing to prevent the *Trident* or the ships astern of her going to leeward of the *Intrepid* and *Princess Louisa*, and so reaching the enemy, except an exaggerated devotion to the theory of the line, to which Durell was only less attached than Cornwall. If, then argued the court, the van did not disobey the signal for line of battle ahead by covering the intervening two miles in line abreast before forming, surely the rear ships should have had no scruple in getting into action as best they could, instead of regulating their speed for at least half an hour by that of the *Intrepid* and *Princess Louisa*. But from here the witnesses' answers became quite contradictory. No obstructions occurred—oh, no, none at all—and yet the rear had to back topsails and wait while the *Princess Louisa* and *Intrepid* dithered in the wind, for fear of breaking the line. Apparently the difficulty of carrying out the tactical idea amounted to a tactical obstruction, though not to a navigational one.

Captain Arthur Gardiner explained how the *Ramillies* had waited about five minutes at the start of the action for the ships ahead of her to get into station, and had then backed her maintopsail when near the *Trident*, because otherwise "the admiral must have gone without his force, which was not his intention." If the signal for the line had been hauled down, and the signal for battle left flying, and the rear had set their topgallants, he thought it might have been a more "speedy" method of bringing on a general action, "but not so regular." A general attack in line abreast, he thought, was "improper," when it was equally possible to go down lasking. When Byng shortened sail the first time, Gardiner said that he had suggested setting more sail in order to encourage the ships ahead to do likewise and so reach the enemy quicker. To this Byng had replied, "You see, Captain Gardiner, that the signal for the line is out, and that I am ahead of the *Princess Louisa* and Durell, and you would not have me, as admiral of the fleet, run down as if I was going to engage a single ship. It was Mr. Matthews's misfortune to be prejudiced by not carrying his force down together, which I shall endeavour to avoid."

Thus Byng had been haunted by the memory of his own judgment on Matthews, and had refused to set more sail and leave his injured ships to windward, although he could easily have done so, as the weather was suitable and none of them was closely engaged.

Cornwall, too, had vivid recollections of the 11th February, 1744. He had seen his cousin killed on the quarterdeck of the *Marlborough*, and had lost his right arm, while Captain Burrish, of the *Dorsetshire*, had been cashiered for holding to windward and not giving them proper support. Thus, twelve years afterwards, the battle of Toulon and its terrible aftermath rose as a ghost from the past and paralysed the initiative of two men whose courage and common sense had never been questioned.

Byng made Lord Robert Bertie agree that the officers and recruits of St. Philip's garrison were of more use on board the fleet than if they had been landed. This was only what was to be expected, as he was a member of the Gibraltar council of war, but coming from a soldier, it was a valuable admission. He was next asked if Byng showed any signs of fear or confusion during the action, and, as this was a delicate question, Byng handed it to the court in writing. "No," said Bertie, "he seemed to give his orders coolly and distinctly, and I did not apprehend he was the least wanting in personal courage."

Lieut.-Col. Marcus Smith and Captain James Edgar, both of the Fusiliers, gave identical answers to these questions, and denied ever hearing a word of discontent against the admiral, as did the six lieutenants of the *Ramillies* and John Lee, the gunner who gave sufficient evidence about the firing to show that they were properly engaged and had had every intention of getting to close quarters.

Byng cross-examined Edward Clarke, the fourth lieutenant, with whom he was well acquainted, and through him was able to bring out that the van need never have put before the wind at all, but could have led down to the enemy on a slanting course, but that if the rear had borne down perpendicularly they would certainly have passed right astern of the enemy, and that bearing down in line abreast was generally inexpedient.

Joseph Belvaird, the master of the *Ramillies*, pointed out that if she had carried more sail it could not have helped her to clear the *Trident*, as the hold-up was unforeseen and might have occurred anyhow, and further hinted that it was inexpedient to crowd sail when going down at half a cable distance to attack an enemy already lying to.

Captain Ward, of the *Culloden*, was expected to give some very important evidence, as his ship was next astern of the *Ramillies*, but although he was questioned for the whole of one afternoon and part of the next morning, he contributed nothing material. He had seen the *Ramillies* near the *Trident*, and had thrown his own topsails aback to avoid falling aboard them, and the *Culloden* being the slowest sailing-ship in the fleet, he had never looked like getting to close action and was never 'designedly' engaged.

James Worth, his first lieutenant, however, was very communicative, and allowed himself to be tied up several times in questions relating to the positions of the ships. He thought it would have been 'utterly impossible' for the *Ramillies* to have gone either to windward or leeward of the *Trident* without first backing astern. On the other hand, both he and Ward tended to create the impression that Byng had prevented the *Culloden* and *Kingston* getting to close action owing to the dense smoke created by the *Ramillies* opening fire so soon, though Worth admitted that "he continued going down all the time," and that even if the *Ramillies* had set all her sail, and so closed the French before they made off, the *Culloden* must have been left behind."

Seeing the witness in this mood, Byng fired off one of his great pompous questions.

"Do you think," he asked, "it would have been prudent in the admiral to have made all the sail he could down upon the enemy, and have left his second behind him, which was one of the principal ships of force in the line, and stationed to support the ship where the honour of His Majesty's flag was most principally concerned, and the enemy at this time lay waiting for us?"

"I should judge very imprudent," replied Worth quite meekly.

As Captain William Parry, of the *Kingston*, had been in the extreme rear, he had never opened fire at all, and had also spent some time in closing up the gap made by the *Deptford* being signalled to quit the line. He was very confident that he could have got to close action if all the ships ahead had set more sail and there had been no 'impediment.'

By four o'clock in the afternoon of 16th January, the evidence for the prosecution was finished, and Byng spent all the next day in preparing his defence, which he presented to the court in writing, to be read by the judge-advocate.

'It is my misfortune,' it ran, 'to have laboured under the disadvantage of a popular and almost national prejudice; for what reasons this spirit has been raised and by what means propagated is not the business of this court to determine, but I have the satisfaction to find the time arrived when I have an opportunity of approving my innocence before judges whose integrity is above corruption, and when my prosecutors are persons (for such indeed are the present) who desire nothing more than equal and impartial justice, and stand indifferent to my condemnation or acquittal. By this means I am at once secured from being borne down by popular clamour, or crushed beneath the weight of an overbearing power.'

Having referred to the 'national reproach' against him, and expressed confidence in the judgment of men of his own profession, Byng went on to define what he considered the two principal charges against him—namely, failure to relieve Minorca and personal cowardice in action—proposing to deal with the first at some length as necessitating counter-charges against 'potent adversaries,' but to treat the charge of cowardice 'with the contempt it deserves.'

He began by showing that the French fleet was superior to his own in every respect, and that 'the *Gazette*, a paper supposed to be published by authority, was prostituted to spread a false list of the strength of both the fleets,' and far from retreating before an inferior force, he claimed to have defeated a superior one.

He then cleverly criticised his instructions by boldly claiming 'that Fighting was the least intentional part of them,' since every project which they suggested, from joining Edgecumbe to landing troops at Minorca, assumed 'the sea to be open and the fleet unopposed.' It was true that the 'destruction of the enemy's main forces ' had never been mentioned, and the Admiralty's calm assumption that fire-ships, tenders, hospital ships and an extra frigate were unnecessary, certainly gave colour to the plea that they never for a moment thought that Edgecumbe's force of frigates might be blockaded at Mahon, or that Byng might have to fight an action. Moreover, Byng declared, ' I was positively assured before my departure, from the highest naval authority, that the enemy could not fit out more than six or seven ships of the line at the most.'

He disposed quickly of the suggestion that he ' loitered ' at Portsmouth, and went on to describe the situation as it appeared to him when the fleet reached Gibraltar. ' Every person there concluded the place [Minorca] lost, and all relief impracticable. . . . I must own there appeared to me no great probability of preserving Minorca at this time, but, however, have the satisfaction to find that the Ministers at home, for once at least, agreed in opinion with me, since the moment intelligence came that the Toulon fleet was sailed, and the troops landed upon the island, there was not a man who did not despair of Minorca.'

A detailed account of the reasons for delay at Gibraltar followed : ' But why (it may be asked) was not Minorca at this time relieved ? I answer, because I was not sent in time enough to prevent the enemy's landing, and that when I was sent, I was not strong enough to beat the enemy's fleet and raise the siege. . . . But after the engagement, it may be said, I might have reattacked the enemy and landed the succours. I might indeed have done the first, with a certainty almost of being defeated; I could not have done the last, though I had been victorious. Had I been defeated, what refuge would have been left for the shattered fleet, what security for Gibraltar, which must have been exposed to the hazard of a sudden siege, without a single ship to defend it? . . . I admit, where orders are positive to fight at all events or all hazards whatever, it is criminal to deliberate; but was I under such orders? Let my instructions speak for me. . . . I, therefore, beg leave to recommend to your particular consideration the different situation of the two fleets at this time, and shall refer you to the minutes of a council of war held on board the *Ramillies* the 24th of May, and when you have duly weighed the opinion of this council, the unanimity of its members, and their characters, what apprehension can I have of my behaviour on this occasion falling under your censure, since it would necessarily imply their guilt? . . . I never retreated from the island till it was impracticable to make any further attempt, and the place was not lost by me, who was too weak to save it, but by those who might have sent double the force two months earlier, and neglected it.'

Having thus replied in general terms to the first charge against him, Byng went on to what he considered the capital but yet contemptible charge of cowardice. After reciting the Twelfth Article of War in full, he urged that failure 'to take or destroy' and 'to assist and relieve' could only be considered criminal if proceeding from 'cowardice, negligence or disaffection,' and that negligence must not be taken to mean 'every sort of neglect and omission, but such gross negligence only as evidently indicates cowardice or disaffection.' Otherwise a tactical mistake, which any commander is liable to make, would be classed as an 'error of judgment.'

Next came a long and detailed account of events from the 19th May onwards, prefaced by two remarkable 'observations':

> '*First.* That success must depend upon execution as well as disposition, and that no commander of a particular ship has a right to deviate from the established discipline and rules of the Navy, contained in the Fighting Instructions and founded on experience and just observation, because if inferior officers may judge for themselves, there is an end to all discipline, and any deviation from orders must tend to disturb and discontent the admiral's plan and throw the whole fleet into confusion.
>
> *Secondly.* That as the French fleet, superior in force, waited the attack, there was no reason to apprehend they would avoid the engagement, and therefore no occasion to hazard a disorder by crowding too much sail and making the attack with precipitation, contrary to the invariable practice of every prudent, good or great officer, heretofore in similar cases.'

He then gave a very clear account of the attempt to open up communications with St. Philip's on

19th May, the action the next day, and the events leading up to the calling of the council of war on 24th May. He included the correspondence with the Admiralty over the second list of witnesses, asked for on 6th September, ostensibly to explain the incompleteness of the evidence due to having no witnesses from the *Captain* and *Princess Louisa*, but really for the opportunity it gave him of showing to the court 'a specimen of the unprecedented oppressions and restriction of privileges I have had to struggle with.'

Byng then called his only two witnesses, Arthur Gardiner and his own secretary, George Lawrence, saying that he would restrict his questions to proving four points:

(1) That there was no unnecessary delay at Gibraltar.

(2) That it was neither possible nor expedient to have landed the officers of the garrison at St. Philip's.

(3) That he showed no backwardness or criminal misconduct during the battle.

(4) That it would have been imprudent and impracticable to have attacked the French after the battle.

Gardiner was asked over sixty questions on these points, to which he gave short and satisfactory answers, and was then cross-examined by the court, but nothing new was brought up, as the whole matter had been threshed out before.

George Lawrence described Byng's refusal to tack till his van was past the enemy's rear, and his annoyance at Captain Andrews not bearing down sooner, after the fleet had gone about, also his anxiety to get to close action and his regret at having no ships left to chase with after the battle.

The hearing of evidence and the prisoner's defence was now over, and the court began to read through the whole of the evidence over again. On 21st January they had finished the reading, and then took six days more to consider their sentence.

CHAPTER XIII

THE SENTENCE

It was a long time since the public had been allowed the luxury of a dramatic trial, and several gentlemen of fashion thought it worth while travelling to Portsmouth, to be present on the spot. Matthews and Lestock had proved very dull stuff; merely two indifferent admirals arguing about each other's tactics; but in Byng's affair there was a spice of political intrigue and persecution that was most alluring. Lord Morton, Lord Willoughby of Parham, Lord Essex and General Skelton were present at the beginning of the trial, as well as the private agents of those politically interested, and in a few days letters began to stream into London describing its progress.

Blakeney's evidence and wordy duel with Byng in court made a very great sensation, and, as usual, Newcastle acted as a general distributing office for all news likely to affect the late Ministers. On 4th January he told Hardwicke that he had had a "very satisfactory" account of West's and Blakeney's evidence, "which seemed almost of themselves sufficient to condemn Mr. Byng." "If it should come out," he continued, as if anticipating some great triumph, "that the fleet was strong enough and sent in time enough to relieve the place, and that the loss was simply owing to the cowardice or fault of the Admiral, how are the Ministers to blame ? ”

Hugh Valence Jones, Hardwicke's nephew, wrote to Newcastle the same day that ‘ Mr. Byng is endeavouring to throw blame upon some of his Captains ; particularly upon Captain Cornwall, who in consequence of it has called down my Lord Effingham ; and also upon three others, who (unfortunately) cannot now speak for themselves, viz. the Captains Catford, Andrews and Noel. Mr. Cleveland seemed to think that things were going on as they should.’ Evidently Mr. Cleveland, the Permanent Secretary to the Admiralty, was in close touch with his old masters, and was taking an *ex parte* view of the affair, but Effingham had been called as a witness by Byng, and Jones's news seems a little exaggerated.

As time went on, the civilian spectators found it increasingly difficult to follow the technical details in the evidence, especially as ‘ the seamen ’ declared ‘ that the soldiers were over necessary on board the fleet, nor was it proper to make delay by landing them.’

By the end of the first week Horace Walpole thought the trial would be ‘ an affair of length ’ and that the reports were ‘ rather unfavourable ’ to Byng. On 17th January he wrote that ‘ it has gone ill for him, but mends ; it is the general opinion that he will come off for some severe censure.’

Lord Morton, however, thought the evidence against Byng ‘ very strong,’ but ‘ will not speak his sentiments till the trial shall be over.’

Hugh Valence Jones was enthusiastic about the behaviour of Captain Moore, 'who puts very proper and sensible questions.' He complained, however, that the trial must take longer than was expected, because Byng 'has laid in for calling again upon almost all the witnesses, who have appeared against him, which Lord Hardwicke thinks should not have been given into, but that Admiral Byng should have been obliged to have put all his questions to the witnesses when first examined, for fear of their being taught to retract afterwards.' Actually, he only wished to recall a few witnesses, and the court showed sufficient jealousy for its own privileges, and humanity for the prisoner, to let him have his way, despite Hardwicke's sinister suggestions.

At the close of the evidence, Mr. Rigby wrote to the Duke of Bedford that 'nobody imagines' that the sentence 'can amount to capital punishment.' Meanwhile, the rumour spread that there were serious disagreements amongst the members of the court. There were only two grounds on which Byng could be condemned; one was for neglect of duty in battle, and the other for neglect to relieve St. Philip's. Although his handling of the battle was open to considerable criticism, it would have attracted little comment at another time, and had it not been connected with the fate of the castle. The Articles of War said nothing about the relieving of castles, and the naval officers forming the court were at a loss to know how to condemn him for failing to carry out instructions involving a combined operation. They agreed that in deserting Minorca he had committed a great strategic crime of which he was expressly charged in the order for the trial, but for which there was no penalty. They therefore determined to find him guilty of neglect of duty in battle, a crime of which he was entirely innocent, in order to bring about his condemnation for a crime of which he was guilty, but which was, at that time, outside the jurisdiction of a naval court martial.

It was then discovered that, as commander-in-chief, the Twelfth Article of War was the only one he could come under, and this was punishable by death. Up till 1749, courts martial had been at liberty to impose a less severe penalty as an alternative, but the general slackness shown in the last war, and the scandalous orgy of trials after the battle of Toulon, led to death being left as the only penalty for neglect of duty.

Byng was the first commander-in-chief to come under the new regulations, and his case presented special difficulties. As the Twelfth Article of War only dealt with neglect of duty in battle by sea, it could not possibly be stretched to include the desertion of Minorca, although that desertion was 'contrary to and in breach of His Majesty's commands.' Therefore, the only sensible solution was for the court to acquit him on the charge of neglect of duty under the Twelfth Article, but to reprimand him severely for disobedience to Admiralty instructions. This course, however, did not commend itself to the court. They could not help feeling that Byng had acted wrongly, and must be condemned on some definite grounds and awarded a definite penalty, but they had no wish to have him executed. Thinking, therefore, that the Admiralty might possibly relax the rigours of the law, they wrote to London to enquire if they might have discretionary powers to inflict a lesser penalty. The Admiralty of course refused, and so they decided to find Byng guilty under the Twelfth Article for his conduct during the battle, and merely to add the desertion of Minorca as an additional and indefinite offence. This would mean that Byng would have to be sentenced to be shot, but they would then send an urgent representation to the Admiralty pointing out the hardness of the law, and recommending him as a fit object for the King's mercy. On receiving such a request, the Admiralty would have to act, and Byng would be reprieved and safely cashiered, after a death sentence which would be shown to be purely formal. What could be simpler? True, the Admiralty themselves had no power to alter the sentence, which must be personally revised by the King, but none doubted the King's merciful heart, and the solution satisfied the waverers.

The court was then thrown open, and the prisoner admitted.

Byng had not the slightest idea of what awaited him as he climbed up the side of the *St. George* to hear his sentence. He looked forward to a handsome acquittal or, at the worst, a reprimand, and perhaps cashiering; his baggage was packed, and his coach was waiting at the dockyard gates. As he reached the deck, a few of his friends, who had been told privately what the sentence would be, stepped forward to prepare him as tactfully as they could to receive the shock. "What, have they broke me?" he asked furiously, as he looked at their glum faces and remembered Matthews. It took him some minutes to realise that it was to be something more than breaking, and when he understood he became quite calm, saying, "Well, I understand; if nothing but my blood will satisfy, let them take it."

The court had prepared its sentence in the form of thirty-six resolutions, of which only fourteen were expressions of opinion, the rest forming a narrative of the facts of the campaign, clearly expressed and very fair to all concerned. The resolutions which dealt with the court's opinion, and therefore dictated the sentence, were as follows:

> Resolution No. 1. That Byng made no unnecessary delay on the voyage out.
>
> No. 5. That on 19th May he 'proceeded properly, upon discovery of the French fleet, to stand towards them.'
>
> No. 7. 'That as so great a number of officers were on board the fleet, belonging to the garrison of St. Philip's, where they must necessarily be much wanted, the Admiral ought to have put them on board one of the frigates he sent ahead, in order to have been landed, if found practicable; and if not landed before he saw the French fleet, he ought to have left the frigate to have endeavoured to land them, notwithstanding he did see the enemy's fleet.'

The court was unanimous in its opinion on all the other resolutions, but on the seventh there was one dissentient, who was of opinion that the general and field officers alone should have been landed.

No. 11. Byng should have tacked when exactly abreast of the French.

No. 19. He 'separated the rear from the van division and retarded the rear from closing with and engaging the enemy, by his shortening sail. . . .'

No. 20. He should instead have signalled the *Trident* and *Princess Louisa* to set more sail, 'and to have set so much himself as would have enabled the *Culloden*, (the worst sailing ship in his division), to keep her station with all her plain sail set.'

No. 25. The *Ramillies* was certainly impeded in going down by the *Trident* and ships ahead of her.

No. 26. Byng acted wrongly in allowing the *Ramillies* to continue firing when not at close quarters, as he thereby wasted ammunition and created dense smoke which prevented him seeing the enemy and his own ships ahead of him.

No. 32. After the action he should have tried to open communications with St. Philip's, 'and to have used every means in his power for its relief, before he returned to Gibraltar.'

No. 33. That he 'did not do his utmost to relieve St. Philip's.'

No. 34. That during the action he 'did not

do his utmost to take, seize and destroy the ships of the French king, which it was his duty to have engaged, and to assist such of His Majesty's ships as were engaged in fight with the French ships, which it was his duty to have assisted.'

No. 35. That by the evidence of Bertie, Gardiner and others he showed no 'backwardness' or 'marks of fear' during the action, but 'seemed to give his orders coolly and distinctly, and did not seem wanting in personal courage.'

No. 36. That he 'appears' to fall under the Twelfth Article of War for not doing his utmost to take or destroy the enemy's ships and to assist and relieve his own.

No. 37. 'That as that Article positively prescribes death, without any alternative left to the discretion of the Court, under any variation of circumstances, that he be adjudged to be shot to death, at such time and on board such ship as the Lords Commissioners of the Admiralty shall direct. But as it appears by the evidence of Lord Robert Bertie, Lieut.-Col. Smith, Captain Gardiner and other officers of the ship, who were near the person of the Admiral, that they did not perceive any backwardness in him during the action, or any marks of fear or confusion, either from his countenance or behaviour, but that he seemed to give his orders coolly and distinctly, and did not seem wanting in personal courage, and from other circumstances, the Court do not believe that his misconduct arose either from cowardice or disaffection; and do therefore unanimously think it their duty most earnestly to recommend him as a proper object of mercy.'

This resolution was obviously a monstrous perversion of justice, as everyone agreed that nothing he had done in the battle made him worthy of death. It remained, therefore, to complete the tale of his crimes, and this was done by pronouncing a sentence including the exact words of resolutions thirty-six and thirty-seven, but adding the words 'and for that he did not do his utmost to relieve St. Philip's Castle, in His Majesty's island of Minorca, then besieged by the forces of the French King, but acted contrary to and in breach of his Command.'

Thus by a piece of honest cunning the sentence was constructed in the form of a legal jigsaw, the real crime, for which there was no penalty prescribed, being added to the fictitious crime, for which there was a penalty, and the whole covered by the statement that the prisoner had disobeyed his instructions, which was also true, but for which there was also no penalty, though this was cleverly veiled by calling Admiralty instructions 'His Majesty's Command.'

The court then drew up an 'urgent representation,' laying before the Admiralty the 'distresses' of their minds, 'in finding ourselves under a necessity of condemning a man to death, from the great severity of the Twelfth Article of War, part of which he falls under, and which admits of no mitigation, even if the crime should be committed by an error of judgment only, and therefore for our own consciences' sake, as well as in justice to the prisoner, we pray your Lordships in the most earnest manner to recommend him to His Majesty's clemency.'

After keeping 'the whole world in suspense for a week,' the court had at last delivered itself in a way that satisfied no one. 'The Monarch is horrid angry with the Court Martial,' wrote Rigby to Bedford, 'who have shoved the odium of Byng's death, if he is to suffer, in some measure off their own shoulders. I wish that puppy Cleveland had sent me the sentence, but it is not yet come and the post will stay no longer.'

The Ministers felt that the 'odium' had also been 'shoved' on to them, while the Board of Admiralty was rent in twain. Lord Temple said that he would not sign the warrant for Byng's execution till he was satisfied that the sentence was legal, and Vice-Admiral Forbes, who had joined the Board in place of John Pitt, was of the same opinion, while Admiral Boscawen was strongly in favour of the execution, and had said quite openly before the trial began, "We shall have a majority, and he will be condemned."

Temple West was at that moment aboard the *Magnanime* at Portsmouth, having been appointed to command a secret expedition, it being quite usual then for Sea Lords of the Admiralty to hold executive appointments. Byng's sentence came as a terrible shock to him, and he wrote off the same day to the Admiralty 'declining the very honourable and distinguished command' to which he had been appointed. 'I must therefore beseech and intreat them to confer it on some person more worthy, since I can only be answerable for my loyalty and fidelity to my king, and resolution of doing what appears to me for his service, which it seems an officer may not want, and yet be capitally convicted for his misconduct or inability of judging right. I am not so presumptuous as to imagine that my actions can always be so rightly governed, nor am I altogether certain that the judgment of others is infallible ; and as in some cases the consequences may be fatal, I must therefore repeat again my most earnest request that their Lordships will be pleased to appoint some other person to my command, and grant me their Lordships' permission to come to town.'

He also wrote to Temple by the same post refusing to serve on terms which subject an officer to the treatment shown Admiral Byng. '. . . Strange reasoning !—to acquit him of the points, cowardice and disaffection, to which that article only can have respect. Since, though negligence is mentioned, yet can only be intended to refer to one or other of these two crimes, negligence proceeding from disaffection or cowardice. And I well remember that was the opinion of the House of Commons, when the Bill was before them ; for which reason no alternative was left in that article, which otherwise there would have been. . . . I shall only make one observation more, in regard to that part of their sentence, wherein he is said not to have done his utmost to relieve St. Philip's Castle, without pointing out which way it could have been relieved by him ; which, indeed, they would have found difficult enough to have done.'

The late Ministers were also dissatisfied. 'The whole world condemns the Court Martial,' wrote Joseph Yorke to Lord Royston,[1] 'and I don't wonder you should be disgusted with the absurdities of those tribunals which indeed pass all understanding.'

Public amazement increased daily, no one being certain what the court really meant by their sentence, many lawyers thinking it illegal, so that when Boscawen went to Portsmouth to hasten some transports he 'alarmed the whole town, who think he has gone to shoot Mr. Byng himself.'

In ignorant circles it was enough that Byng was condemned, and the publication of the sentence was the signal for another outburst of 'Bungiana,' of which the following is a typical example.

ADMIRAL BYNG AND BRAVE WEST

I said unto brave West, "Take the van, take the van,"
I said unto brave West, "Take the van."
I said unto brave West,
"As you like fighting best,
I in the rear will rest;
Take the van."

Oh, woe to cursed gold! Ohon! Ohon!
Oh, woe to cursed gold! Ohon!
Oh! woe to cursed gold;
For Minorca I have sold,
That gallant place of old,
With Mahon!

It's decreed by the King, I do hear, I do hear,
He's decreed it the nation to please,
It's decreed by the King
I'll be shot by my marines,
For the misdeed I have deen,
On the seas.

[1] Hardwicke's eldest son.

On the other hand, the strong personal resentment which many people had originally felt towards him had largely died down. The autumn before, nothing had been too bad for him, but now, after his long imprisonment and trial, it seemed inhuman to shoot him in cold blood, and requests for mercy poured in upon the Admiralty.

Admiral Smith himself took the lead, and wrote to his brothers, Richard and George Lyttelton, 'to beg their interest.' The first named 'was more than ready,' and even the cautious George urged Smith to write at once to the Admiralty, adding, 'I am heartily sorry for the very painful task you have had to go through, but hear with very great satisfaction the honour you have done yourself in discharge of it with so much humanity, justice, and dignity of behaviour.'

Two petitions were then presented to the Admiralty by Byng's nephew, Lord Torrington, 'on behalf of himself and the rest of his afflicted family,' asking to be allowed to present legal arguments against the execution of the sentence. Sarah Osborn, Byng's sister, also worked hard for his reprieve, and got the Duke of Bedford to promise his help if the affair became a Cabinet question. She later sent a petition to Lord Anson asking him to intercede with the King, but naturally he made no attempt to do so.

Support also came from quite an unexpected quarter, for Richelieu, on hearing that Byng was imprisoned and about to be tried, became very indignant, on professional grounds, that he should be treated in this manner, and wrote to his friend Voltaire about it :

'I am very concerned about Admiral Byng. I assure you that, whatever I have seen or heard of him does him honour. He ought not to be attacked in this manner when he has been defeated after doing all that could be expected of him. When two men of honour fight together, one of them must be worsted, but it does not count to his discredit. All Admiral Byng's manœuvres were excellent, the two fleets being at least equal, as the English had thirteen ships and we had twelve, but better equipped and much cleaner. Chance, which controls all battles, and especially those at sea, was more favourable to us, by sending our shots into the English rigging, and I consider that it is generally agreed that had the English persisted in the engagement, they would have lost their entire fleet. There has never been such an act of injustice as that now directed against Admiral Byng, and every officer and man of honour ought to take note of it.'

Voltaire was a man of most generous instincts, and his comment on Byng's execution in *Candide* was never meant to be a 'witticism,' as Mr. P. C. Yorke and many others have supposed. Realising the immense importance of Richelieu's testimony, and thinking it might help Byng in some way, he at once enclosed a copy of it to him, with the following charming letter :

'Sir, though I am almost unknown to you, I think it is my duty to send you a copy of the letter I have just received from the Marshal duc de Richelieu. Honour, humanity, and equity order me to convey it to your hands. This noble and unexpected testimony from one of the most candid as well as the most generous of my countrymen, makes me presume your judges will do you the same justice.'

It is doubtful if these letters ever reached Byng in their original form, as in some curious way they were seized upon by the late Ministers and published in the *Scot's Magazine* for January 1757 and in other periodicals. Hardwicke, in returning copies of them to Anson on 26th January, asks for copies to keep for himself as 'curiosities.' Richelieu's letter he considers is 'an extract only.' 'It begins abruptly, and if the beginning had been added, it would have appeared to be an answer to something, and to have been solicited, as it certainly was. The words "Je vous assure" have the air of an answer. I beg your Lordship would get two facts ascertained:

'1. Whether these letters were shown to the King before they were sent back to Portsmouth?

'2. Whether these letters were sent back to the president of the Court Martial open, so that he might read them and show them; or sent to him sealed up, and directed to Mr. Byng, and only to be delivered to him?'

It is quite certain that the letters were entirely unsolicited, but it is also clear that many people took

Hardwicke's view, and that Voltaire's impetuous generosity, which Joseph Yorke called 'stupid,' 'displeased everybody and seemed calculated to do the prisoner more harm than good.'

The Admiralty were now compelled to make some move; either they must recommend Byng to the King for mercy or they must get the King's permission to issue a warrant for his execution. Temple and the civil lords, however, were very unwilling to adopt either of these courses. They knew that they were weak in Parliament, and that the King, for all his stamping and blustering, was under the thumb of the City merchants, and had pledged himself to the punishment of the 'authors' of the loss of Minorca; while all around stood the ex-Ministers, with their bribes and their boroughs, ready to crush anyone who suggested that Byng was not the sole author of the disaster. On the other hand, they could not well ignore the court's plea for mercy, especially as it was urged in the sentence as well as in the representation. They therefore decided to act in a way we can now only describe as mean and cowardly. On 9th February they presented a 'memorial' to the King stating that they had given the proceedings of the court martial their 'most serious and deliberate consideration, and doubts having arisen with regard to the legality of the sentence, particularly whether the crime of negligence, which is not expressed in any part of the proceedings, can, in this case, be supplied by implication,' they therefore found themselves 'obliged most humbly to beseech' His Majesty for the opinion of the judges.

They then enclosed the sentence and Lord Torrington's petitions, and submitted the whole to the 'Royal wisdom and determination.' The memorial was signed by Temple, Hay, Hunter, Elliot and Admiral Forbes, who was persuaded by them that he was acting for the best. Naturally, the monarch was again 'horrid angry,' as the 'odium' had now been 'shoved' a stage further. He had no power to lighten the sentence, so that it was really a clear issue between pardon and execution; and here were the Admiralty pretending not to be convinced of the 'legality' of the sentence. Still, there was practical wisdom in what they suggested, and twelve judges were empanelled. William Murray, now Baron Mansfield and Lord Chief Justice, presided; he had been Attorney-General in the late Ministry, and was heart and soul in favour of Newcastle, to whom he owed his peerage. Sir John Willes was Chief Justice of Common Pleas, and dated back to the Walpole-Newcastle Cabinet. Sir Thomas Parker had been Baron of the Exchequer since 1742. Of the others, Sir Thomas Denison, Sir Michael Foster, Sir Edward Clive, Sir Thomas Birch, Heneage Legge, Sir Edward Sidney Smythe and Sir Richard Adams were all men who had risen to legal eminence under the Pelham and Newcastle régimes, and might be trusted to remain staunch to the late Ministers. Henry Bathurst was a pronounced Tory and a close ally of the late Frederick, Prince of Walpole, and Sir John Eardley Wilmot was a friend of Pitt's; but they were the two most junior of the twelve, and were quite unable to influence their colleagues in Byng's favour, even if they had been willing to do so. The judges presented their report on 14th February; it was very short, and contained less than a hundred words, in which they declared that they were unanimously of opinion that Byng's sentence was legal. Naturally, there was nothing else they could say, because the legality of the sentence depended on the 'resolutions' of the court, and by the thirty-fourth resolution the court was of opinion that Byng did not do his utmost to defeat the enemy and assist his own ships during the action. This resolution was arrived at by a monstrous perversion of the evidence, but the judges were not concerned with the evidence, nor were they a competent body to adjudicate on it.

At a meeting of the Privy Council held two days later, with all the principal Ministers present except Pitt, who was suffering acutely from gout, it was agreed to send a copy of the judges' report to the Board of Admiralty. This was merely a form, as Temple himself was present at the meeting, and with the judges' report at his back he was in a much stronger position than hitherto, and could order Byng's execution with an easier conscience. He does not seem to have made any personal appeal to the King for mercy till Pitt appeared on the scene, but was content to let the 'casuists of Westminster Hall' deliver their 'opiates.'

On 16th February Temple drew up the warrant, which was addressed to Admiral Boscawen, who was commanding-in-chief at Portsmouth as well as being a member of the Board. It quoted the court martial's sentence, declared that 'His Majesty hath been pleased to consent' to its execution, and ordered Byng to be shot on 28th February by a platoon of marines on board such of the ships as should be thought fit. Lord Temple, Hay, Hunter and Elliot signed, but Temple West and Forbes both refused point blank, and resigned their seats at the Admiralty. Forbes was so furious at the way he had been duped into agreeing to ask for the opinion of the judges that he insisted on putting his reasons for not signing the death-warrant in writing.

'It may be thought great presumption in me to differ from so great authority as that of the Twelve Judges, but when a man is called upon to sign his name to an act which is to give authority to the shedding of blood, he ought to be guided by his own conscience, and not by the opinions of other men.' He then argues that the sentence of the court martial 'does not name the word negligence,' and that even if negligence is implied it cannot be wilful negligence, which itself must proceed from cowardice or disaffection of which he has been acquitted. Byng is declared not worthy of death, but is condemned to death because 'the law admits of no mitigation. . . . I cannot help thinking that, however criminal Admiral Byng may be, his life is not forfeited by that sentence. I do not mean to find fault with other men's opinions, all I endeavour to do is to give reasons for my own.'

The retirement of West and Forbes undoubtedly perturbed the Ministers, but it did not weaken them in Parliament, while the late Ministers, fearful of some great commission of enquiry, had been working their hardest to prepare a proper defence ever since the court martial began. They engaged the services of Mr. Philip Carteret Webb, Secretary of Bankrupts in the Court of Chancery and joint solicitor to the Treasury, an antiquarian of considerable note who possessed a fine collection of manuscripts, coins, marbles and bronzes. He was sent to interview John Cleveland and Philip Stephens, Lord Anson's secretary, and was then instructed by Hardwicke to draw up a paper showing:

> (1) 'That consistently with the probable safety of this country a squadron could not have been sent sooner to the Mediterranean.'
>
> (2) 'That consistently with the probable safety of this country that squadron could not have been made stronger when it was sent.'

The intelligence concerning French preparations at Toulon and on the north coast were then to be divided into periods of time and set side by side.

With these were to be shown the condition of the fleet, the number of seamen, and the duties upon which ships were employed, at times corresponding with the periods covered by the French intelligence. Webb was then to show that Byng's squadron, with Edgecumbe's added, 'was rather superior to M. de la Galissonnière's or any other French squadron with which he was likely to meet.'

By 26th January Webb had finished his task, and Hardwicke thought it 'extremely well done,' and was convinced that the late Ministers were better prepared for the defence than their opponents were for the enquiry. Copies of Webb's work were given to 'trusted friends' under the closest secrecy, for to let the other side know about it in advance would be 'showing our hand at Whist.'

Consequently, when Mr. Hunter officially informed the House of Commons on 17th February that one of their members had been sentenced to death, the 'trusted friends' were ready for emergencies when Sir Francis Dashwood moved for the court martial's representation to be laid before the House. Dashwood was a Leicester House man and founder of the Hell-Fire Club, and his reputation in public life was somewhat unsavoury, but he was by no means bitter or vindictive, and seems to have espoused Byng's cause entirely on humane grounds. In the course of the debate, Pitt, who appeared in the House for the first time since taking office, spoke in favour of the motion, and mentioned an anonymous letter he had lately received, which declared that 'the man that attempts to prevail on H. M. to forfeit his word and pardon Mr. Byng must be no friend to H. M.' 'A distrust already begins to show itself among the merchants and other people of eminence in the City; and they declare publicly that should H. M. be prevailed on to pardon Mr. B. they will never give the least credit to anything that shall hereafter come from the throne.' The letter ended by asking, 'For God's sake, does Mr. Byng deserve so well of his country, as to run the hazard of embroiling the nation on his account?'

Fox fiercely opposed the motion, saying that it

would put a censure on the court martial to discuss the sentence, hinting that Pitt and Temple were trying to shelter Byng. The motion was lost. Posters, too, began to appear in streets, reading: 'Hang Byng; or take Care of Your King!' and the King received anonymous letters stating that there would be no money forthcoming for the defence of Hanover unless Byng was shot.

But the advocates of mercy were not to be browbeaten in this fashion, and on 23rd February Dashwood made a powerful speech in the House when he moved the consideration of the Twelfth Article of War, declaring the sentence to be blundering and absurd, and calling for a special Act of Parliament to absolve the court from their oath of secrecy so that they might disclose what had passed amongst them.

Barrington, of course, opposed, but Alderman Beckford called the sentence cruel, and Pitt suggested that the King might reprieve Byng if left entirely uninfluenced, and did not think the Admiralty ought to interfere. Fox, on the other hand, said any Lord of the Admiralty might approach the King, and urged them to do so, and commented on the words 'It is His Majesty's pleasure' being used in signing the warrant. A violent altercation here arose between Pitt and Fox over the word 'pleasure,' so that the Speaker had to intervene, while Elliot and Hunter gave precedents for its use in former death-warrants.

The same day, Dennis, Moore and Keppel, three members of the court martial, waited on Temple to urge him to get Byng pardoned, and next day Pitt and Bedford interceded with the King, but with no effect. Then seven members of the court martial asked Temple to intercede, which he again did, but again with no effect.

On 25th February, Admiral Norris went to George Grenville, the Treasurer of the Navy, to ask for the court martial to be absolved from its oath of secrecy; but Grenville seemed disinclined to help, though he was again approached by Norris, together with Moore and Keppel.

Horace Walpole tells us he was out of Parliament at the moment, seeking re-election, but hearing of this, and seeing Keppel, who was a member, sitting in the gallery, he rushed up the stairs to implore him to speak out. 'He said he had never spoken in public, and could not, but would give authority to anybody else. The Speaker was putting the question for the orders of the day, after which no motion could be made: it was a Friday, the House would not sit on Saturday, the execution was fixed for Monday. I felt all this in an instant, dragged Mr. Keppel to Sir Francis Dashwood, and he on the floor before he had taken his place, called out to the Speaker, and though the orders were passed, Sir Francis was suffered to speak.' He asked for some way to find out the real opinion of the court martial; Sir John Philipps declared that he was out of order in speaking, but Pitt said that if only Keppel would rise, 'it would be a foundation for him to vote for the Bill demanded.'

Keppel now rose and, conquering his nervousness,

said that he wished to be absolved from his oath of secrecy, as he had something on his mind which he wished to reveal, and read a letter from Admiral Smith to the same purpose. Nicholas Fazackerley, a Tory lawyer, supported him, together with Lord George Sackville, Sir George Lee and eight other most 'noted' speakers of the House. Thornborough 'moved for the Order of the Day's being read, to get rid of Byng's affair, but he was so hunted and roasted by the House that he was glad to withdraw his motion.' George Grenville, with a series of typical hair-splitting arguments, urged Keppel to speak without a Bill, as the oath of secrecy only forbade divulging individual opinions, but this Keppel refused to do, and Pitt agreed that it was impossible, and announced a sitting of the House on Saturday. Keppel was to consult as many members of the court martial as he could during the evening, and if they felt unable to lay their reasons for the sentence before the King, a Bill to absolve them from their oath of secrecy would have to be brought in.

Next morning a special Cabinet Council was held to consider Keppel's request and prepare a Bill, and Keppel, on being called before the Cabinet, said that he could not speak further without such a Bill.

It is probably true that Pitt and Temple wished to save Byng in order to please Leicester House and to 'throw greater blame on the late administration.' 'But to avoid the odium of protecting a man who had been hanged in effigy in every town in England,

they wanted the King to pardon him without seeming to interfere.' Pitt, therefore, went to tell the King that the House of Commons was in favour of a pardon, but received the famous and chilling reply, "You have taught me to look for the sense of my subjects in another place than in the House of Commons." Temple also pressed him strongly, but 'His Majesty persevered and told his Lordship flatly that he thought him guilty of cowardice in the action, and therefore could not break his word, they had forced him to give to his people, to pardon no delinquents.'

The ludicrous idea of the King presuming to be an arbiter of courage in a naval battle which he had not even witnessed struck Temple so forcibly that he lost all sense of politeness and respect, and 'walked up to his nose, *sans autre cérémonie* said, "What shall you think if he dies courageously?"' hinting thereby that the King's conduct at the battle of Oudenarde was not above reproach. 'His Majesty stifled his anger and made him no reply. I think,' said Rigby, 'I never heard such insolence.' No wonder the King thought he was in the hands of 'scoundrels,' and 'that he would rather give his crown to my Lord than live with him another month.'

Anyhow, it was agreed to respite the execution for fourteen days, and on Saturday, 26th February, Pitt read a message for the House from the King saying that he was resolved to let the law take its course, but that as a Member of Parliament and of the court martial desired to be absolved from his oath of secrecy, the execution would be respited, but that it would be eventually carried out unless 'it appeared that Admiral Byng was unjustly condemned.' Here Fox objected to proceedings inside the House being taken notice of by the Crown, but the Speaker excused Pitt, although agreeing that it was a breach of privilege.

Keppel then said that he and four of his brethren had something of weight to tell, but could not do so till they were absolved from their oath. Members at once became doubtful if a sufficient proportion of the court martial were concerned to warrant a Bill, but Nugent spoke in favour of the Bill, however few of the court martial desired it, and said he feared serious riots if the question was not settled at once.

After considerable wrangling, the Bill was brought in by Thomas Potter, Joint-Paymaster, a friend of Pitt's and member of the Hell-Fire Club. Fox asked for the names of those who wanted it, and Keppel told him they were Admiral Norris and Captains Holmes, Geary and Moore. The Bill was agreed to and read a second time, but there was an objection to taking the committee stage as well, all in one sitting. Pitt, however, said it must be done unless Holbourne, Broderick and Holmes were to be detained at home at such a critical time when under orders for sea. The Bill then passed the committee stage, with a typical clause added by George Grenville that the officers were not to be forced to speak if unwilling.

There were strong rumours abroad that day that the Bill would be opposed in the Lords, and Lord

Halifax, a relation of Byng's, wrote to Dodington in great indignation :

> 'In matters of death you will allow patience may come as properly as on any other occasion ; and though I pretend not to move hearts of stone, I am resolved to do what I can towards it. Do our Bishops, who are so careful of their Sunday, wish that blood, probably innocent, should be spilt on Monday ? Will former Ministers wish that blood should be spilt on a supposed crime of negligence ? Will Lords of the law oppose the explanation of a sentence that nobody can understand and they less than any others ? And will common sense and humanity quit the breasts of every other Lord who has not been tied to law or Church ? Fye Fye ! I can't suppose it, but if it is so, as I love you, let me recommend you never to think of us, we are not fit company for you !'

The next day being Sunday, it was rumoured that the four officers cited to Keppel as wanting the Bill now repudiated his statement. These simple sailors had not realised what a political hornets' nest they had aroused, and with the possibility of opposition from Hardwicke and Anson in the Lords they became frightened and tried to back out, Geary telling Sir Richard Lyttelton that it would hurt his preferment to tell what he knew. Horace Walpole was in agonies at the thought that instead of getting Byng pardoned he was 'likely only to add a fortnight to the poor man's misery'! He spent Sunday evening rushing from one house to another, 'to find out and try how to defeat the evil.' First he was at Sir Richard Lyttelton's, and then on to the Speaker, Pitt, Fox, Dodington and Lady Hervey.

On Monday, 28th February, the day Byng was to have been shot, Mr. Potter moved the third reading of the Bill, but Fox opposed it, saying that new information had come to hand. This was a challenge to Keppel, who had to admit that Captain Holmes was now 'easy in his mind' about the sentence and did not want the Bill, and that Geary was neither 'off nor on,' but wished that all should be compelled to speak. But he was able to produce a letter written him by Norris and Moore saying, 'We do authorise you to solicit the Bill.'

Fox now argued as follows: seven of the court martial are in town, and of these, Holbourne refuses to meddle with this affair; Dennis, though a member of the House of Commons, has not appeared during the last few days; Geary won't speak unless all the rest do; and Holmes is easy in his mind about it. Therefore, four out of the seven are against the Bill; therefore, the Bill is unnecessary; let Keppel, Norris and Moore, the minority of three, sign a petition.

Velters Cornwall also opposed the Bill, 'and looking Mr. Pitt full in the face, said that Mr. Byng had been the means of throwing out the old Ministry, and certain he was Mr. Byng would shortly be the means of turning out the new Ministry.'

Keppel then explained as much of his feelings as

he thought he might reveal. When he signed the sentence he thought he had acted rightly, but was uneasy about it, otherwise he would not have signed the 'urgent representation.' 'I do think,' he concluded, 'my desire of being at liberty does imply something great, and what His Majesty should know.'

Proceedings then grew disorderly, owing to Pitt having a violent altercation with Fox, and saying, "I thank God I feel something more than popularity, I feel justice." The Speaker, however, interposed and, order being restored, the Bill was passed for the last time by 153 votes to 22.

Next day being Tuesday, the Bill was brought before the House of Lords, and Mansfield at once opened the attack. Being a Newcastle peer and president of the Committee of Twelve Judges, his conduct is not surprising. Keppel's behaviour is weak and inconsistent, he argues; if the court thought Byng guilty of an 'error of judgment,' it should have acquitted him; if the sentence is wrong, it ought to be annulled; but it is cruel to thrust the onus of it on the King. A Bill such as this is quite wrong, though a Bill of some kind may be necessary; let the members of the court martial be examined on oath at the bar of the House.

Temple, who did not dare treat his fellow-peers as he treated the King, tamely suggested that the court meant 'error of judgment.' Halifax spoke very strongly in favour of the Bill, but Hardwicke opposed, and pressed for the officers to be brought to the bar of the House and asked if they really had anything to tell, supposing they were absolved from their oath, and whether they had not been solicited to raise an agitation by Byng's friends. Sandwich expressed astonishment at the 'unprecedented' Royal message to the Commons, and Hardwicke, taking up the argument, said that the message ought not to be taken notice of in the Lords, as it had not been vouchsafed to that House. He also used every effort to postpone further discussion till Thursday, as an Irish bankruptcy was pending on Wednesday, although some of the members of the court martial were under orders to sail at once. Temple, Bedford, Denbigh and Halifax all pressed for the Bill to be taken next day, and Hardwicke at last consented.

The idea of calling the officers to the bar of the House was first mentioned by Mansfield, probably in concert with Hardwicke, whose purpose it suited admirably. Newcastle was unwilling to do more than 'echo his oracle' with 'busy timidity,' but Hardwicke had sufficient courage to fight openly for his own ends, and carried the burden of the late Ministers' reputation on his shoulders. If judicial bullying was required, then Hardwicke was quite prepared to be a judicial bully, and what better method was there of exercising this art than by bringing the unfortunate members of the court martial to the bar of the Lords and there overawing them. It is unlikely that any private pressure was put on them, as Horace Walpole suggests, as it was so unnecessary. They knew that their promotion depended on the Admiralty, and that Pitt and Temple could not protect them from Hardwicke, Newcastle and Anson, who might return to power at any moment; and they also knew that Anson was Hardwicke's son-in-law. Pitt and Temple did not dare to threaten resignation to obtain Byng's pardon, as they knew that their resignation would be accepted, and Newcastle would return in triumph. The King did not dare pardon Byng, as he had pledged his word to the City that Byng should die, and he would rather that Pitt should resign than that he should have no money to carry on his 'German business.'

Thus, the City merchants held the key to the situation, since they, and they only, could supply the ready money indispensable for carrying on the continental war. Hardwicke and Newcastle only aimed at saving their own skins, but it was to them that the members of the court martial looked.

Hardwicke rightly calculated that, being men of only small private means, they would not risk unemployment and penury in order to disclose the wretched morass of reasoning which had produced their sentence, and when there was no guarantee that such disclosure would save Byng's life.

So, when the seven members of the court previously in town, and the remaining six hastily summoned to London, met at the House of Lords on Wednesday, 2nd March, it only required the atmosphere of that majestic and powerful body to convince them that they had nothing to reveal.

Amongst Lord Hardwicke's papers, now in the

British Museum, there is an interesting draft in his own handwriting of the procedure to be adopted in examining the court martial. Panegyrists of Hardwicke's conduct on this occasion have seldom considered that he was not in office at the time, and that the Great Seal was in the hands of a commission of three judges, Willes, Smythe and Wilmot (three of the famous Twelve), and that they seem to have been quite agreeable to him arranging the procedure as if he were still Chancellor. His scheme for the procedure was as follows:

'1. The members of the court martial to be examined upon oath.

'2. The members of the Court martial to be called in and examined separately.

'3. To begin with such as are under any immediate orders to sail.

'4. The Clerk to be directed to take down the questions and answers in writing at the Bar.

'5. The questions:

'(1) Whether they know of any matter that passed previous to the sentence, to show it to be unjust?

'(2) Whether they know of any matter that may show the sentence to have been given through, or by means of, any undue practice or motives?

'If "Yes" to either of these questions, then

'(3) Whether they apprehend that they are restrained by their oath from disclosing any such matter?

> '(4) What kind of matter or things they apprehend they are restrained by their oath of secrecy from disclosing?'

When the House met, however, the last two questions were altered to read:

> '(3) Whether you are desirous that the Bill now under consideration of the House for dispensing with the oath of secrecy should pass into law?
>
> '(4) Whether you are of opinion, that you have particulars to reveal, relative to the case of, and the sentence passed upon Admiral Byng which you judge necessary for His Majesty's information, and which you think likely to incline His Majesty to mercy?'

Mansfield explained that the four questions would be asked (as amended) and that any member was at liberty to ask other questions.

Admiral Smith was called first; he looked grey-headed, 'comely and respectable,' but 'of no quickness to comprehend the chicanery of such a partial examination'; and like his comrades, was 'awed by the presence of the great persons, before whom they were brought.'

He answered "No" to the first two questions, and said the Bill would "not be disagreeable" to him if it relieved the consciences of his brethren. To the fourth question he answered that he and his brethren were willing to explain the reasons which induced them to recommend Byng to the King's mercy.

To Hardwicke's original third question he answered, "The application for mercy was unanimous. I think I am at liberty to give the reasons why I requested that mercy." But nobody asked him the reasons—presumably Byng's friends "lest it should interfere with the necessity of the Bill," and his enemies because they had no wish for the reasons to be made public.

Holbourne answered "No" to everything. Norris seemed terrified, and begged to be excused answering the first and fourth questions while under oath of secrecy, and said "No" to the second, but yet wanted the Bill. Broderick gave a 'short and steady negative,' and Holmes an 'explicit' one.

At that moment Halifax stated that Norris had more to say, so he was recalled and said, "At the time that I said I desired the Act might pass, I thought we should have an opportunity of explaining our reasons for signing the sentence." Nobody seemed interested in what this meant, and he again withdrew.

Geary, Boys and Dennis answered in the negative to all the questions. Moore answered "No" to the first two questions, but wanted the Bill, though he did not think himself at liberty to answer the fourth question, but said, "I could give better information what were my motives for signing that sentence and letter." This was tame enough after what had been expected, but the greatest surprise was Keppel. He answered "No" to the first two questions, but

"Yes, undoubtedly" he desired the Bill, to the third. To the fourth he answered, "I think that I cannot answer that question without particularising the reasons for my vote and opinion." To the further question, "Do you understand that these particular reasons are asked now?" he simply answered "No."

All the officers having been examined, Temple moved that they should be absolved from further attendance and their evidence read. He was still in favour of the Bill in order 'to indulge the conscientious' and clear the doubts of others, remarking that although the sentence now appeared to be just, Keppel had not said half as much as he did in the Commons. Hardwicke at once opposed, expressing his great contempt for the Bill and its sponsors in the Lower House. Halifax, Byng's staunchest supporter amongst the peers, had to admit that the examination was a depressing anticlimax, though he urged the merits of the Bill, but Hardwicke wound up the debate by carrying a motion to print the examination and reject the Bill. Far from pleading 'against Byng like little attorneys,' he and Mansfield had taken a firm line, and their evil cause had triumphed.

The officers, who had looked forward to giving a satisfactory explanation of their conduct before a small and sympathetic gathering in some intimate chamber, were overawed and bewildered when faced by the whole assembly of 'the great persons,' with their robes and ribbons.

Parliament had taken up Admiral Byng and

dropped him again; Pitt and Temple were disinclined to risk their popularity further; and unless something intervened he would be shot on 14th March.

There was one more effort made to save him. For some days past, in the City, Byng's fate had been looked upon 'as a trial strength between the old and new Ministry, in which the latter have greatly lost themselves and exposed their weakness.' But Paul Whitehead, who had continued to work for Byng ever since his imprisonment, tried to pierce the grim indifference of such comments by circulating copies of the trial as recorded by Mr. Cooke, Byng's shorthand man. The majority of the merchants considered that the loss of Minorca was an indelible blot on our prestige and a great danger to our Mediterranean trade, and that the King should be held to his promise to punish the scapegoat with the threat that he should have no more money if he relented. Consequently, a storm of opposition was roused by Whitehead's humane propaganda, and on 1st March a manifesto was issued 'To the worthy merchants and citizens of London,' stating that 'Mr. Byng has in most solemn manner been tried, convicted and condemned by the proper legal court martial. All the unprecedented steps which have been taken to raise doubts about the sentence, have only confirmed it. . . . This is not a contest between Minister and Minister, but between an injured nation and their admiral who has betrayed them. . . . Is this a time, when we are singly engaged in a most dangerous war and our all is at stake, to relax the discipline of our Navy? It matters not to us whether this man or that man is Minister. If our colonels and admirals are to refuse to fight when their duty calls them, this nation is ruined, and it will be too late to call them to account when the next shall run away from Plymouth under pretence of covering Portsmouth. His Majesty has been graciously pleased to promise us that he will not spare the guilty, and it is he only that can redress our grievances. Though the throne were beset by advocates for the criminal, yet His Majesty's ears are always open to the cry of his people. To him let us therefore petition for justice, and the execution of a sentence, upon which our very being as a nation may, hereafter, very possibly depend.'

As an example of well-timed propaganda, this manifesto could hardly be bettered. It cleverly disassociated the King from his Ministers, and held him relentlessly to his former promise by making Byng's death a necessity for the safety of the State.

Nevertheless, on 11th March, some of the aldermen went to the Lord Mayor to ask for a Common Council to be called in order to organise a petition recommending Byng to the King's mercy. They were headed by Matthew Blakiston, Lord Mayor in 1761, and seem to have consisted of only four Tory aldermen, so that Pitt's City friends must have been told to take no part. Marshe Dickinson, the then Lord Mayor, was, however, well under the thumb of the late Ministers, and Hardwicke was able to tell Newcastle the same day that he had refused to help the petitioners. So by their control over the law lords, the merchants, and the Navy, which they had exercised triumphantly for many years, the late Ministers were able to gain their immediate ends, even when temporarily displaced from power. No more far-reaching example exists of the extent and diversity of Whig patronage than this tale of the gates of mercy being shut against Byng. Even the City merchants, with their great independent power, at last became convinced that financial stability could only exist under a Pelham and Yorke régime, and obediently found in Byng the sole 'author' of disaster, while the King was forced to play the part of an unscrupulous bully. His grandson, George III, broke the power of the Whigs and seized their patronage, but his use of it added little to our public credit, and the Whigs, chastened by secessions and distant wanderings, became the political ancestors of the advocates of Parliamentary reform.

CHAPTER XIV

THE EXECUTION

"HAVE they broke me?" Byng had asked when he first stepped on to the deck of the *St. George,* and realised from the glum looks of his friends that something had gone wrong. When they told him, he showed extraordinary self-control, and was the only man present in the Great Cabin who remained apparently unmoved while the judge-advocate read out the sentence. After this ordeal he went ashore to his lodgings with the same air of composure, and refused to listen to any suggestions that he might be pardoned, saying, "What satisfaction can I receive from liberty to crawl a few years longer on the earth, with the infamous load of a pardon at my back? I despise life upon such terms, and would rather have them take it."

A few days after, he was sent on board the *Monarque,* where Captain John Montague treated him with great consideration, and very differently from Isaac Townshend. He was confined in the captain's cabin, where divine service was performed for him every morning and in which he spent the rest of the day, being visited by his friends and arranging his family affairs. After the warrant for his execution arrived he was guarded very carefully, his friends being obliged to leave him at dusk, and their names and the times at which they came and went being noted in a journal, presumably to prevent any attempt at escape in another person's clothes. For the same reason the lieutenants of the ship had to take it in turn to be in the Great Cabin day and night, so that he was never alone except when in the stateroom, and at night extra marines watched on deck, calling " All is well " to each other every five minutes, while a guard-boat rowed round and round the ship. There is no evidence, however, that these precautions were initiated by Captain Montague, who seems to have tried to make his confinement as little irksome as possible.

As the Cabinet only decided to respite his execution on 26th February, Byng did not hear of it till the 27th, which was the day before the one on which he expected to die. Nevertheless, he did not appear the least surprised or pleased, and merely conveyed his compliments to Admiral Boscawen, through whom the order came, remarking with great truth, " I think it is become an affair entirely political."

His curious temperament, which had driven him to expose the shortcomings of Gibraltar and to acquiesce in Fowke's refusal to supply troops, had been so influenced by long weeks of imprisonment that he appeared to be unaffected by the most sudden gusts of fortune. Obstinacy was changed by persecution to supreme indifference, and in the end he showed, like Socrates, a most perfect example of simple courage.

As soon as the Bill to absolve the court martial from their oath was rejected by the House of Lords, he knew that his last chance had gone, as there were too many people interested in allowing the law to take its course. Only once did he display any violent feeling, and that was on the day before his death, when he learnt that as an unnecessary humiliation Boscawen had ordered him to be shot upon the forecastle. "Is not this putting me on the footing of a common seaman?" he exclaimed with great indignation. "Is not this an indignity to my birth, to my family and to my rank in the service? I think I have not been treated like an officer in any instance since I was disgraced, excepting in that of being ordered to be shot."

His friends hastened to quiet him by pointing out that one place was as good as another, but he continued to object, saying, "It is very true, the place or manner is of no great importance to me, but I think living admirals should consult the dignity of the rank, for their own sakes. I cannot plead a precedent; there is no precedent of an admiral, or a general in the Army, being shot. They make a precedent of me such as admirals hereafter may feel the effects of."

Byng was correct; his execution was a precedent, but one that has never had to be followed since in either service.

He spent his last day after the true fashion of the Stoics, receiving the Communion, and then entertaining his friends and relations to a simple dinner, followed by tea. As the day wore on, he watched the wind carefully, hoping, as he said, that it might continue westerly, and so keep those of the court martial under orders to sail in harbour, and allow them to be present next morning. That evening, by special permission of Boscawen, his friends were allowed to stay as long as they liked, but Byng himself asked them to go at eight. He first ordered a small bowl of punch and, when they had all filled their glasses, said, " My friends, here is all your health, and God bless you all. I am pleased to find I have some friends still, notwithstanding my misfortunes." He then drank to them, and continued, " I am to die to-morrow, and as my country requires my blood, I am ready to resign it, though I do not as yet know what my crime is. I think my judges, in justice to posterity, to officers who come after us, should have explained my crime a little more, and pointed out the way to avoid falling into the same errors as I did. As the sentence and resolutions stand now, I am persuaded no admiral will be wiser hereafter by them, or know better how to conduct himself on the like occasion." He then asked them into the stateroom one at a time, and embraced and took leave of them, saying, " I have not a heart of stone. I am a man, and must feel at parting with my friends, but you will not see me discopmosed to-morrow."

They then went ashore, and one of them waited on Boscawen and represented the indignity involved in ordering the execution to take place on the forecastle. Boscawen at first pleaded definite Admiralty orders, but soon relented, and agreed to let him be shot on the quarterdeck.

That night Byng slept soundly, and next morning, being Monday, 14th March, he rose at five and was ready to exchange his usual joke with Mr. Brough, the Admiralty marshal, at being the first up of the two. Like all famous victims of capital punishment, he made a careful toilet for his last appearance, putting on a white waistcoat and stockings, a plain grey coat and breeches, and a large white wig, and requested to be put into his coffin fully clad. While dressing, he took off his gold sleeve-buttons and exchanged them for his valet's, saying as he did so, "Wear these for my sake; yours will do to be buried with"; and then, realising that the valet might afterwards be accused of stealing them, he called in the marshal and a servant to witness the exchange. As soon as he was dressed, he spent some time alone in the stateroom, and then breakfasted with the marshal. At nine he was ready to greet four of his friends who came to pay him their last respects, the relations being asked to stay on shore. He now learnt that the quarterdeck was appointed for his execution, at which he was greatly pleased. He then made some adjustment in his will, and heard morning service, after which his friends began to dissuade him from his original intention of being shot with his face uncovered, to which he kept answering, "No; it is my fate; I must look at it and receive it."

At last, however, they persuaded him to cover his eyes with a handkerchief, representing that otherwise the marines would be confused and embarrassed by looking at him, and might not kill him at the first volley. He then suggested taking off his coat, lest it should be said that he was afraid to receive the bullets, but they told him that that was unnecessary and that it would be more decent to keep it on. "Well, then," he said, "if it is more decent, no alteration shall be made."

"Curiosity is strong," he remarked as he took a telescope and looked out of the cabin window at the crowds of boats bobbing about round the *Monarque* and the swarms of men on the shrouds and yards of every ship within sight, "but their curiosity will be disappointed; where they are they may hear, but they cannot see." This was true, for although half Portsmouth had come out to see him die, even the captains' boats of the warships, which were ordered to attend by standing regulations, lay to on their oars and did not board the ship, as it would have made too great a crowd.

He then took a paper from his pocket and, addressing the marshal, said, "Sir, these are my thoughts on this occasion. I shall give them to you that you may authenticate them, and prevent anything spurious being published, that might tend to defame me. I have given a copy to one of my relations."

By this time it was nearly twelve, the appointed hour, and outside, the marines were being drawn up on the poop and the gangways of the waist. The firing-party, consisting of a platoon of nine, were drawn up in three ranks along one side of the quarter-deck, the first two ranks having their bayonets fixed, as was customary on such occasions.[1] They were then told what signal the admiral would make, and

[1] In the illustration the third rank are wrongly shown with their bayonets fixed.

that they would receive ten guineas "to encourage them to behave properly." Opposite them was put a heap of sawdust and a cushion.

At a few minutes to twelve an officer came to the Great Cabin to warn Byng's friends that it was nearly time. He at once withdrew to the state-room for about three minutes and then came out, 'with a stately face and composed countenance'; he had put off his easy, congenial manner of the last few days, and was once more John Byng, son of Lord Torrington and Admiral of the Blue.

"Come along, my friend," he said to the marshal, as if inviting his company in leading the way in a great State function, and bowing gravely to his friends, he walked out on the quarterdeck, followed by Mr. Daniel, Mr. Brampton, Mr. Melliquet and Mr. Machen.

Then, bowing again to the marshal, he said, "Remember, sir, what I have told you relating to this paper," and handed it to him.

It contained a short affirmation of his entire innocence of any crime, and prophesied that justice would be done him in the future, when 'the manner and cause of raising and keeping up a popular clamour and prejudice against me shall be seen through. I shall be considered (as I now perceive) a victim, destined to divert the indignation and resentment of an injured and deluded people from the proper objects. My enemies themselves must now think me innocent. . . .' Speaking of his judges, it continues: 'If the error of judgment should be on their side God forgive them as I do, and may the

THE EXECUTION
March 14th, 1757

[p. 282

distress of their minds and the uneasiness of their consciences, which in justice to me they have represented, be relieved and subside, as my resentment has done. The Supreme Judge sees all hearts and motives, and to Him I submit the justice of my cause.'

It was blowing a gale and there was a heavy sea running as he stepped forward and knelt down on the cushion, holding two white handkerchiefs. One of these being ready folded, he began to tie over his eyes, gently repulsing one of his friends who came forward to help him. "I am obliged to you, sir, I thank God I can do it myself; I think I can; I am sure I can." "God bless you," said he, taking his friend by the hand; "don't stay longer here; they may shoot you."

The marines advanced two paces and presented their muskets, the front rank kneeling with their bayonets nearly touching his chest, the second rank ready to fire over their heads, and the third rank held in reserve in case the first volley was unsuccessful. He continued kneeling in prayer for something over a minute, holding the second handkerchief in his hand. Then he dropped it, and they fired.

'At twelve the Admiral was shot upon the quarter-deck,' says Lieut. Richard Filkins in the log of the *Monarque*, and next day 'at half past nine p.m. sent the corpse of Admiral Byng ashore, with all his baggage to the Dockyard.'

In April the long-promised 'enquiry' into the loss of Minorca was held. Hardwicke had had the free run of all Government papers in the meanwhile, and his own personal correspondence contains hundreds of pages of notes on the subject.

Horace Walpole's description of the affair is by far the best.

> 'They send for cart-loads of papers from all the offices, leaving it to the discretion of the clerks to transcribe, insert, omit whatever they please, and without enquiring what the accused Ministers had left or secreted. Before it was possible for people to examine these with any attention, supposing they were worth any, the whole House goes to work, sets the clerk to read such bushels of letters that the very dates fill three-and-twenty sheets of paper. . . . We sat six days till past midnight. Mr. Pitt broke out a little the second day and threatened to secede and tell the world the iniquity of the majority, but recollecting that the majority might be as useful as the world, he recomposed himself, professed meaning no personalities, swallowed all candour as fast as it was proposed to him, swallowed camels and haggled about gnats, and in a manner let the friends of the old Ministry state and vote what they pleased. They were not modest, but stated away. Yet on the last day, on their moving that no greater force could have been sent to the Mediterranean than was under Byng, the triumphant majority sank to seventy-eight, many absenting themselves, and many of the independent sort voting with the minority. This alarmed them so much that the pre-determined vote of acquittal or

approbation was forced to be dropped, and to their great astonishment the late Cabinet is not thanked Parliamentarily for having lost Minorca.'

It was certainly a pity no serious investigation of the campaign was ever attempted, though all incriminating evidence was certainly destroyed, and the papers used at the 'enquiry,' published by the Navy Records Society, are merely taken from a volume in the Admiralty library, incompletely copied from Hardwicke's private papers in the British Museum.

Little can be said of the influence of Byng's trial on the future careers of the officers chiefly concerned, as the accession of George III in 1760 upset the Whig system, and for some time Ministries and Admiralties changed with bewildering suddenness, and later, the Tory tone of some of Byng's supporters found adequate recognition under North and Sandwich. Temple West, Boscawen and Anson all died before the end of the war, leaving Hawke supreme, but Forbes lived to be Admiral of the Fleet in 1781. Edgecumbe and Hervey prospered, but Arthur Gardiner was killed in the act of capturing the *Foudroyant* in 1758.

The fortunes of the court martial varied without being affected by Byng; only Keppel, the most junior, rose to great distinction, and his action off Ushant in 1778 was fated to be the third of the battles of the eighteenth century to provoke a popular scandal and a remarkable trial.

Philip Carteret Webb continued to prosper till he

fell foul of Wilkes ; David Mallet received a pension ; and Mr. Charles Fearne became deputy secretary of the Admiralty. Isaac Townshend continued to tyrannise in Greenwich Hospital, and eagerly accepted Byng's seat in Parliament for Rochester, which Admiral Smith indignantly refused.

On the north side of the church at Southill, in the County of Bedford, is a vault containing the remains of various members of the Byng family, amongst them Lord Torrington. There are holes for the coffins to be slid into place endwise, when they are then covered by a tablet with the usual inscriptions.

On one of these, however, in bold lettering are the following words :

To the Perpetual Disgrace
Of Publick Justice,
The Honourable John Byng, Esq.,
Admiral of the Blue,
Fell a Martyr to Political Persecution,
March 14th, in the Year MDCCLVII ;
When Bravery and Loyalty
Were Insufficient Securities
For the Life and Honour
Of a Naval Officer.

INDEX